Hamilton County, Indiana

Will Book B

1835–1844

෴

Frances T. Ingmire

Heritage Books
2025

HERITAGE BOOKS

AN IMPRINT OF HERITAGE BOOKS, INC.

Books, CDs, and more—Worldwide

For our listing of thousands of titles see our website
at
www.HeritageBooks.com

Published 2025 by
HERITAGE BOOKS, INC.
Publishing Division
5810 Ruatan Street
Berwyn Heights, MD 20740

International Standard Book Number
Paperbound: 978-0-7884-7763-8

HEIRS OF THOMAS MARSHILL

Inventory of the Goods and Chattles of the Minor heirs of Thomas Marshill, late of Hamilton County, Indiana, deceased. Taken November 18th, A.D. 1835 by David Mc Kinney and John Barber.

One Mantle Clock	$12.00	
One Bed and Bedding	2.00	
One Bed and Bedding	6.00	
One Lot of Bed Clorothes	4.50	
One Bed Stead and Cover	2.00	
One Bed Stead	.25	
One Cradle	.25	
One Churn	.75	
Two Meal Bags	.55	
One Meal Seive	.50	
Three Glass Bottles	.50	
One pair of Wool Cards	.37	1/2
One pair of Cotton Cards	.50	
One pair of Weavers Gears	.06	1/4
Flat Iron	.37	1/2
One Table	.75	
One Oven and Bale	.62	1/2
One Skillet and lid	.75	
One Stew Kettle	.37	1/2
One Sugar Kettle	3.50	
Iron Pot hooks and bails	1.25	
One Washing tub	.50	
One Fire Shovel	.25	
One Set of Candle Molds	.20	
One lot of Crocks	.30	
Six Table Spoons	.25	
One Lot of Cutlers	.12	1/2
Three Phials	.18	3/4
Seven Pewter Plates	2.00	
Six Delf Plates	.37	1/2
One Lot of Earthen Ware	.25	
One Coffee Pot	.25	
Three Glass Bottles	.50	
One Coffee Mill	.50	
One Looking Glass	.62	1/2
One Lot of Books	.50	
Chairs	11.00	
One Sheet and Bedtick	1.50	
One Sugar Tub	.50	
One Salt Barrel	.12	1/2
One Brlac (?) Tray	.20	
One Large Box	.25	
Pounds of Wool	3.75	
Fax Wheel	.25	

One Bed Stead	$ .12 1/2
Pounds of Carded Cotten	.80
One Ink Stand	.12 1/2
One Lot of Old Iron	.12 1/2
Carpenters Compass	.12 1/2
One Peck Measure	.12 1/2
One Keg	.37 1/2
One Lot of Thread	.15
One Lot of Coopers Tools	.25
One Lot of Spools	1.00
One Sickle	.50
One Pair of Drawing Chains	.75
One Log Chain	1.00
One Colter Plough	.70
One Bull Plough	1.00
One Axel	1.25
One Axel	1.00
One Weeding Hoe	.50
One Pocket Compass	.37 1/2
One Tablecloth, Towel and Small Bag	.50
Fat Tub	.75
One Iron Wedge	.37 1/2
One Salt Barrel	.12 1/2
One Old Trunk	.18 3/4
One Pickeling Tub	.50
One Small Base	.75
One Lot of Books	.50
One Iron Pitchfork	.20
Two Shettles and a Woden Compass	.25
One Razor and Brush	.20
Haims and Collar	.37 1/2
One Tin Horn	.18 3/4
One Slead	.50
One Tablecloth	.25
One Door Latch, handle and hinges	.25
One Pair of Spectackles and gimblet	.25.
One Shot Pouch	1.50
One Lot of Flax	1.62 1/2
One Lot of Wool	.75
One Lot of Wool	1.75
One Clevis and Boalt	.25
Two and a half bushels of Wheat	1.87 1/2
One Mattock	1.50
One Bell	.50

We do hereby certify that the above is A true list of appraisement of and Chattles of said heirs.

David Mc Kinney
John Barber

State of Indiana)   I, hereby certify that David Mc Kinney and John Barber
Hamilton County)   was duly qualified Before the entered into the above
appraisement By Me, given under my hand and seal and
futher that the made a just and true appraisement to the best of their

2

knowledge.

Given under my hand and seal.
Benjamin Wheeler, J.P.

A List of the Sale of the Goods and Chattles of Thomas Marshill, deceased, made this the 28th day of November, A.D. 1835.

Zachariah Reece	Three Pans	$ .10
do Do	One Churn	.45
Nathan Bales, Sr.	One Bag	.45
Joshua Marshill	One Seive	.50
Isaac Well	One Bottle	.17
Do Do	One Bottle	.17
Jonathan Cary	One Bottle	.10
Jonathan Marshill	One Pair of Cards	.21
John Barker	One Wool Cards	.38
Joshua Marshill	One Flatiron	.30
Do Do	One Oven	.53
Charles F. White	One Skillet	.95
Joshua Marshill	One Kettle	.37 1/2
Isaac Wells	One Pair of Hooks	.34
Joshua Marshill	One Pot	.76
Do Do	One Washing Tub	.31
Do Do	One Fire Shovel	1.17
Charles F. White	One Pair of Candlemolds	.20
John Barker	Two Crocks	.12 1/2
Do Do	One Crock	.03
David Baldwin	Thevials	.06
Isaac Wells	One Set of Spoons	.20
Joshua Marshill	Four Pewter Plates	.91
William Osborn	Three Pewter Plates	.73
Dinah Marshill	One Set of Plates	.40
Isaac Baldwin	One Coffee Pot	.18 3/4
David Baldwin	One Coffee Mill	.60
Andrew Cain	One Looking Glass	.75
Samuel B. Wells	One Lot of Books	.60
Joshua Marshill	Two Chairs	.64
Do Do	Two Chairs	.64
Levi Reese	One Peck Measure	.25
Joshua Marshill	One Keg	.06 1/2
Isaac Williams	One Lot of Twine	.44 1/2
Isaac Baldwin	One Lot of Cooper Tools	.46
Samuel B. Wells	One Sickle	.60
Zachariah Reese	One Bucket	.32
John Barker	One Bucket	.33
Joshua Marshill	One Plow	3.46 1/4
David Baldwin	One Coulter Plow	.71
Jonathan Cary	One Axe	.56 1/2
Jonathan Paris	One Axe	1.21
Isaac Wells	One Hoe	.52
Samuel B. Wells	One Pocket Compass	.41
Isaac Baldwin	One Towel	.06 1/4
Joshua Marshill	One Table Cloth	.07
Charles F. White	One Sack	.21

3

Isaac Baldwin	One Fat Tub	$ .43 3/4
Moraecar	One Goard	.01
David Baldwin	One Iron Wedge	.70
Isaac Wells	One Box	
Nathan Bales, Sr.	One Pickling Tub	
Joseph Marshill	One Box	
Dinah Marshill	One Lot of Books	
Charles F. White	One Pitchfork	Amounts
Zenas Cary	Two Shuttles	
Nathan Davis	One Razor	Unreadable
David Baldwin	One Bugle	
Joshua Marshill	One Table	
Isaac Wells	Three Tin Cups	
Do Do	Four Tin Cups	
William Osborn	Three Saucers	
Dinah Marshill	One Pound of Wool	
Levi Reese	Two Pounds of Wool	
James Wise	Two Pounds of Wool	
Joshua Marshill	One Sheet	
Do Do	One Bed Tick	
Andrew Cain	One Tub	
William Reynolds	One Clock	
Charles F. White	One Set of Spools	
Dinah Marshill	One Quilt	
Do Do	One Quilt	
Do Do	One Covelet	3.37 1/2
Do Do	One Counterpin	.77
Do Do	One Counterpin	.75
Do Do	One Bed	4.00
Joshua Marshill	One BedStead	1.50
William Osborn	One Quilt	.65
Charles F. White	One Sheet	1.00
Joshua Marshill	One Sack	.95
William Osborn	One Bedstead and Bed	12.40
Joshua Marshill	One Quilt	1.33
Do Do	One Quilt	.87 1/2
Do Do	One Quilt	.64
Zachariah Reese	One Quilt	.32
Dinah Marshill	One Sheet	.75
Do Do	One Quilt	.25
Levi Reese	One Cradle	.10
Jonathan Paris	One Salt Barrel	.07
Isaac Wells	One Tray	.25
Jonathan Paris	One Salt Barrel	.12 1/2
Zachariah Reese	One Sack	.50
William Osborn	One Flax Wheel	.35
Joseph Marshill	One Ink Stand	.18 3/4
Nathan Bales	One Heckle	3.00
David Baldwin	One Compass	.12 1/2
Benjamin Wheeler	One Lot of Iron	.13
John Barker	One Log Chain	1.00
Joshua Marshill	One Pair of Gears	1.17
Isaac Baldwin	One Kettle	2.78 3/4
James Wise	Two Pounds of Wool	.62

4

Jonathan Paris	One Pound of Wool	$ .42 1/2
Moraicar Cloud	Three Dishes	.21
Isaac Wells	One Set of Knives and Forks	.31 1/4
Jonathan Parris	One Lot of Rags	.25 3/4
Owen Williams	One Lot of Books	.10 1/4
Jonathan Paris	One Lot of Rags	.13
James Wise	One Pair of Weavers gears	.03
James Wise	One Lot of Cotton	.40

David Mc Kinney, Clerk

State of Indiana)
Hamilton County)   I, hereby certify that David Mc Kinney was duly qualifyed according to law, that this is a true List of the property sold of the heirs of Thomas Marshill, deceased, given under my hand and seal this November 28th, A.D. 1835.

Benjamin Wheeler, J.P.

EDWARD ESSEX' ESTATE

September 17th, 1836

One Mare	$50.00
One Colt	35.00
One Cow	10.00
One Heifer	5.00
One Calf	2.00
Four Borrows	8.00
Two Sows	5.50
Three Acres of Corn	4.50
Seventy-five Bushels of Corn	15.00
Twenty-five Bushels of Corn	5.00
Forty Bushels of Corn	4.00
One Ploough Eary	5.00
One Shovel Plough	3.00
Stretchers and Clips	1.50
One Iron Wedge	.75
Hand Saw	1.00
Sickle	.50
One Saddle	4.00
Two Sets of Gears	8.00
Two Blind Bridles	10.50
Two Meat Tubs	.50
One Matick	1.50
One Shugar Kittle	2.50
Aples Trees	.45
One Ax	1.00
Horse Shoes	.12 1/2
One Spinning Wheel	1.00
One Hog	1.50
Bed and Bedding	10.00
One Bedstead	.37 1/2

State of Indiana)
Hamilton County) To Wit: This day came before me, Henry Davis, a justice
                of the Peace in and for said County, Robert Barnhill,
administrator and Mary Essex, administratrix of the Estate of Edward Essex,
deceased after being Duly sworn saith that the within is a true Inventory
of the personal estate, goods, Chattles rights, Credits, monies and effects
of said Essex so far as the same has come to their knowledge, ~~sworn-to-and~~
~~subscribed-before-me-this-14th-day-of-October,-1836.~~

                              Robert Barnhill
                                   her
                         Mary   X   Essex
                                  mark
Sworn to and subscribed before me this 14th day of October, 1836.

                              Henry Davis
                              Justice of the Peace

SALE BILL

James Hoover	One Mare	$66.00
Elias Bishop	One Colt	46.00
Widows Claim	One Cow	10.00
Do Do	One Heifer	5.00
Do Do	One Calf	2.00
Do Do	Four Hogs	8.00
Thomas Olophant	Four Sows	4.37 3/4
Widows Claim	Three Acres of Corn	4.56
Henry Davis	25 Bushels of Corn at $.18 3/4 per.	4.68 1/2
James Hamer	25 Bushels of Corn at $.18 1/2 per	4.62
James Hamer	25 Bushels of Corn at $2.00 per	3.00
Mary Essex	25 Bushels of Corn at $.18 3/4 per	4.68 3/4
Widows Claim	40 Bushels of Corn	4.50
Alexander Brown	One Plough Cary	5.57 3/4
David Ellis	One Plow Shovel	3.00
Reuben Parish	Strechers & Clips	1.62 1/2
James Hamer	One Iron Wedge	.93 1/4
Alexander Brown	One Handsaw	1.37 1/2
Daniel Ellis	One Sickle	.56 1/4
John Essex	One Saddle	6.00
N. B. Webber	Set of Gears	4.75
Eli Harison	Blind Bridle	.87 1/2
Widows Claim	Two Meat Tubs	.50
Thomas Olophant	One Mattock	1.87 1/2
Widows Claim	One Sugar Kettle	2.50
Widows Claim	One Axl	1.00
Widows Claim	One Spinning Wheel	1.00
Ephraim Bowers	One Hog	2.50
Widows Claim	Bed & Bedding per	10.00
Widows Claim	One Bedstead	.37 1/2
Widows Claim	Household and Kitchen Furniture	3.50

George Hardin	Shoemaking Tools	$ 1.87	1/2
Widows Claim	Four Bushels and 1/4 of Wheat	2.12	1/2
Eli Harrison	One Set of Gears	4.93	3/4
George Hardin	One Blind Bridle	.87	1/2
John Cruse	Two Horses	.12	1/2
Ephraim Bowen	One Sow	2.93	3/4
Widows Claim	Fruit Trees	.45	
Widows Claim	One Dollar & Fifty Cents	1.50	

$237.24

Deduct Amount Selected by Widow   61.45

$169.79

I do certify the foregoing a correct Bill of the property of Edward Essex, deceased, disposed on the day of sale, September 20th, 1836.

Nathaniel B. Webber,
Clerk of the Sale

I do certify that Nathan B. Webber was duly qualifyed as Clerk of the Sale of the above named property of Edward Essex, deceased, Henry Davis, Justice of the Peace, Hamilton County, Indiana, September 20th, 1836.

The Appraisement of the remainder of the property of Edward Essex, deceased.

One Sow	$10.00
Five Shoats	7.00

Samuel Morrow
Henry Cruse
The Widows Claim

State of Indiana)
Hamilton County) Personally appeared before me the undersigned, one of the Justice of the Peace of the County aforesaid, Samuell Morrow and Henry Cruse after being duly sworn deposeth and saith that the foregoing Appraisement is true to the best of their Judgement and was all the property shown them by the administrators, December 8th, 1836.

Henry Davis, (Seal)
Justice of the Peace

State of Indiana)
County of Hamilton) Personally appeared before me the undersigned, on of the Justice of the Peace of the County aforesaid Robert Barnhill, Administrator and Mary Essex, administratrix of the Estate of Edward Essex, deceased, after being duly sworn saith that the above is a true inventory of all the property of the above Estate that has come to their knowledge, December 8th, 1836.

Henry Davis, (Seal)
Justice of the Peace

CHARLES A. DAVIS ESTATE

An Inventory of the Goods and Chattles of Charles A. Davis, deceased, taken by Riley Glasgo, administrator and James D. Smith and Parnick George, Appraisors:

One Plough	$ 4.37 1/2
One Pair Hames Chains & Collar	2.75
DO DO DO DO	3.12 1/2
One Pair of Hames	.37 1/2
Doubletree and Clevis	1.75
Saddle and Bridle	2.25
One Square	2.50
Turning Lathe	4.50
One Axe	.75
One Kettle and Bales	1.75
One Skillet	7.25
Cupboard Ware and Table	7.25
Lot of Hardware	3.50
Bed and Bedding	4.00
Keg of Nails	.62 1/2
Three Chairs	.75
Two Hatchets	1.50
One Lot of Files	.50
Two Gimblets & Screwdrivers	.37 1/2
3 Augurs	1.37 1/2
Lot of Chisels & One Punch	2.37 1/2
1 Square	.50
One Lot of Plains	4.00
One Rabbit Plain	1.00
Two Table Plains	.75
Gauge and Curry Comb	.25
One Saw	1.50
One Tenant	1.50
Old Saw	.75
Two Pipes	. __
One Coalt	32.00
One Old Mare	2.00
Corn in the Field	2.00
Oats	.50
One Hatchet	1. __
One Hammer	.37 1/2
One Plough Plain	1.75
One Jack Plain & Fore Plain	2.12 1/2
One Smoothing Plain	1.00
One Chisel	.50
One Chisel and Compass	1.8_
One Mallet	.2_
One Oil Stone	.5_
One Shash Plain	1.25
One Square	.75
One Stew Pot	2.00
One Brow and Bits	3.27 1/2
One Work Bench Screw	6.00
One Gague	.12 1/2

(Amount too Dim to Read)

8

```
A Lot of Hinges, Locks & Sundries    $ 2.00
3 Horse Shoes                           .7_
Beadted Screws                          .5_        (Amount too
1 Sash Cramps                           .7_          Dim  to
1 Bed Plain                             .3_          Read)
1 Chest and Plain Stocks               9.00
1 Grindstone                           1.12 1/2
One Crosscut Saw                       3.00
```

Given under Our hands this 2nd day of January, A.D. 1837.

                                    Parnie   X   George
                                           his mark

State of Indiana)
Hamilton County)   Personally appeared before me, John W. Plummer, a Justice
              of the Peace in and for said County, Riley Glasgo, Admin-
istrator of the Estate of Charles A. Davis, deceased and Parnick George and
James D. Smith, Appraisors of said Estate and being duly sworn the George
and Smith, say that within Inventory and appraisement is signed by them is
a just and true Inventory of and valuation of the Goods, Chattles and Effects
of Said Charles A. Davis to the Best of their Judgement and the said Riley
Glasgo, says the above is a true Inventory of the Personal Estate of said
Davis, deceased, so far as the same has come to his hands to be administrated.

                                    John W. Plummer, (Seal)
                                    Justice of the Peace

Sale Bill of the Personal Estate of Charles A. Davis, Deceased:

```
Samuel Dale        Match Plains          $  .12
   Do    Do        One Plain                .03
   Do    Do        One Plain                .06 1/4
James Hushmar      Plain                    .12 1/2
Samuel Dale        One Bench Plain          .25
James Hushmar      Plain Stock              .09
   Do    Do        Moulding Plain           .25
Samuel Dale        One Plain Stock          .02
James Hushmar      Match Plains Stocks     2.06 1/2
Samuel Dale        Plain Stocks             .06 1/4
   Do    Do        Plain Stocks             .26
N. W. Reynolds     Plain Stocks             .62 1/2
Samuel Dale        Plain Stocks             .04 3/4
Samuel Dale        Plain Stocks             .12 1/2
James B. Reynolds  Horse Shoes              .25
Samuel Dale        Plain Stocks             .06 1/2
Samuel Dale        Plain Stocks             .02 1/2
J. S. Ross         Plain Stocks             .06 1/4
J. S. Ross         Plain Stocks             .03
Samuel Dale        Plain Stocks             .10
Samuel Dale        Plain Stocks            1.37 1/2
Samuel Dale        Plain Stocks             .25
J. S. Ross         Plain Stocks             .18 3/4
Riley Glasgo       Turning Lathe           2.00
Samuel Dale        Tool Box                1.37 1/2
J. B. Reynolds     Mahogony                 .01
```

J. A. Groves	Whetstone	$ .75
Riley Glasgo	One Horse	6.00
N. W. Reynolds	1 Brow & Bitts	2.88
Riley Glasgo	3 Augurs	.89
Riley Glasgo	Curry Comb	.01

Riley Glasgo, Admrs.

Test: Jacob Robbins, Clerk of said Sale

The above named Jacob Robins, makes oath that the above is a Just and true account of the sale of the personal estate of Charles A. Davis, late of the County of Hamilton, and State of Indiana, deceased, sworn before Me, a Justice of the Peace of Said County, the 7th day of February, A.D. 1837.

John W. Plummer, (Seal)
Justice of the Peace

THOMAS HAIR'S ESTATE

Inventory and Appraisement of the Personal Estate of Thomas Hair, late of Hamilton County, Indiana, deceased, Taken by Polly Hair and James Mahin with the assistance of Silas Jagoe, Philip Stoops, Jr., Lewis V. Keller, which was duly sworn to make true appraisement of the Same.

One Ox Waggon	$ 70.00
One Bel Cow	15.00
One Brinde Cow	15.00
Three Calves at $3.00 each	9.00
One Spotted Cow	14.00
One Pair of Black Steers	30.00
One Buck & Spark Yoke Cattle	55.00
One Golden & Berry Yoke Cattle	55.00
One Black Heifer	8.00
Two Red Steers	11.00
Two Yearling Calves at $4.00 each	8.00
Two Red Heifers	5.00
One Roan Colt, 2 years old past	25.00
One Black Mare Coalt	25.00
One Black Mare	45.00
One Sorrel Mare	25.00
One Sorrel Colt	15.00
One Bay Filly, 3 years old	40.00
One Bay Filly, 2 years old	30.00
One Horse, 3 years old	40.00
One Bay Colt	20.00
Two Log Chains ($1.37 1/2 & $4.00)	7.75
One-Twelve Gallon Kettle	3.75
One-Ten Gallon Kettle	2.18
One Cary Plow	2.50
One Windmill	20.00
One Lot of Flax	2.00
Hay on Floor	4.00
One Lot of Oats in Sheaf	7.00
Hay on Barn Floor (Upper)	2.00

One Box of Grass Seeds	$ 1.00
One Pick Fork	.37
One Barrel and Wooden Forks	.37
Orchard Corn and Fodder	17.00
Corn in Field, South East of Hairs	34.00
Old Saddle and Bridle	2.00
New Mans Saddle & Cover	12.00
One Meal Sive	.25
One Box of Grain	.50
One Bell and Sprouting Hoe	1.25
One Bedstead and Cord	2.00
Boxes and Barrels	2.00
Potatoes in the Hole	1.25
Haims, Brace and Square	1.00
Three Sickles	.75
Three Bedsteads	3.50
One Bedstead	2.00
One Lot Shotes 16 in number, $1.25 each	20.00
Five Fat Hogs	45.00
Six Head of Sheep	10.00
One Pair of Steel Yards	1.25
Two Pair of Gears	6.00
One Lot of Tools, Mattock, augurs and Knifes	2.50
One - 1/2 Crosscut Saw	2.43
One Shovel Plow	1.25
One Barrel	.50
One Pitchfork	.25
One Round Point Shovel	1.00
One Choping Axe	1.50
Two Old Axes	1.25
One Peacock Plow	4.00
One Mantle Clock	8.00
One Beaureau	9.00
One French Post Bedstead and Bedding	27.00
One Plain Bedstead and Bedding	25.00
One Trunnel Bed and Stead	8.00
Seven Chairs, Split Bottom	1.75
One Oven and Led	1.25
One Copper Kettle	1.50
One Pair of Tongs and Shovel	1.00
Two Sad Irons	.75
One Cradle and Clothing	4.00
One Breakfast Table	3.00
One Pot Metal, 2 Stewpots, 2 skillets	3.00
One Grass Sithe	2.00
Three Hoes	.37
One Griddle Gridiron and Coffee Stand	2.00
One Conk Shell	1.00
One Half Bushel	.25
One Tea Kettle	.50
One Lot of Quilts and Blankets	30.00
One Looking Glass	1.00
One Pair of Timber Wheels	20.00

One Bull		$ 10.00
One Large Breeding Sow and Pigs		8.00
One White Sow and Three Shoats		4.00
Two White Borrows		5.00
One White Sow		5.00
Six Acres of Wheat, $1.50 per Acre		9.00
One Plow		1.80
55 Bushels of Wheat, $.75 per Bushel		41.25
Two Hay Stacks, $5.00 Dollars each		10.00
1/2 of a Hay Stack		2.50

Philip Stoops, Jr.
L. V. Keller
(Appraisors)

Personally appeared Before me the undersigned, a Justice of the Peace, the within named Philip Stoops and L. V. Keller, who was duly qualifyed that the within was a true appraisement Bill of the Property of Thomas Hare, deceased as presented to them by the Administrator, February 14, 1837.

James Mahin, (Seal)
Justice of the Peace

December 15th, 1836   Page 1

A List of Articles belonging to the Estate of Thomas Hare, deceased, appraised by Philip Stoops, Jr., Silas Jagoe and Lewis V. Keller and Sold by Order of the Administrators.

Buyer	Article	Amount
Joseph J. Nicholas	Bell on Collar	$ .37 1/2
Amon Shall	Clevis Hoe	1.00
William D. Carlin	Hames Square	.75
Jacob Mahin	Bedstead	1.08 1/2
Philip Stoops	Spade	.75
Anthony Hamble	3 Sickles	.37 1/2
Andrew Frybarger	Mowing Sythe	1.75
James Selley	Axe	1.12 1/2
Wm. S. Davidson	Box of Iron	.25
J. Cottingham	Sive	.31
Michael Reveal	Saddle & Bridle	.81 3/4
Philip Hare	Brace	.93 3/4
Isaac Cottingham	Auger & File	.68 1/4
James Mahin	Conk Shell	1/31 1/4
Mary Hare	Clock	5.00
Do	Bureau and Bed	8.00
Do	Bed	12.00
Do	Bedstead	9.00
Do	Bedstead	4.00
Do	Table	2.50
Do	Looking Glass	.50
Do	7 Chairs	1.75
Isa Mc Daniel	Quilt	1.62 1/2
Isaiah Mc Daniel	Quilt	.75
Isaac Cottingham		1.93 3/4

Isaiah Mc Daniel	Quilt	$ 1.00	
Isaac Cottingham	Quilt	.25	
James Ridgeway	Bedstead	.75	
James Mahin	Plow	1.06	1/2
James Mahin	Plow	4.81	1/4
William Davidson	One Book	.75	
Jacob Mahin	Two Books	.43	
James Mahin	Two Books	1.68	
Isaac Cottingham	Two Books	.50	
James Mahin	Two Books	1.68	3/4
Jacob Mahin	Two Books	.68	
James Mahin	Four Books	1.00	
Peter Paswater	2 Books, Boxes Marlyrs	1.87	1/2
Philip Hare	1 Beehive	3.12	1/2
Peter Paswater	1 Beehive	1.50	
Philip Stoops	1 Cradle	1.50	
Charles Hare	Saddle	10.62	1/2
John Grilby	2 Books	.50	
Anthony Hamble	Mattock	1.00	
Pernod Cottingham	Plow	2.31	
J. D. Cottingham	Waggon	67.00	
David Uhl	Yoke Red Oxen	50.00	
J. D. Cottingham	White Cow	15.25	
Philip Karr	Bull	11.06	1/4
Thomas Reveal	Yoke Black Oxen	37.00	
Michael Reveal	Yoke Red Oxen	17.12	1/2
Joshua Cottingham	3 Calves	12.00	
Andrew Frybarger	Heifer	4.50	
Andrew Frybarger	Red Heifer	5.13	
Anthony Frybarger	Heifer	8.05	1/2
A. B. Jones	1 Fat Hog	8.06	1/2
Abram Richhart	White Sow	6.31	
George Beddick	Sorrel Mare	25.06	1/2
Nathaniel Hall	Bay Mare	41.50	
W. D. Carlin	Bay Mare	30.06	1/2
Anthony Hamble	Black Colt	23.00	
Philip Stoops	Rone Colt	20.12	1/2
Anthony Hamble	Bay Colt	18.00	
Samuel Monroe	Sorrel Colt	15.06	1/2
Philip Hare	Log and Wheels	13.00	
Chester D. Granger	Log Chain	5.81	
Amon Shall	Crosscut Saw	6.37	1/2
James Mahin	Windmill	19.00	
James Mahin	Lot of Flax	1.00	
James Ridgeway	Six Hogs	14.06	1/2
James Mahin	Timothy Sythe	1.75	
John Frybarger	Tar Bucket	.71	
Philip Hare	One Log Chain	45.00	
Philip Hare	One Yoke of Oxen	55.00	
		$632.99	

We, solemly sware that the above contains a correct amount of the property and the amounts sold for Belonging to the Estate of Thomas Hare, deceased, come to me as Clerk of thd Sale.

Elijah Cottingham

Sworn to and Subscribed before Me, this 14th day of February, 1837.

James Mahin, (Seal)
Justice of the Peace

November the 14th, A.D. 1837

An additional Inventory of the Property of Thomas Hare, deceased, his Intrusts in a certain Store, known By the firm of J. Mahin and Company; the half of the aforesaid Establishment belonging to Jacob Mahin, Thomas Hare and James Mahin the other half, belongs to D. Yanders and E. T. Porter, the whole of the Stock in the aforesaid Establishment, estimated at Twenty Six hundred dollars, the one sixth of which belongs to the Estate of Thomas Hare, deceased, amounts to four hundred and thirty three dollars and thirty three cents.

The same Charged to the administrator, James Mahan one of the administrators.

ALEXANDER HACKER'S ESTATE

The following is the Appraisement Bill of the Property of Alexander Hacker, late of Hamilton County, deceased.:

1 Shovel Plow	$ 1.37 1/2
1 Hovel Plow	2.00
1 Carey Plow	3.00
1 Pair of Horse Gears	2.87 1/2
1 Pair of Horse Gears	1.50
1 Pair of Doubletress	1.50
1 Mattock	1.25
2 Axes	2.50
1 Weeding Hoe	.18 1/2
1 Wedge	.75
1 Lot of Auger	1.25
1 Saw and Drawing Knife	1.50
1 Lot of Tools	1.50
1 Smoothing Iron	.50
1 Mason Trowel	.50
1 Lot of Old Iron	.37 1/2
1 Tea Kettle	.50
1 Stew Kettle	.75
2 Ovens	2.00
1 Skillet	1.00
2 Sugar Kettle	5.75
2 Pot Trammels	.75
1 Lot of Books	3.50
1 Lot of Chains	2.00
1 Lard Can	.12 1/2
1 Churn	.31 1/4
1 Table	.75
1 Dresser and Ware	10.00
2 Spinning Wheels	4.00

1 Coffee Pot and Bucket		$ .87
1 Beal		1.25
1 Man Saddle		12.00
1 Lot of Flax Seeds		.75
1 Crout Tub		.25
1 Loom		6.00
1 Bed and Bedding		8.00
2 Beds and Bedding		5.00
1 Mantle Clock		19.00
1 Lot of Hogs		40.00
1 Lot of Corn		25.00
1 Colt		8.00
2 Calves		4.00
2 Cows		35.00
1 Share of Sein		3.00
1 Barrel		.50
1 Lot of Flax		3.00
50 Apple Trees		1.50
1 Bell		.75
1 Coffee Mill		.75
1 Clock		100.00

This property praised by Alexander Irwin and Isom Cloud, this 9th day of January, 1837.

I, do certify that I did duely qualifed Isom Cloud and Alexander Irwin, as Appraisers of the Property of Alexander Hacker, Deceased.

In testimony there of I have hereunto set my hand and Seal/

                                F. Redwin, (Seal)
                                Justice of the Peace
                                January 9th, 1837

Sale Bill of the property of Alexander Hacker, deceased ,this 14th day of January, A.D. 1837:

Joseph Kirkendall	1 Lot of Old Iron	$ .12	1/2
Absallam Hacker	1 Clevis	.18	3/4
Joseph Kendle	1 Drawing Knife	.53	
Wm. Bradley	1 Iron Wedge	.75	
Do	1 Lot of Gears for Horse	2.00	
G. W. Kerkendall	1 lot of Dubbletress	1.00	
James Morrow	1 Trowel	.62	1/2
Joseph Kirkendall	1 Carpenter Square	.62	1/2
G. K. Hacker	1 Sugar Kettle	12.25	
Joseph Kirkendall	1 Saddle	12.56	1/2
Wm. Hazle	1 Clock	.12	1/4
Jesse Ratliff	1 Mantle Clock	12.50	
Geo. W. Kirkendall	1 Lot of Flax Seeds	.70	
Absolem Hacker	1/8 part of a Sen & Canoe	1.00	
Anthony Uhl	1 Book	1.00	
The Widow	2 Chissels	.31	1/2

The Widow	1 Handsaw	$ .37 1/2
Do	1 Bell	.06 1/2
Do	1 Shovel Plow	.25
Do	2 Pot Trammals	.12 1/2
Do	1 Barrel	.12 1/2
Do	1 Loom	1.00
Do	1 Lot of Flax	.50
Do	1 Book and 1 Bow	5.07
Do	1 Lot of Hogs	10.00
Do	50 Apple Trees	.57 1/2
Do	1 Sugar Kettle	.50
Do	1 Clevis	.18 3/4
Do	1 Hammer	.50
		$ 54.52

I do hereby certify this to be a Bill of all the Property that was sold to the best of my knowledge.

Isaac Hurlock

State of Indiana)
Hamilton County) Personally appeared before Me the undersigned, Justice of the Peace, Isaac Hurlock who being by me duely sworn says that the within is a true Sale Bill of the Personal Property of Alexander Hacker, deceased as the same was Sold on the 14th day of January, 1837.

Isaac Hurlock

Sworn to and subscribed this 9th day of May, A.D. 1837.

John W. Plummer, (Seal)
Justice of the Peace

CHARLES LACY'S WILL

The Last Will and Testament of Charles Lacy of Hamilton County and State of Indiana.

I, Charles Lacy, being of sound disposing mind and memory do make and publish this my last will and Testament in manner and form following that is to say.

First, to my four Daughters, Elvira, Nancy, Sarah, and Minerva, I give and bequeathe One Hundred Dollars each to be paid out of my personal Estate.

2nd., I give and bequeathe to my wife Mary, One hundred dollars to be paid out of my personal estate.

3rd., I give and bequeathe unto my wife, Mary, One Bed and Bedstead and bedding being the same which She had when we were married.

4th., I will and devise unto my three sons, William Lacy, John H. Lacy, and Jackson Lacy all my Real Estate in fee simple to them and their heir forever - In case there should be any difficulty with my sons in the divisions of my said Real Estate, I desire that the Probate Court shall appoint three Competens persons to divide the Same, who shall be sworn to make an Equitable division. I also will and direct that My said Wife, shall have no dower in my Real Estate.

5th., I hereby Will and bequeathe unto my said three sons, all the residue of my personal Estate after the payment of all my debts and legacies in this My Last Will and Testament, mentioned the said personal Estate to be equally divided among them.

I do herby appoint Jacob Robbins, the Executor of this my Last Will and Testament hereby revoking all former Wills by me made.

In Witness whereof I have hereunto set my hand and seal this 13th day of December, A.D. 1836.

his
Charles   X   Lacy, (Seal)
mark

Indiana To Wit)
Hamilton County) Personallly came before me the undersigned Clerk of the Hamilton County Probate Court, John Stoops and John Beal, Two of the Subscribing witnesses to the foregoing Will, who after being duely Sworn saithe that the foregoing instrument of writing was Signed, Sealed and delivered by the above named Charles Lacy as and for his Last Will and Testament and that the Assigned their Names thereunto as Witnesses in his presence and in the presence of each other and further that they beleave he was of perfect mind and memory at the time of the execution thereof.

Intestmony thereof I have hereunto set my hand and Seal this 9th day of January, A.D. 1839.

Jno D. Stephenson,
Clerk Hamilton County Probate
Court

An Inventory of the Goods and Chattles of Charles Lacy, late of Hamilton County, deceased taken by Jacob Robbins, Executor and appraised by John Beal and John Stoops:

1 Mantle Clock	$ 20.00
1 Set of Windsor Chairs	12.00
5 Split Bottom Chairs $.37 1/2 each	1.87 1/2
6 Old Windsor Chairs $.37 1/2 each	2.25
1 Sugar Desk	5.00
1 Stand	3.00
1 Bureau	5.00
1 Table	7.00
1 Oil Cloth	1.00
2 Brass Candlesticks $.50 each	1.00
1 Cloth Brush	.37 1/2
1 400 Reed	.50
1 Looking Glass	.75
1 Jug and Bottle	.37 1/2
1 Bottle of Terpentine, PinchersShears and Whetstone	1.12 1/2
1 Ball Candlewick	.75
Shaving Box and Razor and Strap	1.00
1 File and Slate	.31 1/2
1 Coat Pattern and Trimming	8.00
1 Carpet	5.00
1 Bed and Bedding	18.50
1 Bed Stead	1.50
1 Set of ann Irons	.50

```
1 Set of Gears                                    $  2.50
1 Box of Old Iron                                     .50
1 Bedstead                                           8.00
1 Bed and Bedding                                   18.00
1 Bed and Bedding                                   13.00
1 Bedstead and Cord                                  1.50
1 Cupboard                                           8.00
1 Table                                              3.00
1 Set of Andirons                                    2.50
1 Lot of Potmettle                                   4.50
1 Large Kettle                                       4.00
1 Kettle and Pot                                     4.25
2 Smoothing Irons                                     .37 1/2
2 Shovels                                            1.50
1 Lot of Tinware                                     2.12 1/2
1 Wooden Bucket                                       .50
8 Crocks                                              .50
Wooden Bowl                                           .12 1/2
1 Lot of Cupboard Ware                              1.75
1 Lot of Plates                                       .75
6 Glasses $.12 1/2 each                               .75
1 Lot of Glassware                                  1.87 1/2
1 Bottle Glass                                        .37 1/2
2 Large Dishes                                       1.50
1 Lot of C. Ware                                      .87 1/2
Spoons, Knives and Forks                            2.37 1/2
Sythe Stone, candlestick and bottle                  .25
1 Keg of Lard                                        9.00
1 Lot of Meat                                       52.00
3 Barrels (Meat)                                      .75
1 Barrel of Soap                                     3.25
1 Bench                                               .50
20 Bushels of Apples                               10.00
1 Saddle                                            10.80
1 Bell and Strap                                     1.50
1 Pair of Steel Yards                               2.00
1 Bed and Bedstead                                  7.00
Two Wheels                                           2.00
Lard, 10 lbs.                                         .90
1 Table                                               .50
                                                  ─────────
                                                   141.27 1/2

1 Gun and Shotpouch
1 Toaster                                            1.00
1 Gun and Shotpouch                                11.00
1 Lot of Sundries                                   1.22
1 Sive and 1 Churn                                  1.00
Barrel and Flour                                    3.25
1 Barrel and Salt                                   2.50
3 Bags                                               .75
1 Lot of Cooper Tools                               7.25
1 Iron Wedge and hammer                             1.00
1 Grubing Hoe                                         .50
1 Crosscut saw                                      5.00
1 Scraper                                            .50
```

1	Box of Old Iron	$ .25	
	Saw Brush, Hook and Drawing Knife	1.25	
4	Axes	3.00	
3	Hoes and One Spade	1.25	
1	Halter	.50	
1	Blanket (Saddle)	.50	
3	Augers	1.25	
2	Bridles	2.00	
1	Sheepskin	.50	
4	Sickels	1.00	
1	Lot of Buck Wheat	8.00	
2	Lythes	3.50	
	Singletrees	.50	
1	Pair of Geers	3.50	
2	Collars	.75	
2	Half Bushels	.50	
	Cutting Box	2.12	1/2
2	Pitch Forks	1.37	1/2
3	Log Chains	8.00	
		78.12	1/2
1	Lot of Hay	5.00	
1	Stack of Hay	8.00	
3	Stacks of Hay and Straw	9.00	
2	Shovels Ploughs	7.50	
1	Plough and doubletree	8.00	
1	Plough	1.00	
1	Plough	3.00	
1	Clevis	.37	1/2
1	Harrow	1.75	
1	Waggon	85.00	
1	Black Mare	30.00	
1	Bay Mare	50.00	
1	Black Mare	50.00	
1	Sorrel Colt	25.00	
1	Sorrel Colt	35.00	
1	Sorrel Mare	35.00	
1	Cov Horse	100.00	
1	Yoke of Cattle	75.00	
1	Yoke of Cattle	55.00	
2	Cows at $18.00 each	36.00	
3	Cows at $20.00 each	60.00	
1	Heifer	15.00	
1	Heifer	6.00	
9	Sheep at $3.00 each	27.00	
4	Steers at $6.00 each	24.00	
1	Bull	7.00	
7	Calves at $3.00 each	21.00	
4	Sows at $8.00 each	32.00	
25	Hogs at $2.50 each	62.50	
15	Ghoats at $1.25 each	18.75	
1	Lot of Potatoes	.25	
		$892.87	1/2
5	Beehives	11.00	
	Wheat Fan	18.00	
1	Blind Bridle and lines	1.75	

```
1 Watch                                              $   5.00
                                                        35.75
1 Lot of Corn                                          175.00
1 Lot of Oats                                           75.00
1 Lot of Beans                                           4.00
1 Lot of Potatoes                                        3.75
                                                     $1548.33 1/2
```

John Stoops
John Beal

State of Indiana)
Hamilton County) Personally appeared before me the undersigned, a Justice
              of the Peace in and for said County, John Stoops and John
Beal who being duly sworn say that the foregoing appraisement of the Personal
goods of Charles Lacy, deceased is a true and Just Calculation there of to
the best of their Judgement.

     Sworn to and Subscribed before me this 11th day of July, A.D. 1837.

                                        John W. Plummer
                                        Justice of the Peace

Account due the said Estate:

```
        Charles Morrow, Dr., as is supposed but
                            amount unknown        $    .
        James Tharp                                   2.00
        John F. Greenning                             2.00
        Leonard Medsker                               3.00
               Reddick                                2.00
        Cilas Moffit                                  2.00
        Silas Moffit                                  2.00
        Wm. Reddick                                   2.00
        One Note on James M. Stewart given to
                     Alexander Mitchell               2.06 1/4
        One Note on James A. Groves                  20.00
        Wm. Archer and J. Robbins, one Note         212.50
        Wilburn Davis, One Note                     220.00
        F. B. Cogswell, one Note                     50.00
        Receipt of Note for Collection by
                            J. W. Plummer             22.75
        One Note on Alexander Mills with interest     25.00
        One Note on Joseph Rich to E. Jasper           5.00
        One Note on J. & G. Buckingham               18.00
        One Note on George Messick                  104.50
                                                   $690.31
```

                                        Jac. Robbins

State of Indiana)
Hamilton County) Personally appeared before Me the undersigned, a Justice
              of the Peace in and for said County, Jacob Robbins, the
Executor of the Estate, Will and Testament of Charles Lacy, deceased, who

being by me duly sworn upon his oath says that the foregoing Inventory of the Personal Property and the foregoing Debts are all of the Personal Estate that Will of said Deceased that has come to his actual knowledge.

Samuel Dali, (Seal)
Justice of the Peace

Account of Sales of the Personal Property of Charles Lacy, late of the County of Hamilton and State of Indiana, deceased at a Public Auction held at the Late Dwelling House of the said Deceased on the 8th day of February, A.D. 1837:

William Lacy	1 Black Cow	$ 14.00
George Metsker	1 Black Bull	9.00
Geo. W. Kirkendall	2 Steers	19.31 1/2
Do Do	2 Steers	14.25
William Wallace	1 Heifer	7.13 3/4
William Anthony	42 Bushels of Oats at $.12 1/2	12.15
Thadius Baxter	1/3 of Sheaf Oats $.16 cts per doz.	8.04
William Lacy	1/3 of Sheaf Oats $.16 cts per doz.	
Thomas Anthony	1/2, Third of Sheaf Oats 16	
John Johnson	1/2, Third of Sheaf Oats 18	
William Lacy	1/3 of Corn, $.29 per bushel	
John Lacy	1/3 of Corn, $.29 per bushel	
Stephen Carey	1/2, Third of Corn $.28 per bushel	
Elisha Wall	1/2, Third of Corn $.28 1/2 per bus.	
John Lacy	1 Lot of Beans	1.31 1/4
William Lacy	1 Fanning Mill	10.18 3/4
William Lacy	1 Lot of Hay $.15 cts per hundred	
Joseph Moor	4 Calves	20.00
Uriah Kirkendall	1 Cow	20.00
Samuel How	1 Red Cow	25.25
A. P. Casler	3 Calves	11.00
Abraham Ross	1 Cow	19.30
Vincent Tharp	1 Cow and Calf	35.50
Wm. Richardson	1 Yoke of Oxen	57.00
James A. Groves	1 Yoke of Oxen	55.75
Levi C. Keller	1 Cow and Calf	16.50
William Lacy	10 Hogs (1st Choice)	70.00
John D. Cottingham	10 Hogs (2nd Choice)	45.50
John Lacy	Last Lot of Hogs, $2.60 per head	
Anthony Fryberger	4 Sheep (1st Choice)	15.01 1/2
Anthony Fryberger	5 Sheep (2nd Choice)	15.50
William Lacy	1 Covering Horse	60.00
John Lacy	1 Black Mare	50.00
Sinnet Fallis	1 Sorrel Colt	47.00
Sinnet Fallis	1 Horse Colt	30.00

Jacob Vanlerslys	One Bay Mare	$ 50.50	
John Lacy	One Black Mare	13.00	
Benjamin Shoemaker	One Sorrel Mare	37.50	
Isiah Mc.Daniel	One Waggone	100.81 1/4	
John Lacy	One Plough	7.00	
William Fisher	One Plough	9.50	
William Lacy	One Shovel Plough	2.25	
John Lacy	One Shivel Plough	3.50	
Abraham Rose	One Peacock Plough	6.37 1/2	
William Lacy	One Harrow	1.12 1/2	
John W. Flower	One Sow	10.25	
John Tharp	One Stack of Hay	9.25	
John W. Flower	One Sow and Pigs	14.75	
John W. Flower	One Sow	12.87 1/2	
John D. Cottingham	One Runaway Sow	7.00	
John Perine	One Saddle	10.18 3/4	
John D. Cottingham	Six Chairs Windsor	12.57 1/4	
David M. Anthony	One Iron Wedge	.87 1/2	
John D. Cottingham	One Carpet	3.00	

State of Indiana)
Hamilton County)   To Wit: The above named James Castler makes oath that
            the above is just and true of the Sale of the Personal
Property of Charles Lacy, deceased.

Sworn to Before me, a Justice of the Peace of said County, the 10th
day of February, 1837.

John W. Plummer, (Seal)
Justice of the Peace

A Sale Bill of a Part of the Personal Estate of Charles Lacy, deceased
sold at his late Residence in Hamilton County, Indiana on the 4th day of
March, 1837:

Robert Stewart	Lot of Cooper Tools	$ 3.93	
William Lacy	Feather Bed, Straw Bed and Bedding	26.00	
John Lacy	Cover Lit	5.00	
William Lacy	Blanket	4.00	
John F. Greening	Blanket	1.68	
Jackson Lacy	Feather Bed and Straw Bed	14.00	
Sally Tharp	Feather & Straw Bed	8.00	
William Lacy	5 Split Bottom Chairs	1.50	
Wm. Richardson	Breakfast Table	4.50	
John F. Greening	Sugar Desk	5.75	
Wm. Lacy	Dining Table	6.25	
Wilder B. Potter	Table Covering	1.12 1/2	
James Tharp	Spaid	.50	
Thos. G. M. Sally	Hoe	.56 1/4	
Wm. Lacy	Brush Sythe	.37 1/4	
John Greening	Drawing Knife	.31	

Wm. Slater	Coat Pattern & Trimings $	9.62	1/2
James Tharp	Box of Old Iron	.25	
Wm. Rickerson	Stand and Cover	3.12	1/2
Samuel Monroe	Rifle Gun	10.56	1/2
James Tharp	4 Ark Baed	.56	1/2
Charles Head	Brass Candlesticks Pair	.50	
Roswell Buress	Brass CandleSticks	.50	
John Lacy	Brush	.25	
Richard Gooden	Looking Glass	.87	1/2
Wm. Slater	Bottle of Turpentine	.83	
Wm. Lacy	Ball Candle Wick	.50	
Esquire Brock	Pair of Shears	.43	
Charles Heady	Pair of Whetstone	.18	3/4
James Tharp	Jug	.18	3/4
Geo. W. Kirkendall	Bottle	.19	
Wm. Lacy	Razor Strap	.25	
John F. Greening	SALE	.06	1/4
Esquire Brock	Farmers Manuel	.93	
Thaddeus Baxter	Gazetteer	.62	1/2
Wm. Lacy	Bead Steat	10.00	
John Lacy	Mantle Clock	6.00	
Jonas Bradfield	Bureau	6.75	
John Lacy	Bedstead	1.00	
Robert Gilbreath	Bedstead	1.25	
Wm. Slater	Pair of Andirons	3.06	1/4
Esquire Brock	Pair of Andirons	.81	
Wm. Lacy	Shovel	.75	
Wm. Lacy	Walking Cane	.12	1/2
Wm. Lacy	Cupboard	10.25	
Wm. Lacy	Table	.43	
Wm. Lacy	Set of Cups and Saucers	.43	
James Tharp	Sugar Bowl & 2 Soup Bowls	.50	
Wm. Lacy	Spoons, Knifes & Forks	1.75	
Robert Still	4 Plates	.43	
Wm. Lacy	Pitcher	.37	1/2
Jonas Bradfield	Teapot	.43	
Wm. Gilbreath	Bowls & Plates	.50	
Alexander Johnson	Teapot	.31	1/4
John Jackson	Quart Pot & Spoons	.62	1/2
Wilder B. Potter	4 Glasses	.37	1/2
Wm. Lacy	Plates, Mugs Etc.	.75	
James A. Groves	Set of Glassware	1.56	1/4
Wm. Lacy	Dish	1.00	
James Tharp	DIsh	.75	
Wm. Slater	Cream Pot	.13	
Wm. Lacy	Platter, Pot, Etc.	.31	
Wm. Lacy	Shovel	.75	
Wm. Lacy	Tea Kettle	1.00	
John Lacy	Fryingpan	.75	
John F. Greening	Bucket	.68	
Wm. Lacy	Coffee Pot, Etc.	.25	
Esquire Brock	Susagestuffer	.31	
Wm. Lacy	Pair of Smoothing Irons	.75	
Wm. Lacy	Sugar Kettle	.25	

```
1 Pair of Haims & Etc.          $  2.00
1 Collar                           1.00
1 Blind Bridle                      .50
1 Halter                           .37 1/2
1 Neck Band                        .75
1 Bell and Strap                   .75
1 Neck Band and Rope               .25
1 Curry Comb                       .12 1/2
1 Lot of Potatoes at 12 1/2
         cts per lb.              1.31 1/4
1 Rifle                          12.00
1 Pouch                            .25
2 Cows $10.00 each               20.00
2 Calves $3.00 each               6.00
1 Calf                            2.00
1 Colt                           12.00
1 Colt                           30.00
1 Mare                           45.00
1 Fat Hog                         3.50
1 Lot of Hogs                    10.50
1 Lot of Pork                     3.50
  Boards 750 Feet                 6.56 1/4
8 Chois, 16 Fat Logs 3 by 8       1.00
4 Crocks                           .25
1 Lot of Cupboard Ware            3.00
1 Pot, 1 Smoothing Iron and
         Fire Shovel              1.50
1 Skellet                          .50
1 Clock                           5.00
1 Looking Glass                    .06 1/4
4 Chains                          1.00
2 Rocking Chairs                   .25
1 Tub for Crout                    .37 1/2
1 Beaureau                        6.00
1 Table                           2.00
  Steelyards                      1.00
1 Sive, 2 Bedsteads, Bedding
  for 3 Beds, 1 Bag and 3 Acres
  of Wheat in the Ground         31.75
1 Apple Butter Stand, 1 Lot of
  Hogs, Shoe Making Tools        10.37 1/2
1 Vinager Barrel, 1 Spinning
  Wheel, 1 Reel, 1 Hagel and
  Tobacco                         5.37 1/2
1 Axe Handle, 1 Umbrella, 2
  German Books                     .65
                               $246.00 3/4
```

George Kloepper)
) Apprs.
Peter Schenbach)

24

Thomas Dumgs	Bell	$ 1.25	
Roswell Burress	Crosscut Saw	6.00	
Wm. Lacy	Auger	.43	
Jno. D. Cottingham	2 Augers	.93	
Aurther Hobson	Grubbing Hoe	.62	1/2
James Tharp	Shoe Hammer	.12	1/2
John Lacy	Saw and Drawing Knife	.12	1/2
Wm. Lacy	Hand Saw	.50	
James A. Groves	Scraper	.77	
James Tharp	Oven & Lid	1.00	
John Lacy	Oven & Lid & Bowls	1.25	
Wm. Gilbreath	Stew Kettle & Etc.	1.39	
Mark Hedy	Froe	.62	1/2
Synoe Fallis	Bridle	.89	
John Jackson	Axe	1.12	1/2
Wm. Lacy	Axe	.62	1/2
Esquire Brock	Axe	.75	
John Jackson	Pair of Steelyards	2.19	
Anthony Hammel	Spinning Wheel	2.00	
John F. Greening	Cotting Wheel	1.50	
Wm. Slater	Wooden Bowl	.12	1/2
John W. Kirkendall	Churn	.50	
R. L. Still	Box and B Flour	.75	
John F. Greening	Frunnel	.81	
Jno. D. Cottingham	5 Bushels of Wheat	5.50	
Wm. Lacy	5 Bushels of Wheat	5.43	
John Lacy	Barrel and Flour	2.00	
Jno. D. Cottingham	Large Kettle	2.31	
Jno. Lacy	Barrel of Salt	2.00	
Esquire Brock	Wooden Bowl	.12	1/2
Esquire Brock	Bowls & Etc.	.78	
R. Burress	Quart Bottle	.06	1/4
Wm. Rickason	Log Chain	4.00	
Thad. Baxter	Log Chain	4.00	
S. Fallis	Log Chain	2.00	
Wm. Gilbreath	Sickle	.25	
T. P. Tharp	Sickle	.36	1/4
Wm. Roberts	Sickle	.37	1/2
John Lacy	Barrel of Meat	13.00	
Francis Booker	Barrel of Meat at 7 cts. per lb.		
Francis Booker	Barrel of Meat at 8 cts. per lb.		
John Lacy	Barrel and Soap	3.50	
Wm. Lacy	Keg of Lard	10.00	
Richard Gooding	Barrel of Meal	.25	
Wm. Lacy	Bee Stand	1.00	
P. F. Greening	Bee Stand	1.26	
Geo. Metseker	Bee Cass	3.00	
J. D. Cottingham	Bee Cass	1.00	
Jno. Veal	Bee Cass	.50	
Wm. Lacy	2 Collars	2.25	
Wm. Lacy	Gears	3.00	
Jas. Tharp	Pair of Gears	4.06	1/4
Jas. Tharp	Cutting Box	1.43	

Wm. Lacy	Sythe and Snead	$ 1.12 1/2
Wm. Slater	Syhte and Snead	1.00
R. Burress	Pitchfork	.90
Wm. Lacy	Pitchfork	.41
S. Fallis	Pair of Collars	.25
J. D. Cottingham	Tar Can	.31 1/4
Jas. Ridgeway	Box of B. Wheat 54 cts. per B.	
Jonas Bradfield	Box of B. Wheat 62 cts. per B.	
Wm. Lacy	Hole of Potatoes	2.25
Wm. Lacy	Hole of Potatoes	.31
Jno. Lacy	Pair of Bed Stead	.25

D. E. Davis, Clerk

Jacob Bobbins, Executor

State of Indiana)
Hamilton County)   The above named, Daniel E. Davis, makes oath that the above is a Just and true account of the Sale of Personal Estate of Charles Lacy, late of said County, deceased, So far as the same was Sold on the 4th day of March, 1837.

Sworn before me, a Justice of the Peace of said County, the 4th day of March, 1837.

John W. Plummer, (Seal)
Justice of the Peace

GEORGE MESSICK'S ESTATE

An Inventory of the Goods and Chattles of George Messick, Deceased. Taken by the assistance of Samuel Beaty, and Andrew Fryberger on this Twenty-eighth day of November, 1837.

4 Bredding Sows, 18 Shotes with 9 Sucking pigs	$ 20.00	
1 Cast Plough	7.50	
1 Shovel Plough	1.50	
Bottom of an old Waggon	.12 1/2	
6 Fating hogs	13.50	
1 Dung Fork	1.00	
1 Sythe and Cradle	2.50	
1 Stack of Wheat	18.00	
1 Lot of Corn in the husk, supposed to be 20 bushels	6.00	
110 Feet of Cherry Boards	1.00	
1 Stack with a Shock of Oates at	13.68 3/4	
Cow and Calf	19.00	
1 Field of Corn, Subject to Rent	7.50	
1 Log Chain	3.00	
1 Spaid	1.00	
1 Lot of Gears	1.50	

2 Sets of Gears	$ 6.00	
2 Halters with Straps	2.00	
1 Saddle and bridle with blanket	8.00	
1 Lot of Shingles	1.50	
1 Lot of Bricks	.25	
1 Hay Fork with barrel and lot of eags	1.25	
2 Boxes, 12 1/2 cts each with 3/4 Augur		
with small chain	.43	3/4
2 Hoes and 2 Rakes	1.00	
2 Large Sugar Kettle and 2 Small ones	10.00	
2 Chopping Axes	3.00	
1 Wash Tub and Board	1.25	
2 Buckets	.62	1/2
Spider Stewkettle, Tea Kettle and Dutch Oven	4.00	
Large Stew Kettle and Spider	2.75	
Waffle Iron	1.00	
Iron Square	.50	
Tailor Goose	1.50	
	$161.87	1/2
Shovel and Tongs	1.00	
3 Flat Irons	1.20	
1 Pair of Tailors Shears	1.00	
1 Churn	1.00	
1 Table	4.00	
6 Chairs	3.00	
1 Map of the United States with Roler	1.50	
Sythe Stone at 18 3/4 cts., 7 Spelling Books		
15 cts each	1.25	
Market Casket with a Split Basket	1.25	
Large water 25 cts., Lot of Chany Ware $4.00	4.25	
3 Tin pans $1.00, 3 Tin pans with dipper 62 1/2 cts.	1.62	1/2
1 Water Pbucket	.50	
1 Lot of Cupboard Ware	2.00	
2 Brass Candlesticks 75 cts, 1 tin Candlestick 12 1/2	.87	1/2
1 Mantle Clock	20.00	
1 Bureau	11.00	
1 Large Cedar Wash Tub	1.25	
1 Bed and Bedding with Stead and Cord	18.00	
1 Large Trunk	3.00	
1 Pair of Vests	4.00	
10 Pairs of Suspenders	4.00	
4 Cards of Vest Buttons	2.00	
2 1/2 Yards of Fine Cloth	15.00	
Plaid Cotton Drillens	2.75	
1 Chest, 50 cts., Small Chest, 25 cts	.75	
Carpet, 16 yrds, 25 cts per yard	4.18	1/2
Trunnel Bed Stead	1.50	
1 Straw Bed	.25	
1 Bed and Bedding with Stead and=cord	20.00	
1 Bed and Bedding with Stead and Cord	25.00	
2 White Marsails Cownter Panes	5.50	
Pattern of Beddtick	3.60	
1 Old Single=Coverlet	.25	
Quilt Calies	3.00	

1 Pair of Cotton Sheets 25 cts, 1 Pr. of Sheets 25¢	$ .50
	170.08 3/4
1 Pair of Cotton Sheets	1.00
1 Pair of Cotton Sheets	1.50
1 Pair of Old Blankets	1.25
1 Blanket	2.50
Pewter Dish and Meal Sive	1.62 1/2
Mal Cag and fower Barrell	.25
Coffee Mill	.25
24 Yards of Carpeting at 25 cts per yard	6.00
1 Pair of Hand Irons	2.00
Brass Cast and Irons	3.00
Strawberry Roan Mare, 4 years old last spring	45.00
Lot of Potatoes	3.00
Small Bed Stead	.12 1/2
Small Waggon	45.00
	$112.50

We Andrew Fryberger and Samuel Beaty being called upon by John D. Cottingham, Administrator of the Estate of George Messick, Deceased to appraise the Property of said Deceased, being duly sworn by J. W. Plummer, a Justice of the Peace do say that the amount a next to each article is its true value of the goods and Chattles and effects of the said George Messick, Deceased, according to the best of our knowledge, so far as the same has come to our hands to be administraed.

Sworn and Subscribed this before me, the 28th day of November, 1837.

J. W. Plummber (Seal)   Andrew Fryberger
    Justice of the Peace   Samuel Beaty

Property inventoryed on day of Sale by the Same appraisers, Samuel Beaty and Andrew Fryberger and the amount of each article in cash attached. this 16th day of December, 1837.

1 Blind Bridle	$ .62 1/2
Curricomb and old Bell	.25
Large Family Bible	2.50
1 Iron Skimmer	.25
1 Fine Hat	4.00
1 Chisel	.13 1/4
Lot of Planks	.37 1/2
1 Black Cow	12.00
	$ 20.93 1/4

An Inventory of notes and accounts Due to George Messick, Deceased to Collected in Delaware, Maryland and Indiana. Inventoried by Joshua Cottingham, Administrator of said Deceased, November the 30th, A.D. 1837

John A. Hopper, Delaware City and Delaware State
    1 Note on demand for $97.93, dated
       May 23rd, A.D. 1837 $ 97.93
Richard S. Bell, Constable in Willington, Kent
       County Maryland, Receipt for Sundry

```
                notes and accounts the amount of
                   Which is                              $175.00
An Account against Elizabeth Pillips for                   12.00
An Account against Pleasant Williams Paid                    .37
An Account against William Cannum for                       2.25
F. W. Emmons note and order to W. Emmons                    8.75
Note on George Burget for 100 Bushels of Corn
                   with a credit of 19 Bushels
                   and 10 Dollars cash.  Balance           10.25
Note on Daniel Gungon for 27 Cords of Wood at
                   37 1/2 cts per Cord with a
                   Credit of $2.93 1/2, Balance             7.37 1/2
Check on the Bank of Baltimore for                         55.00
Note on J. D. Stephenson for                               31.00
Judgment on the Docket of Esquire Plummons
                   against George Uhl in favor
                   of the Estate for                       11.00
                                                         $411.04 1/2
```

     The Following is the Appraised Value of Property Selected by the Widow of George Messick, Deceased as Her Hundred Dollars for which She is not to account. Taken this 8th day of December, A.D. 1837. Delivered by Joshua Cottingham, Administrator of said Deceased to said Widow, Hester Messick.

```
1 Fat Hog, Last Choice                                   $  1.25
1 Wash Tub with Washboard                                   1.25
1 Bucket and Dipper                                          .75
  Spider Stewkettle, Tea Kettle and Dutch Oven             4.00
  Tailors Goose                                            1.50
  Fire Shovel and Tongs                                    1.00
3 Smoothing Irons                                          1.20
  Tailors Shears                                           1.00
1 Table and 6 Chairs                                       7.00
1 Market Basket                                            1.00
  Large Water                                               .25
  Set of China Tea Cups and Saucers, Half Dozen             .75
3 Tin pans with dipper                                      .62 1/2
  Lot of Cupboard Ware                                     2.00
2 Brass Candlesticks, 75 cts., 1 Tin Candlestick
                   $.12 1/2                                 .87 1/2
1 Bureau                                                  11.00
  Cedar Wash Tub                                           1.25
1 Bed and Bedding with Stead and Cord                     18.00
  Large Chest, 50 cts; Small Chest .25 cts                  .75
  Carpet 16 3/4 yards at .25 cts per yard                  4.18 3/4
  Trunnel Bedstead                                         1.50
1 Bed and Bedding with Stead and Cord                     20.00
  Bed Tick Pattern                                         3.60
  Single Coverlet Old                                       .25
2 Pairs of Old Bottom Sheets                                .50
1 Pair of Old Blankets                                     1.50
  Pewter Dish and Meal Sive                                1.62 1/2
1 Pair of Cast Fire Irons or Hand Irons                    2.00
```

4 Bushels of Corn		$ 1.00	
4 Bushels of Wheat		4.00	
		$ 95.61	1/2
2 Bushels of Potatoes		.50	
1 Big Dish		.75	
1/2 Dozen Small Plates		1.00	
Lard Keg or Lard Firken		.25	
1 Barrel and four Kegs		.25	
2 Old Tin Buckets		.25	
1 Fat Hog, First choice		1.37	1/2
		$ 5.37	1/2
		95.62	1/2
		$100.00	

Received of Joshua Cottingham, Administrator of the Estate of George Messick, Deceased, the foregoing Property at the Appraisement of the same, it being One Hundred Dollars for which I am not to account. Received this 8th day of December, A.D. 1837 by Hester Messick, widow of the said Deceased.

A Sale Bill of the Personal Property Belonging to the Estate of George Messick, Deceased, Sold on the 16th day of December, 1837.

Samuel Beaty	Box and Regs	$ .06	1/4
James Ridgeway	2 Hoes and 2 Rakes	.50	
Andrew Fryberger	Bucket	.37	1/2
Andrew Fryberger	2 Halter Chains	1.12	1/2
James Mahin	2 Bridles	.75	
James Mahin	Basket	.37	1/2
James Mahin	Spade	.68	3/4
Jessa Willson	Log Chain	2.00	
Samuel Beaty	1 Set of Gears	1.75	
James Mahin	1 Set of Gears	1.76	
Henry Seearce	1 Set of Gears	.62	1/2
Andrew Fryberger	Auger and Chisel	.26	
Jessa Willson	1 Axe	1.25	
James Ridgeway	1 Axe	1.37	1/2
James Morrow	1 Saddle	6.00	
James Ross	Steelyards	.56	1/4
Jabez Ross	Lot of Brick	.06	1/4
James Ross	Lot of Shingles	.70	
A. B. Cole	Lot of Plank	.25	
James Mahin	Sugar Kettle	.43	
Samuel Beaty	1 Sugar Kettle	1.75	
James Mahin	1 Sugar Kettle	1.75	
Jacob Mahin	Lot of Corn .21 cts per bushel	.75	
James Ridgway	Sugar Kettle	1.81	1/4
		$ 29.83	3/4
Joshua Cottingham	Map of U.S.	1.12	1/2
Joshua Cottingham	1 Large Bible	2.37	1/2
Joshua Cottingham	Set of China Ware	3.00	
James Carpenter	2 Spelling Books	.12	1/2

Peter Weaver	2 Spelling Books	$	.13	
Jesse Willson	4 Spelling Books		.26	
Samuel Dale	Iron Square		.32	
A. B. Cole	Wousul Iron		1.50	
Thomas Demoss	1 Axe		.25	
Joshua Cottingham	1 Brass andiron		2.00	
Joshua Cottingham	Stew Kettle		.87	1/2
Jesse Willson	Pewter Basen, Tin Pan		.63	
J. G. Burns	2 Blankets		4.50	
James Ross	2 Blankets		3.37	1/2
Joseph Messick	1 Pair of Sheets		.56	1/2
Joseph Messick	2 Sheets		.56	1/2
James Ross	1 Coverlet		3.26	
Joseph Messick	1 Coverlet		2.76	
Joseph Messick	1 Quilt		2.00	
Joseph Messick	1 Quilt		3.12	1/2
Joshua Cottingham	1 Spider and Lid		1.00	
Peter Weaver	1 Mat		1.90	
Joseph Messick	1 Bed		20.00	
Joseph Messick	1 Straw Bed		.25	
Jonathan Colborn	1 Bed Stead		4.00	
Joseph Messick	1 Straw Bed		.33	
Joshua Cottingham	1 Clock		9.50	
Jessa Willson	1 Bed Stead		1.31	1/4
Joseph Messick	2 Cards of Brass Buttons		.31	
Peter Strait	2 Cards of Brass Buttons		.31	
			$ 71.58	

William Ross	Suspenders	.37	1/2
James Ridgway	Suspenders	.26	
William Carran	Suspenders	.26	
Joseph Messick	Suspenders	.28	
James Carpenter	Suspenders	.27	
Charles White	Suspenders	.18	
Jabez Ross	Suspenders	.37	1/2
Jesse Stoops	Suspenders	.25	3/4
Joshua Cottingham	Suspenders	.31	1/4
Joseph Messick	Suspenders	.26	
Moses Burk	Suspenders	.25	
Andrew Fryberger	8 Yards of Cotton Drilling .26 cts per yard	2.08	
A. B. Jones	2 Yards of Cloth $4.68 3/4 per yard	9.37	1/2
Samuel Dale	Vest	.65	
Andrew Fryberger	1 Vest	.76	
Joshua Cottingham	1 Trunk	3.00	
Joshua Cottingham	1 Carpet, 24 yds. 20cts per yd.	4.80	
Edmund B. Hutchenson	4 Fat Hogs	10.00	
James J. George	1 Black Calf	4.25	
Edmund B. Hutchenson	1 Red Cow	15.00	
Andrew Fryberger	1 Black Cow	11.00	
Andrew Fryberger	Shick of Oats	2.62	1/2
Andrew Fryberger	Oats Stack	14.00	
Jabez Ross	1 Lot of Plank	.75	
Peter Weaver	1 Sow and Pigs	2.12	1/2

James Carpenter	1 Sow	$ 3.50	
Jabez Ross	1 Sow	2.06	1/4
Peter Weaver	1 Sow	1.31	1/4
Jabez Ross	16 Shoats, 75 cts each	12.00	
Andrew Fryberger	1 Wheat Stack	13.31	1/4
James Ridgway	Sythe and Cradle	7.75	
		$115.81	1/4

Andrew Fryberger	Waggon Bottom	.06	1/2
Samuel Beaty	Shovel Plough	1.00	
James Ridgway	Plow	7.00	
Jessa Willson	Lot of Corn	4.18	3/4
Moses Burk	1 Waggon	20.50	
Samuel Beaty	S. Ware	21.25	
W. D. Carband	Potatoes, 5 bushels at 11 Cts. per Bushel	.55	
		$271.96	1/4

I, Elijah Cottingham, being duly sworn do say that the amount affix to each article is the true amount for which each article was bid off at and placed to the proper person bidding of the Same.

Elijah Cottingham
Clerk of the Sale

Sworn to and Subscribed before Me on the 12th day of January, A.D. 1838.

J. W. Plummers (Seal)
Justice of the Peace

PETER HANNAMAN'S ESTATE

The following is a list of the Personal Property belonging to the Estate of Peter Hannaman, deceased, appraised by us as follow, to Wit:

1 Cow	$ 20.00	
1 Mare Poney	40.00	
1 Axe	1.00	
1 Bedstead	5.50	
16 lbs. of Sugar at 10 cts.	1.60	
6 1/2 Tallow at 10 cts.	.60	
1 Razor & Strap & Box and Brush	1.25	
1 Candle Stand & 1 Lot of Iron in the _____	1.25	
1 Lot of Cups and Saucers	1.50	
3 Sets of Plates	1.75	
3 Plates	.62	1/2
1 Set of Glass Plates	.28	3/4
1 Oval Dish	.50	
1 Set of Knives and Forks	.75	
1 Set of Bretana Spoons.	.37	1/2
1 Set of Tea Spoons	.25	
1 Ball of Candle Wick	.06	1/4
1 Tea Pot, 1 Sugar, 1 Creamer	2.25	
1 Large Pitcher	.50	

```
2 Bowls at .25 cts each            $   .50
1 Teapot, creamer, pepper box and
                        salt set       .37 1/2
2 Tumblers, 1 Decanter                 .25
2 Pans                                 .75
1 Candle Stick, Bread Bowl             .75
1 Canister, 1 Cup, 1 Sand Box, and
                        1 Pepper Box   .62 1/2
1 Barrel with some Meat              2.01
1 Keg of Meat                          .62 1/2
1 Bed Cord                             .37 1/2
1 Keg of Soap                        1.00
1 Saddle Blanket                       .37 1/2
1 Basket                               .50
                                   $ 88.99 1/4
1 Table                              4.00
2 Tin Buckets, 1 Copper Bailer       1.25
1 Mantle Clock                      15.00
7 Chares                             3.00
1 Stew Kettle (Large)                2.00
1 Stew Kettle (Small)               11.25
1 Tea                                1.00
1 Skillet (Small)                    1.00
1 Skillet (Large)                    1.00
1 Bed and Bedding & Bedstead & Curtings 30.50
1 Coffee Mill                        1.00
1 Fire Shovel and Tongs              1.75
1 Shaving Glass                        .62 1/2
  CASH                               4.00
                                   $156.48 3/4
```

Zeneath Beckwith)
Henry Ferguson)
                    Appraisers

J. W. Plummer, Administrator

State of Indiana)
Hamilton County) To Wit
          Personally appeared before Me, John Colis, a Justice of the
          Peace in and for said County, J. W. Plummer, Administrator
of Peter Hannaman, deceased and Zenis Beckwith and Henry Ferguson, Appraisors
of Said Estate and being duly Sworn, Zenin Beckwith and Henry Furguson, says
that the above Inventory and Valuation of the Goods, Chattles and Effects
of Said Peter Hannaman, Deceased to the best of their Judgment and the said
J. W. Plummer says that the above is a true Inventory of the Personal Estate
of the said Peter Hannaman, so far as the same has come to his hands to be
Administered.

                            John Colips, (Seal)
                            Justice of the Peace

     Invoice of the Goods and Chattles of Peter Hannaman's, sold by J. W.
Plummer, Administrator of said Estate, To Wit:

Samuel H. Colips	1 Set of Plates	$	.56 1/4
Jacob Brull	1 Set of Plates		.43 3/4
James Demoss	5 Plates		.62 1/2
Isaac Stevens	1 Set of Cups and Saucers		.25
David Froman	3 Plates		.12 1/2
James Pelles	1 Set of Tablespoons		.40
Joseph Arnold	1 Set of Common Cups		.37 1/2
Ketchum Walls	Part Set		.37 1/2
James Kelly	1 Coffee Mill		.75
Henry Jones	1 Tin Pan		.38
Henry Jones	1 Tin Pan		.51
David Fromer	1 Coffee Pot		.40
Alonzo Steming	1 Tin Bucket		.62 1/2
Jacob Mock, Jr.	1 Tin Bucket		.50
Jacob Brull	1 Tea Canister		.43 3/4
Henry Jones	1 Pray		.25
David S. Master	1 Set of Knives and Forks		.62 1/2
George Peck	1 Set of Teaspoons		.25
Joseph Arnold	5 Tea Plates		.20
Isaac Stevens	1 Bowl		.16
Isaac Stevens	1 Bowl		.14
Joseph Arnold	1 Tea Pot		.75
Joseph Arnold	1 Sugar Bowl		.43 3/4
Joseph Arnold	1 Cream Mug		.28
George Peck	1 Dish		.50
Alonzo Seoning	3 Plates		.75
Alphew Robert	1 Dish, salt and pepper Box		.43 3/4
Austin Feakeway	2 Tumblers		.18 3/4
Bicknel Cole	1 Tin and Pepper Box		.08
Jacob Colip	1 Sand Box		.25
Parnick George	1 Brass Candlestick		.43 3/4
			$ 13.79
David S. Masters	1 Decanter		.31 1/4
David Komer	1 Lot of Candle Wick		.08
Parnick George	Shovel and Tongs		2.43 3/4
Ira Kingsbury	1 Set Bedstead		5.68 1/4
James Jelly	Sugar Box and Sugar		1.50
Joseph Arnold	Lot of Tallow		1.00
Martha Hannaman (Widow)	Razors and Box		.25
Ditto	Razor Strap		.25
Henry Jones	1 Door Sath		.12 1/2
James Jelly	1 Saddle Blanket		.63 1/4
Jacob Tyason	1 Basket		.83 3/4
Martha Hannaman (Widow)	1 Candle Stand		3.06 1/4
John P. Speern	1 Barrel and Bason		1.62 1/2
David Axeman	1 Bag, 1 Barrel and Meal		.37 1/2
Charles Nells, Jr.	1 Dinning Table		4.56 1/2
Martha Hannaman (Widow)	1 Mantle Clock		10.62 1/2
David S. Master	1 Tea Kettle		1.81 1/4
Isaac Stephens	1 Skillet		1.00
William Murphy	1 Skillet		.62 1/2

William Murphy	1 Stew Kettle	$	.87 1/2
Becknal Cole	1 Tea Kettle		.81 1/4
Jacob Ayson	1 Chair		.64
Wm. Whycoff	1 Chair		.50
Jacob Ayson	1 Chair		.65
Alanzo Semming	1 Chair		.66
John Colip	1 Chair		.76
John Colip	1 Chair		1.06
Duncan Hannaman	1 Chair		1.31 1/4
Jacob Ayson	1 Axe		.62 1/2
Alphews Roberts	1 Bed Cord		.25
Ira Kingsbury	1 Cow and Calf		25.00
S. Roll	1 Lot of Lime		.37 1/2
			$ 84.16

I do hereby certify that the Above is a true Statement of the Goods and Chattles of said Estate, sole by said Administrator on the 24th day of June in the year 1837. Given under my Hand and Seal.

Jacob Colip   (Seal)
Clerk of Said Sale

State of Indiana)
Hamilton County) To Wit:
Jacob Colip, makes oath that the above is a true account of the Sale of the Personal Estate of Peter M. Hannaman, Deceased, late of said County.

Sworn to and Subscribed before Me, a Justice of the Peace this 24th day of June, 1837.

Jacob Colip, (Seal)
Justice of the Peace

The Following are Notes and Accounts of Said Peter M. Hannaman, Deceased, To Wit:

1 Note on Charles Brooks, due in February, 1840	$	65.23
1 Note on Joseph Williams		25.00
1 Note on John Williams, Jr.		5.00
1 Note on T. Popjoy (Doubtful)		2.50
1 Note on Joseph Fouts		21.62 1/2
William Popejoys Account		30.90
		$150.25 1/2

State of Indiana)
Hamilton County) Vs. Hamilton County Probate, November Term, 1837:

Personally appeared in Open Court, John W. Plummer, Administrator of the Estate of Peter M. Hannaman, Deceased, who being duly sworn says that the foregoing Sale Bill and Accounts are all except amount taken by Widow at the Appraisement and further saith Not.

WILBURN DAVIS' WILL

This My Last Will and Testament:

That after my death, I bequathe to Nancy, My wife all my personal property and all moneys after my debts are paid to be under her absolute control and direction as long as she remains a Widow, Provided that should She marry. Then and in that case the said Property shall be valued and sold and the proceeds to revert to my heirs to be divided amongst them equally. Likewise I bequeath to my Wife, ten acres of Land to be selected by her out of any of the Land I now hold. The same to be under and regulated by the above provisions.

I bequeath to my Sons, Newton P., Albert C., Hannibal and William Davis and to my Daughters Dulcined and Cordelia Davis, Forty acres (Each) of my Real Estate and the remainder of my Realty to be divided amongst my heirs in such a manner as to make them as nearly equal as may be taken in to consideration the value of the Parcel Set apart for Each.

And I hereby appoint Jasper N. Davis, my sole Executor.

Intestimony where of I hereunto set My Hand and Seal, this 13th day of July, 1837.

Wilburn Davis   (Seal)

Signed and Sealed in Presence of

Paul Davis
Jasper N. Davis

State of Indiana)
Hamilton County)   Personally appeared before me the undersigned Clerk of
the Hamilton County Probate Court at my Office in Noblesville on the Eighteenth day of September, A.D. 1837,
Jasper N. Davis, one of the Subscribing Witnesses to the
within Will of Wilburn Davis and after being by Me duly
Sworn according to Law upon his oath says that he Saw
Wilburn Davis, sign the foregoing Will and heard him de-
clare it to be his Last Will and Testament and further
says that the said Wilburn Davis was of Sound Mind and
disposing Memory at the time of Signing the Same and
further that He signed his name there to as a Witness
in the presence of the Testator and further saith not.

In Testimony where of I, do hereunto set my Hand and affix
the Seal of the Said Court the date above.

John G. Burns, (Seal)
Clerk H. C. P. C.

An Inventory and Appraisement of the Personal Estate of Wilburn Davis of Hamilton County, Deceased made the 9th day of November, 1837:

5 Head of Horse Breasts	$120.00
6 Head of Meat Cattle	50.00
25 Head of Hogs	40.00
3 Plows	1.50

3 Hogs and 1 Mattock	$ 1.00
2 Axes	1.50
1 Hand Saw	.50
4 Augers	1.00
1 Square	.50
1 Waggon	5.00
2 Pair of Harness	4.00
2 Guns	8.00
2 Sugar Kettle	1.50
Kitchen Furniture	8.00
2 Bureaus	8.50
3 Bed Steads	6.00
4 Bed & Bedding	30.00
1 Clock	3.00
2 Tables	4.00
11 Chairs	3.00
1 Loom and Weaving Apparatus	5.00
Library	10.00
1 Crosscut Saw	3.00
	$315.00

I do hereby Certify that John Querry and Joseph Horne were severally Sworn previous to appraising the above described Property of the Late Wilburn Davis, Deceased in said County and State of Indiana, also were Sworn that the above Inventory is just and true according to the best of their understanding.

Given under my hand and seal this 10th day of November, 1837.

Joseph Horne   James A. Sackey   (Seal)
John Querry   Justice of the Peace

An Inventory of the Notes, Accounts and Monies belonging to the Estate of Wilburn Davis of Hamilton County, Deceased, made the 14th day of November, A.D. 1837.

Peter Smith	Note	$400.00
Demoss & Adams	Note	150.00
J. D. Cottingham	Note	85.00
John Dale	Note	45.00
Samuel Dale	Note	32.39
Bryan & Hare	Note	20.00
John D. Stephenson	Note	50.00
Jonathan Colburn	Note	5.93 3/4
John Toppins	Note	4.00
Joseph Kirkendall	Note	2.80
Samuel Garriott	Note	2.62 1/2
William West	Note	.43 3/4
Jas. W. Kirk-		
patrick	Note	1.00
Dow Wells	Note	.59
Abijah Reed	Note	1.64 1/2
Charles Speaks	Note	.68 3/4
		$802.00 3/4

Philip Hare	Note	$ 3.56
J. K. Lemming	Note	2.28
John Dale	Note	25.80
Amos Palmer	Note	1.37
Zur Acord	Note	.25
Pleasant Williams	Note	2.37
Henry Seearce	Note	1.25
Harlem Bones	Note	.37
Wm. B. Mathison	Note	3.66
Andrew Johnson	Note	3.00
Wm. Emmons	Note	1.00
Joseph Williams	Note	.25
John Dicksons Est.	Note	1.43
Rial Adams	Note	1.75
Charles W. Whichel	Note	.25
William Whichel	Note	.25
		$850.26 1/4

Names of Debtors Accounts

John S. Burg	$ 2.50
Andrew Robe	.78
Joshua Wheeler	3.00
James Mahin	6.00
James Hare	2.50
Garret Wall	.12
Edward Coverdale	.31
Lewis Jones	.12
Leonard Midsgar	.06
Samuel Garriott	1.75
Robert Still	1.08
John Fisher	.12
A. Bowman	.12
Dudly Willson	2.00
John Wallace	.37
Jacob Collop	.18
John Tharp	.31
Richard Curry	.06
David F. Heaton	.75
Harvy Stears	1.94
John Mc Clelland	.50
Lewis Rice	.12
James Parker	.25
James Tharp	.56
Philip Hare, Jr.	2.73
John Hays	.47
Reuben Stinson	.44
Peter Townsand	5.33
Joshua Abney	.18
Samuel Pryor	.25
John Hare	.81
Thomas Spencer	.15
John Robberts	1.44
Jonathan Hougham	.19

Barton Wall	$ .81
Curtis Mallory	12.93
Wm. Moor	1.69
Nancy Cottingham	8.44
George Burget	.25
Charles Snodgrass	.25
	$903.52 1/4
R. L. Blackmore	1.47
Wm. Hillory	.31
H. M. Goe	1.12
Isaac Cottingham	14.72
Charles Lacy	19.87
James Williams	6.25
Thomas West	.18
Edward Jackson	.12
James Johnson	.50
Seth Bacon	1.56
Rossel Burris	.18
James Hughey	12.10
Joseph Willson	6.85
Abijah Reed	.62
H. W. Clark	10.87
Thomas Morris	.12
John Blanch	.31
Jordon Peyton	5.40
Peter S. Shall	10.37
Henry Hill	.18
John Kirkendall	.25
Samuel Morris	.18
Josiah West	.12
John Applegate	.37
Amon Shall	.12
Samuel Stewart	3.31
John Colborn	.12
John D. Cottingham	15.48
George Abney	.75
Jesse Wilson	1.18
Elizabeth Shannon	1.00
Stephen Robinett	.12
Phineas Carpenter	.12
Purnal Cottingham	.18
Stephen Jones	.25
Samuel Ross	1.87
Peter Paswater	.12
Thomas O. Sprigg	1.25
Ebenezer Hurlock	.12
Jacob Applegit	3.13
	$1026.19 1/4
Washington Collop	1.18
Robert Colborn	1.31
Thomas Demoss	.50
Jacob Kirkendall	1.75
Samuel Dale	.25
Thomas Hare	.56

```
Eli Heaton                          $  1.25
A. B. Cole                              .87
Wm. Conner                              .25
Senate Fallis                          7.37
James Selby                             .62
James Caster                            .50
James Ross                              .25
Joseph Carlin                           .25
John D. Stephenson                      .75
John Greening                           .54
James Irwin                            3.00
Collected of Wm. H. Bryon             17.30
                                 $1064.68 1/4
```

                                        Jasper N. Davis

State of Indiana)
Hamilton County)   Hamilton County Probate Court
                    November Term, 1837
     Personally come into Open Court, Jasper N. Davis, the Executor of the
Last Will and Testament of Wilburn Davis, Deceased and after being duly
sworn saith that the foregoing is a correct Inventory of the Personal Pro-
perty of Said Estate, so far as the Same has come to his hands to be
Administrated.

     Sworn to this 14th day of November, 1837.
                                        Att. John G. Burns, Clerk.

GEORGE A. WILL'S WILL

     The Last Will and Testament of George A. Will of the County of Hamilton
and State of Indiana.

     I, George A. Will being weak by reason of bodily infirmety, but of
sound disposing mind and memory do make and publish this My Last Will and
Testament in manner and form following (that is to say)

     First, That all my debts and funeral expences be duly payed out of My
personal property or out of cash Which I have now on hand.

     Secondly, I give and bequeath unto my beloved Wife, Marcella Will all
My personal Property, monies, rights, credits and Effects to be held and
enjoyed by Her forever. And I do herby appoint my said Wife, Marcella Will,
Executrix of this My Last Will and Testament hereby revokeing all former
Wills by me made.

     In Witness whereof I have hereunto set My Hand and Seal the Twenty-eight
day of April in the Year of Our Lord One Thousand Eight Hundred and Thirty-
Seven

                                        George A. Will, (Seal)

     Signed, Sealed, Published and declared by the above named George A. Will

to be his Last Will and Testament in the presence of Us, who have hereunto
Subscribed our Names, as Witnesses in the presence of the said Testator.

> John D. Stephenson
> Jacob Robbins
> F. W. Finch

State of Indiana)
Hamilton County) Personally came before Me, the undersigned Clerk of the
Hamilton County Probate Court, on this first day of June
A. D. 1837, John D. Stephenson, Jacob Robbins and Fred-
erick W. Finch, the subscribing Witnesses the foregoing
Will who after being duly Sworn Saith that the foregoing
Instrument of Writing was Signed, Sealed and delivered
by the within named, George A. Will and for his Last Will
and Testament and that they Signed their Names there to
as Witnesses in his presence and in the presence of each
other And further that they believed he was of perfect
mind and memory at the time of the Execution thereof.

Given under My Hand and Seal, the date above.

> John G. Burns, Clerk.

WILLIAM REYNOLDS' WILL

I, William Reynold at this tirre. residence in Hamilton County and
State of Indiana do make and ordain this my Last Will and Testament in the
following manner and form.

First, I order that all my just debts be paid together with my funeral
charges and all charges arising from the execution of this Will empowering
my execution hereafter named to sell as much of my personal Estate at Public
Sale as will defray the above charges if need be.

I Will and bequeath unto my Wife, Nancy, the West half of the Southwest
Quarter of Section No. Twelve in Township No. Eighteen North of rance no.
Three East and the Southeast Quarter of the Southeast of Section No. Eleven
in Township No. Eighteen North of Range No. Three East and my mare named
Kate, so long as She remains to be my Widow. Then to be disposed of as
hereafter named and my mare named Polly, Side Saddle and bridle and such
one of my Cows and such an Heifer as She shall make choice and my Lot of
Sheep, also all my household and kitchen furniture and Ten Dollars in Money
and to have so much of the produce of my farm as may be necessary to suffice
Her until time to raise another crop. And in case She should die, my Widow
it is my Will that the above named personal property (Except my Mare named
Kate shall be divided equally between My two Daughters, Namely Sally and
Nancy Reynold.
  I will and bequeath unto my Son, Lewis Reynold, my Waggon and Harness.
  I will and bequeath unto my Daughter, Deborah Doan, ten Dollars.
  I will and bequeath to my Grandson, William R. Bundy, ten Dollars.
  I will and bequeath unto my son, Emsley Reynold the East half of the
South West quarter of Section No. Twelve in Township Eighteen, North of Range

Three East and the North West Quarter of the North West Quarter of Section No Thirteen in Township No. Eighteen North of Range T ree East, Provided however that he shall pay unto my Daughter Sally Reynold the Sum of Twenty-five dollars, lawful money when the said Sally arrive at the full age of Eighteen years old. And I also Will and bequeath unto Said Emsley, my Mare named Jewel, a Saddle and bridle.

I Will and bequeath unto my Son, William Reynolds the West half of the South West Quarter of Section No. Twelve in Township Eighteen North of Range Three East and the South East Quarter of the South East Quarter of Section Eleven in Township No Eighteen North of Range Three East.

It is my Will that said William shall not inherit the above said Land untill my Wife Nancy Shall relinqueshed Her right by death or otherways it also is my will that said William Shall pay unto my Daughter Nancy Reynolds the sum of Twenty-five Dollars lawful money, when She the said Nancy arrives to the full age of Eighteen years old.

I also Will and bequeath unto the said William My Mare named Kate to have and to hold as soon as My Wife, Nancy relinguish her rights by death or other-ways. I also Will and bequeath unto the said William, My farming tools pro-vided however that My Wife Nancy have the use of them while She remains to be my Widow. It is my Will that the remainder of My Personal Estate be equally divided amongst my Children, Nancy, Lewis, Deborah, Emsley, William, Sally and Nancy Reynolds.

I nominate and appoint my Son, Emsley Reynolds to be My Executor to this My Last Will and Testament. Signed, Ordained and Established this the Twenty-third day of the ninth month in the year One Thousand Eight Hundred and thirty Seven.

William Reynolds

Attes: Isaac Baldwin
       Moses Coffin

State of Indiana)
Hamilton County) SS:
            Personally appeared before Me the undersigned Clerk of the Probate Court of the County of Hamilton in the State of Indiana at my Office in Noblesville, on the 23rd day of April, A.D. 1838, Isaac Baldwin and Moses Coffin, the subscribing Witnesses to the foregoing Will of William Reynolds and after being by me duly affirmed according to Law upon their affirmation, Say that they heard William Reynolds acknowledge the signing of the fore-going Will and heard him declare to be his Last Will and Testament. And further say that the Said William Reynolds was of sound mind and deposing memory at the time of Signing the same and further say Not.

In testimony where of I have hereunto Set My Hand and affixed the Seal of Said Court, the date above.

John G. Burns, Clerk

(S E A L)

An Inventory of the Goods and Chattles and effects William Reynolds,

Deceased, late of Hamilton County, Indiana. Taken by Emsley Reynolds, Executor of the Estate of said Deceased with the assistance of Moses Coffin and Isaac Baldwin, Appraisers, called and duly affirmed for that purpose.

14 Hogs	$ 20.00	
1 Brindle Cow and Calf	18.00	
1 Whiteback Steer	12.00	
1 White Steer	5.00	
1 Raw Hide Murrin	2.50	
1 Broad Axe	3.00	
1 Hand Saw	.62 1/2	
1 Rawhide Slaugtered	3.00	
2 Sheep Skins	.25	
1 Mans Saddle	3.00	
1 Iron Square	.50	
1 Crosscut Saw	2.50	
1 Frow	.50	
	$ 78.87 1/2	

Given under Our Hands the 4th Month and 24th day, 1838.

Moses Coffin)
) Apprs.
Isaac Baldwin)

State of Indiana)
Hamilton County)   To Wit
Personally appeared before Me, Benjamin Wheeler, a Justice of the Peace in and for said County, Emsley Reynolds, Executor of the Estate of William Reynolds, Deceased and Moses Coffin and Isaac Baldwin, Appraisers of said Estate and being duly affirmed the said Moses Coffin and Isaac Baldwin say that the above Inventory and appraisement as assigned by them is a just and true Inventory and valuation of the Goods, Chattles and Effects of said William Reynolds to the best of their judgment. And the said Emsley Reynolds that the above is a true Inventory of the Personal Estate of the Said Wm. Reynolds, so far as the Same has come to his hands to be administrated.

Benj. Wheeler, (Seal)
Justice of the Peace

An Account of the Sales of the Personal Property of William Reynolds, Deceased, late of Hamilton County, Indiana, Sold the 19th of the 5th Month (May), A.D. 1838.   (Amounts of the Following are too dimn to read)

Lewis Reynolds	1 Iron Wedge	$ .5
Nancy Reynolds	1 Frow	.2
Nancy Reynolds	1 Hand Saw	.37 1/2
Emsley Reynolds	1 But Saw	.2
Thomas Clayton	1 Man's Saddle	1.84 3/4
Nancy Reynolds	1 Brindle Cow & Calf	8.37 1/2
Emsley Reynolds	1 Broad Axe	4.3
Thomas Clapper	2 Shotes (first Choice)	2.6

(Amounts are too dimn to read)

Jesse Reece	2 Shotes (Second Choice)	$ 2.87
Isaac Baldwin	2 Shotes (Third Choice)	1.7
Thomas Clayton	2 Shotes (4th Choice)	1.2
Solomon Stembrough	2 Shotes (5th Choice)	1.3
Robert Mendenhall	6 Shotes (last Choice)	3.1
Robert Mendenhall	1 Sow	2.9
Nancy Reynolds	2 Shotes (1st Choice)	2.3
Robert Mendenhall	4 Shotes (last Choice)	3.00
Robert Tailor	1 Black Steer	8.
Robert Mendenhall	1 White Steer	6.3
Andrew Scott	1 Whiteback Steer	7.5
Robert Tailor	2 Sheep Skins	.0
Robert Tailor	1 Rawhide Beef	2.68 3/4
Sarah Smith	1 Rawhide Murrin	1.50
Nancy Reynolds	1 Pair of Saddle Bags	1.75

Attes: Isaac Baldwin, Clerk   Emsley Reynolds, Executor

State of Indiana)
Hamilton County) SS: The Above named Isaac Baldwin, makes affirmation
that the above is a just and a true account of the
Sale of the Personal Estate of William Reynolds,
late of said County, deceased.

Affirmed before Me, a Justice of the Peace of said
County, the 2nd day of the 6 month (June), 1838.

Benjamin Wheeler (Seal)
Justice of the Peace

MICHAEL MAPPIS' WILL

In the name of God, Amen. I, Michael Mappis of Hamilton County, Indiana being weak in body, but of sound mind and memory do hereby make and ordain this My Last Will and Testament, revoking all others to part.

I will and bequeath unto my beloved wife Susannah Mappis all my estate both real and personal, that I may be possessed of at my death -- to do with and dispose of for her maintainance and support as She may think proper during her lifetime and at the death of the said Susannah Mappis it is my will that if then shall remain any of my said Estate it shall be equally divided among my children - And I also hereby appoint My Wife Susannah Mappis, sole executor of this my Last Will and Testament.

In Testimony whereof I have hereunto set My hand and Seal this seventh day of April in the year of Our Lord, One Thousand Eight Hundred and thirty Six.

his
Michael   X   Mappis, (Seal)
mark

Signed, Sealed and Delivered in presence of:

Amos Palmer
James Mc Neal

State of Indiana)
Hamilton County) Personally appeared before me the undersigned, Clerk of
the Hamilton County Probate Court, James Mc Neal and
Amos Palmer the subscribing Witnesses to the within Will
who after being duly sworn sayth that the within instrument of writing was Signed, Sealed and Delivered by the
within named Michael Mappis as and for his Last Will and
Testament and that the signed his name thereto as Witness
in his presence. And further he believing he was of perfect mind and memory at the time of the execution thereof.

In Testimony whereof I have hereunto Set My Hand and Seal
this 4th day of June, A.D. 1836.

John D. Stephenson, Clerk
by J. G. Burns

JOSEPH FOUTS' ESTATE

An Inventory of the Goods, Chattles, Effects of Joseph Fouts, late of
Hamilton County and State of Indiana, Deceased. Taken by Ira Kingsbury,
Administrator of the Said Estate of the Deceased with the assistance of
Becknel Cole and Horace Stowell, Appraisers called and duly sworn for that
purpose.

1 Roan Mare & Colt	$ 60.00	
1 Strawberry Roan Mare	55.00	
1 Cow and Calf	2.00	
2 Set of Gears	14.00	
1 Ladle	1.00	
1 Chest	1.25	
1 Log Chain	2.30	
1 Pair of Boots	2.00	
2 Axes	2.00	
2 Fat Cans	1.75	
1 Meal Bag	1.50	
1 Waggon Cover	3.00	
1 Iron Hooped Bucket	.87 1/2	
1 Lot of Old Iron	1.00	
7 Books	2.00	
5 Skans Tow Thread	.50	
1 Razor and Tools	.50	
1 Shirt Pattern	.56	
1 Iron Square	.25	
1 Drawing Knife	.75	
7 Horse Shoes	1.25	
1 Keg	.50	
1 Funnel	.18 3/4	
3 Augers	1.37 1/2	
2 Chizels	.75	
1 Curry Comb	.64	
5 Tin Cups	.50	
1 Stew Kettle	.50	
1 Tin Horn	.18 3/4	

```
        1  Wire Sive                              $    .50
        1  Half Bushel Measure                          .37 1/2
        1  Two Horse Waggon                       40.00
        4  Case Knives                                  .25
        2  Wall Paper                                   .12 1/2
        1  Wedger                                       .58
        4  Iron Hoops                                   .25
        1  Gallon Timothy Seed                          .25
        1  Tad Lock                                     .25
        1  Bridle                                  1.50
        1  Tea Bottle                                   .50
        1  Tin Bucket                                   .37 1/2
        1  Basket                                  1.50
        1  Hand Saw                                     .13
        1  Pint Bottle                                  .18 3/4
        1  Pot Hook
        1  Halter Chain                            1.50
        2  Crocks                                       .25
        1  Bed and Bedding                         8.00
        1  Pan
        1  Looking Glass                                .75
        1  Bottle                                       .18 3/4
        1  Pair of Spectacles                           .37 1/2
        1  Bowl                                         .50
        1  Shinel Plain                            1.50
        2  Shoes                                   1.00
        1  Mattock                                 1.25
        2  Chairs                                       .50
        6  Yards of Linen                          1.75
        1  Bell                                         .63
        2  Beds and Bedding                       10.00
        1  Tin Kettle                                   .50
        1  Oven                                    1.25
        1  Stew Kettle                             1.25
        4  Plates                                       .58
      1/2  Set of Tea Cups and Saucers                  .65
        1  Coffee Boiler                                .63
       57  lbs of Bacon at 10 cts per lb.          5.70
        1  Singletree                                   .87
        1  Gun, Shot Pouch and Bullet Mole        11.00
        1  Tin Pan                                      .18 3/4
        1  Clevis                                       .25
        1  Pot                                          .08
        1  Pair of Upper Leather                   1.75
        1  Two Horse Plow                          3.75
        1  Field of Corn, 12 acres $3.00
                          per acre               36.00
```

Invoice of the Goods, Chattles and effects of Joseph Fouts, Deceased
late of Hamilton County and State of Indiana, sold by Ira Kingsbury, administrator of said Estate. To Wit:

```
        Parnick George        1 Stew Kettle        $    .50
        Nehemiah Dean         1 Tea Kettle              .75
```

Name	Item	Price
March Tucker	1 Pot	$ .56 3/4
March Tucker	1 Bucket & Clevis	1.06 1/4
March Tucker	1 Singletree	.25
Nehemiah Dean	1 Tin Bucket	.37 1/2
John Collip	1 Tin Pan	.08 3/4
Parnick George	1 Tin Bucket	1.00
Wm. Murphy	1 Seive	.39
Wm. Murphy	1 Tin Pan, bugle and 5 Tins	.26
Peter Achenback	1 Half Bushel	.43 3/4
William Ward	2 Crocks	.14
Charles Freel, Jr.	1 Pr. of Horse Shoes Curry	.57 1/2
Charles Freel, Jr.	1 Pr. DO DO DO	.37 1/2
Parnick George	3 Horse Shoes	.40
Parnick George	1 Keg	1.06 1/4
Nehemiah Dean	1 7 qt. Auger	.75
Christian Shell	2 Augers and 1 Chezle	1.18 3/4
Austin Fukeway	1 Log Chain	3.38
William Ward	1 Bottle	.15
William Ward	3 Yards of Linen	1.31 1/4
March Tucker	1 Shirt Pattern	.32
William Murphy	Iron Hoops, Clevis, and Old Iron	1.13
John Osborn	1 Razor Box and Specks	.50
James Goodpaster	1 Bell	.12 1/2
William Freel	Some Thread	.37 1/2
Austin Fukeway	1 Iron Wedge and Horn	.57
March Tucker	Timothy Seed	.32
William Ward	1 Halter Chain and Hooks	1.62 1/2
William Freel	1 Pair of Boots	1.00
William Murphey	1 Iron Square	.25
Elizabeth Fouts	1 Lot of Dutch Books	.56 1/4
William Freel	1 Bottle & Window Paper	.12 1/2
Alonzo Learning	1 Side of Upper Leather	3.06 1/4
Benjamin Lee	1 Chest	1.75
William Murphey	1 Mattock	1.62 1/2
William Ward	1 Keg	.38
John Mooney	2 Shoes	.57
William Ward	1 Shaving Knife	.63
William Ward	1 Firkin	.81 1/4
Elizabeth Fouts	1 Looking Glass	.12 1/2
William Freel	1 Strap	.18 3/4
Alonzo Learning	1 Basket and Lumber	.68 3/4
Parnick George	1 Pad Lock	.81 1/4
John Mooney	1 Old Bridle	.43 3/4
Parnick George	1 Axe	1.00
March Tucker	1 Hammer & Chains	1.37 1/2
Charles Freel, Jr.	2 Bridles	2.00
Wm. Freel	1 Hammer & Chains	2.15
Charles Freel, Jr.	2 Horse Collars	1.25
James Simpson	1 Pant Pattern	.56 3/4
William Ward	1 Set of Harness	9.50
Thomas Murphey	1 Plough	3.62 1/2
Benjamin Lee	1 Shovel Plough	1.56 1/2

Martha Fouts	1 Gun	$ 6.76	
Benjamin Lee	1 Tub & Corn	.71	
William Freel	1 Lot of Bacon	2.75	
William Freel	1 Bed	3.05	
William Freel	1 Quilt	.25	
Elizabeth Fouts	1 Counterpin	.76	
Christian Shell	1 Breast Chains	.75	
Benjamin Lee	1 Waggon Cover	2.51	
George Peck	1 Waggon	45.00	
Martha Fouts	2 Chairs	.50	
Charles Freel, Jr.	1 Tar Bucket	.51	1/2
James Goodpasture	1 Belt	.25	
William Freel	1 Hand Saw	1.50	
William Freel	1 Axe	1.00	
Parnick George	1 Pitch Fork and Hammer	.50	
Charles Freel, Jr.	1 Roan Mare	50.00	
Charles Freel, Jr.	1 Lot of Corn in Field	15.31	1/2
		$188.57	3/4

SARAH MURPHY'S ESTATE

Appraisement Bill of the Property of Sarah Murphey, Deceased, as taken
by John Guilkce and Aron C. Finch.

1 Barrel of Pork	$ 14.00
1 Pot and Lard	3.00
2 Sheep	5.00
1 Basket and Bell Collar	.50
4 Reeds and Geers	2.75
2 Bedsteads	2.00
Roles and Wool	1.00
1 Cow and Bell	20.00
1 Red Heifer	6.50
1 Lot of Cubboard Ware	1.50
1 Calf	3.50
1 Horse	55.00
1 Mare	22.50
1 Colt	12.00
1 Sow and Pigs	4.50
12 Stock Pigs	24.00
74 Bushels of Corn at 25 cts	18.50
12 Bushels of Wheat	1.50
8 Acres of Wheat	16.00
1 Wheel	1.00
1 Bed and Bedding	10.00
1 Straw Bed	1.00
1 Lot of Bed Clothes	12.00
7 Tables	1.50
1 Coffee Mill	.50
1 Lot of Pot Metal	5.00
2 Table Clothes	2.00
1 Loom and Warpenmill	4.00
Salt and Churn	1.50

```
                        Carried Over      $242.25
        Lard and Fat                          .50
2 Kegs of Sugar & Leather                    1.51 1/2
3 Axes                                       4.00
2 Ploughs                                   10.00
2 Pairs of Gears                             8.00
1 Harrow                                     3.00
1 Plough and Hoe                             1.75
1 Clevis and Pot Hooks                       8.87 1/2
1 Slate and Pumpkin Seeds                     .75
  Cotton Thread                               .50
5 Chairs                                     1.20
2 Bridles                                     .50
2 Sickles and 1 Auger                        1.00
1 Doubletree and Singletree                  1.50
  Potatoes                                   1.50
1 Tin Bucket and Lard                         .50
  Candles                                     .18 3/4
1 Shoat                                      1.25
1 Pair of Shuttles and Temples                .62 1/2
1 Cowhide, 4 Calf Skin in Cobb
        ones ___ Yard                        3.25
  F. B. Cogswell                             1.00
  A. B. Cole                                  .75
  Aaron O. Finch                             1.75
                                           _____
                                           $289.74
```

Given under our hands and se~~al~~s- making in all, this 28th day of February, 1838.

                                Aaron O. Finch)
) Appraisors
                                John Guilkey   )

Given under My Hand and Seal this 28th day of February, 1838.

                                Philip Stoops, Jr.
                                Administrator

State of Indiana)
Hamilton County) Personally appeared before Me, Samuel Dale, a Justice
                  of the Peace in and for said County, Philip Stoops,
                  Administrator of the Estate of Sarah Murphey, Deceased
                  and Aaron O. Finch, John Guilkey, Appraisors of said
                  Estate and being duly sworn the said Finch and Guilkey
                  say that the above Inventory and Appraisement as Signed
                  by them is a just and true Inventory and Valuation of
                  the Goods, Chattles and Effects of the said Sarah Murphey,
                  Deceased to the best of their Judgment and the said
                  Philip Stoops, says that the above is a true Inventory
                  of the rest of the Estate of the Said Sarah Murphey,
                  so far as the same has come to his hands to be Administ-
                  rated.

                                Samuel Dale, (Seal)
                                Justice of the Peace

Sale Bill of the Property of Sarah Murphey, Deceased, which was Sold at Public Sale at Her late residence on Saturday, the 10th day of February, A.D. 1838.

John Colbourn	1 Wash Board	$	.30
John Gilkey	1 Pot		.62 1/2
Philip Stoops, Jr.	1 Dutch Oven & Lid		1.25
Henry T. Burcham	1 Small Skillet		.18 3/4
Philip Stoops, Jr.	1 Bucket & Horn		.50
Robert Darson	1 Coffee Pot & Strainer		.12 1/2
Robert Darson	1 Lot of Cup & Saucers		.25
Robert Darson	1 Lot of Cubbard Ware		.20
Aaron O. Finch	1 Crock & Sundrys		.25
Philip Stoops, Jr.	1 Lot of Knives & Forks		.25
William Dickson	1 Lot of Pumpkin Seed		.15
Samuel Perdam	9 Harrows Teeth		2.68 3/4
Peter Paswaters	1 Shovel Plough		.41
Henry H. Burcham	1 Cicle		.06 1/4
Henry H. Burcham	1 Cicle		.14
J. W. Kirkpatrick	1 Sugar Kettle		2.50
William Dickson	1 Pot Hooks		.25
Phillip Stoops	1 Spinning Wheel		1.12 1/2
John Colbourn	1 Lennen Sheet		.78
Philip Stoops, Jr.	1 Table Cloth		.62 1/2
Jesse Colbourn	1 Table Cloth		.50
John Guilkey	1 Bed Spread		1.50
Philip Stoops, Jr.	1 Blanket		.50
John Wheeler	1 Quilt		.87 1/2
Peter Paswaters	1 Quilt		1.00
Luticia Mincer	1 Blanket		1.56 1/2
Harrison Bryan	1 Cover Lid		4.00
Peter Paswaters	1 Cover Lid		3.82
James Babcock	1 Doubletree & Tree		3.00
Edward Furl	1 Single Tree		.80
John Simpson	1 Lot of Cotton Yarn		.20
Peter Paswaters	1 Tea Pot and Auger		.30
John Wheeler	1 Churn		1.00
Philip Stoops, Jr.	1 Reed		.68
Philip Stoops, Jr.	1 Reed		.87 1/2
John Wheeler	1 Table		1.57 1/2
John Colbourn	2 Chairs		.68 3/4
John Wheeler	1 Small Chair		.25
John Colbourn	2 Chairs		.68 3/4
Aaron O. Finch	1 Reed and Sundrys		.74
Aaron O. Finch	1 Bottle		.13
Ebenezer Hurlock	1 Coffee Mill & Bridle		.73
Philip Stoops, Jr.	1 Lot of Books		.31
J. D. Cottingham	1 Axe		2.12
John Guilkey	1 Axe		1.20
J. D. Cottingham	1 Axe		.50
Rheuben Coverdale	1 Barrel		.37
Harrison Bryan	1 Feather Bed & Bedding		10.25
Peter Paswaters	1 Bed, Bedding & Stead		.75
James Babcock	1 Bedstead		.75

Philip Stoops	1	Bucket & Barrel	$ .37
John Colbourn	1	Box and Wheat	1.43
Luhoia Minner	1	Lot of Candles	.14
Aaron O. Finch	1	Troff and Sale	.12 1/2
Johnathan Fox	1	Pr. of Warping Bars	.51
Aaron O. Finch	1	Lot of Soap Fat	.12 1/2
Smith Goe	1	Clevis	.18 3/4
Aaron O. Finch	1	Lot of Potatoes	.81 3/4
John Fisher	1	Cow	27.43
John Fisher	1	Bell and Collar	1.12 1/2
John Story	1	Heiffer	7.00
Clement Paswaters	1	Calf	3.94
James D. Stoops	1	Black Horse	51.00
Harrison Colbourn	1	Mare	20.00
Thomas Demoss	1	Colt	10.25
James Babcock	1	Bridle	1.25
Daniel Johnson	30	Bushels of Corn 50 cts.	15.00
Daniel Johnson	26	Bushels of Corn 51 cts.	13.26
Wm. Dickson	1	Plough	7.50
James Babcock	1	Shovel Plough	2.87 1/2
Rheuben Coverdale	1	Blind Bridle	.68
Daniel Johnson	5	Hogs (1st Choice)	12.12 1/2
Daniel Johnson	6	Hogs (2nd Choice)	9.37 1/2
Daniel Johnson	1	Hog (2nd Choice)	1.00
Jacob Mahin	8	Acres of Wheat in ground	18.25
James D. Stoops	1	Loom	.50
N. D. Shoemaker	3	Head of Sheeps	9.06 1/4
Aaron O. Finch	1	Lot of Gears	4.12 1/2
Louis Jones	1	Lot of Gears	4.66 1/4
Aaron O. Finch	1	Bell, Collar & Basket	.41
Philip Stoops, Jr.	1	Lot of Wool	1.50
Phillip Stoops, Jr.	1	Pot and Fat	1.87
John Colbourn	45 1/2	lbs of Meat, 12 1/2 cts.	5.71 1/2
Wesley Burget	50 1/2	lbs of Meat, 08 1/2 cts.	4.08
Wesley Burget	22 1/2	lbs of Meat, 09 cts.	2.02 1/2
Wesley Burget	167 1/2	lbs of Meat, 05 3/4 cts/	8.74
William Dickson	1	Sow and Pigs	4.18 3/4
Aaron O. Finch	1	Leather Line	.38
Walter Murphey	1	Slate	.12 1/2
J. W. Kirkpatrick	1	Old Bucket	.25
Peter Paswaters	2	Bags	.63
Aaron O. Finch	2	Bags and Leather	1.31 1/4
			$307.60

State of Indiana)
Hamilton County)   Personally appeared before Me, the undersigned, a Justice
of the Peace, Ebenezer Hurlock, Clerk of the within Sale
Bill and being by Me, duly sworn says the within Sale
Bill is true to the best of his knowledge, this 21st day
of February, A.D. 1838.

Samuel Dale, (Seal)
Justice of the Peace

ELIZA GRIFFITH'S ESTATE

An Inventory of the Goods, Chattles and Effects of Eliza Griffiths, Late of Hamilton County and State of Indiana, Deceased, taken by Sarah Griffith and William S. Goe, with the assistance of Joseph Waddle and Richard G. Goe, Appraisors called and duly sworn for that purpose.

1	Speckled Cow	$ 15.00
1	Bull	8.00
1	Red Cow	20.00
1	Spotted Heiffer	8.00
1	Black Cow and Calf	18.00
1	Red Heiffer	5.00
1	Sorrel Mare and Colt	63.00
1	Chestnut Sorrel Mare and Colt	66.00
6	Large Hogs	25.00
43	Stock Hogs	75.00
29	Geese	10.87 1/2
1	Plough Shear	3.12 1/2
1	Sythe	1.25
2	Stacks of Wheat, 50 Bushels	37.50
1	Wind Mill	20.00
1	Large Tub and Box	
1	Sugar Kettle	3.00
90	Lbs. of Bacon	7.00
1	Cubboard	14.00
1	Set of Cubboard Ware	5.00
1	Clock	10.00
1	Bed, Bedstead and Bedding	20.00
1	Bed, Bedstead and Bedding	15.00
1	Bell	3.00
1	Spinning Wheel	3.00
	Kitchen Furniture	6.00
1	Gun	5.00
10	lbs of Feathers	13.93
1	Shovel	1.00
1	Hoe	.37 1/2
1	Sickle	.37 1/2
1	Account on Edward Laten	1.00
1	Sheep	2.00
1	Note on Frances G. Reynolds	18.07
1	Note on Nathan Caster	20.00

Whole Amount $524.25

Joseph Waddle)
) Appraisors
Richard Goe)

State of Indiana)
Hamilton County) Personally appeared before Me, Joseph Carlin, a Justice of the Peace in and for said County, Sarah Griffith and William S. Goe, Administrators of the Estate of Eliza Griffith, Deceased and Joseph Waddle and Richard J. Goe, Appraisors of Said Estate and being duly sworn the said

Joseph Waddle and Richard L. Goe say that the above Inventory and Appraisement as Signed by them is a Just and true Inventory and valuation of the Goods, Chattles and Effects of the said Eliza Griffith, to the best of their Judgment and the said Sarah Griffith and Wm. S. Goe, say that the above is a true Inventory of the Personal Estate of the said Eliza Griffith, so far as the same have came to their hands to be Administraed.

Joseph Carlin, (Seal)
Justice of the Peace

An additional Inventory of the goods, Chattles and Effects of Eliza Griffith, late of Hamilton County and State of Indiana, Deceased, taken by William S. Goe and Sarah Griffith, Administrators of the Estate of the Said Deceased with assistance of Joseph Waddle and Richard F. Goe, Appraisors called and duly sworn for that purpose, August 31st, A.D. 1838.

10 Hogs $ 13.00

Joseph Waddle (Seal)
Richard F. Goe (Seal)

Account of Sale of the Personal Property of Eliza Griffiths, Late of the County of Hamilton and State of Indiana, Deceased at a Public Auction, held at the Late dwelling of the Said Deceased on the fifth day of September, A.D. 1838.

Sarah Griffith	1 Cup Board	$ 10.00
Sarah Griffith	1 Gun	2.00
Sarah Griffith	1 Mowing Sythe	1.00
Stephenson Hair	1 Lot of Geese	5.37 1/2
Sarah Griffith	1 Pided Calf	2.75
Sarah Griffith	1 Blush Cow	15.75
Sampson Caster	1 Pided Cow	13.00
Semour Shirts	1 Brindle Bull	7.00
Semour Shirts	1 Red Cow	18.00
Sarah Griffith	1 Sorrel Mare	25.00
Thomas West	1 Sorrel Colt	20.00
John Lacy	1 Sorrel Mare	35.50
John Wheeler	1 Bay Colt	19.62 1/2
	Whole Amount	$175.50

Joseph Lutz

State of Indiana)
Hamilton County) The above named Joseph Lutz, makes oath that the above is a true and Just Account of the sale of the Personal Estate of Eliza Griffith, late of said County, Deceased.

Sworn before Me, a Justice of the Peace of said County, the 1st day of October, 1838.

Samuel Dale (Seal)
Justice of the Peace

JACOB WEESE'S ESTATE

An Inventory of the Goods, Chattles and Effects of Jacob Weese, late of Hamilton County and State of Indiana, deceased. Taken by Samuel S. Mc Grew and Sarah Weese, Administrators of the Estate of the Said Deceased, with the assistance of James Edwards and John Wallace and George W. Kirkendale, called and duly sworn for that purpose.

1 Yoke of Oxen	$ 70.00
10 Head of Sheep	20.00
1 Sow and Shoat	4.00
9 Head of Hogs	9.00
1 Old Cow and Calf	12.50
1 Young Cow and Calf	15.00
1 Heiffer	6.50
1 Plough Share	1.50
1 Iron Wedge	.75
1 Well Bucket	1.00
1 Barrel	.50
1 Kettle	3.00
1 Pot, Oven and Tea Kettle	2.75
1 Kettle	3.00
1 Oven	1.00
3 Axes	2.00
1 Iron Square	.37 1/2
1 Bridle and Martingill	.75
1 Pair of Chains	1.25
1 Back Band and Bell Collar	.65
1 Lot of Iron	1.25
1 Tub and Meat	3.50
1 Wash Tub	.50
1 Pack of Wool	1.75
1 Cickle	.50
1 Scythe	2.00
1 Rifle Gun	8.00
1 Mantle Clock	16.50
1 Dresser Ware	2.50
1 Table	.25
1 Spinning Wheel	1.00
1 Churn	.50
6 Chairs	.50
1 Seive and Tray	.50
1 Box of Books	4.00
1 Razor and Box	1.25
1 Bed and Bedding	10.00
1 Bed and Bedding	4.00
1 Lot of Flax	1.00
1 Knot Marol (?)	.50
Whole Amount	$218.50 1/2

Given under our hands, this 24th day of April, 1838.

John Wallace, Appraisers

```
                                   his
                        James    X   Edwards
                               mark
                                   his
                        George   X   Kirkendall
                                mark
                             (Appraisers)
```

     Personally appeared before Me the undersigned, Justice of the Peace,
John Wallace, James Edwards, and George W. Kirkendale, the above named
Appraisors and was duly Sworn that the within was a Just and true Inventory
of the Goods, Chattles and Effects of Jacob Weese, according to the best
of their Judgment.

     Given under My Hand, this 20th day of May, 1838.

                              Eliza Brock,   (Seal)
                              Justice of the Peace

     Account of Sales of the Personal Property of Jacob Weese, late of the
County of Hamilton and State of Indiana, Deceased at a Public Auction held
at the Late dwelling House of the Said Deceased on the 15th day of May,
A.D. 1838.

George W, Kirkendall	1 Manl (?)	$	.37 1/2
George W. Kirkendall	1 Iron Wedge		.25
Leonard Medsker	1 Cickle		.25
Joseph W. Heaton	1 Cickle		.12 1/2
Leondard Medsker	1 Pr. Traces, Backband		1.26
John Weese	1 Bridle & Martingills		.75
Joseph W. Heaton	1 Axe		.61
Greene Lanham	1 Axe		.37 1/2
Geo. W. Kirkendall	1 Plough		.75
John Weese	1 Bell Collar		
John Kirkendall	1 Sythe		2.12 1/2
Geo..W. Kirkendall	1 Oven		1.00
Geo. W. Kirkendall	1 Barrel		.31 1/4
Sarah Weese	1 Barrel of Meat		1.00
Uriah Kirkendall	1 Glass		.19
Uriah Kirkendall	1 Gun		8.24
Uriah Kirkendall	1 Kettle		2.62
Samuel Stuart	1 Shot Pouch		.16 1/2
Sarah Weese	1 Lot of Looking Vessels		1.00
Ditto	1 Kettle		2.25
Ditto	1 Clock		7.00
Ditto	1 Axe and Hachet		1.50
Ditto	1 Box of Books		2.00
Ditto	1 Bed and Bedding		4.00
Ditto	1 Bed and Bedding		4.00
Ditto	1 Lot of Hogs		10.62 1/2
Samuel T. Mc Grew	1 Cow and Calf		11.00
John Weese	1 Yoke of Oxen		69.00
Samuel Stuart	1 Razor and Box		1.25
			$133.89

May 15th, A.D. 1838   Attest: David Heaton, Clerk of Sale
                            Samuel T. Mc Grew)
                            Sarah Weese   ) Administrators

State of Indiana)
Hamilton County)   The above named, David Heaton, makes oath that the above
is a true and just account of the Sale of the Personal
Estate of Jacob Weese, late of Said County, Deceased.

Sworn before me, A Justice of the Peace of Said County,
this 15th day of May, A.D. 1838.

Eliza Brock, (Seal)
Justice of the Peace

THOMAS CHAPPELL'S ESTATE

An Inventory of the Goods, Chattles and Effects of Thomas Chappell, late of Hamilton County and State of Indiana, deceased, taken by Benjamin Chappell administrator of the Estate of the Said Deceased with the assistance of Levi Hains and Asa Bales, Appraisers of Called and duly affirmed for that purpose.

1 Beawear	$ 15.00
1 Mantle Clock	10.00
6 Windsor Chars & Setter	7.00
1 Saddle, Rope and Blanket	8.75
1 Bridle and Martingills	1.50
1 Bedstead and Cord	3.50
1 Pair of Saddle Bags and Lock	3.00
1 Lot of Books (7 in number)	1.87 1/2
2 Pocket Books	.75
1 Umbrella & Horse Whip	.37 1/2
1 Pair of Match Planes	3.00
1 Single for Do Do	1.25
1 Double Smooth Plane	1.25
2 Bead Plane	1.50
1 Jack and Smoothing Plane	2.00
1 Slitting, Gage & Thumb Gage	.50
1 Steel Blade and Square	1.00
1 Tenor Saw	1.50
1 English Rule	.75
1 Set of Table Planes	1.50
1 Rabbit Plane	.50
1 Foot Box	.31 1/4
	66.81
1 Lot of Building Timber	5.00 .
	71.81 1/4
1 Slate	.25
Whole Amount	$ 72.06 1/4

Given under our Hands, this 10th day of the Ninth Month, 1838.

Levi Haines)
Asa Bales) Appraisors

To the foregoing, May be added One Receipt on Benjamin Bates for
Note left with him in Ohio for Collection Amounting to $ 33.17 1/2

An Account on Benjamin Chappell   2.87 1/2
                                                                  $ 36.05

Given under My hand this 10th day of the 9th Month, 1838.

                                        Benjamin Chappell,
                                            Administrator

State of Indiana)
Hamilton County) To Wit:
                  Personally appeared before Me, Benjamin Wheeler, a Justice
                  of the Peace in and for said County, Benjamin Chappell,
                  Administrator of the Estate of Thomas Chappell, deceased
                  and Levi Hains and Asa Bales, Appraisors of Said Estate
                  and being duly affirmed the said Levi Haines and Asa Bales
                  say that the above Inventory and Appraisement as Signed
                  by them is a Just and true Inventory and Appraisement of
                  the Goods, Chattles and Effects of the said Thomas Chappell,
                  to the best of their Judgement. And the said Benjamin
                  Chappell, says that the above is a true Inventory of the
                  Personal Estate of the said Thomas Chappell, so far as the
                  same has come to his hands to be Administered.

                                        B. Wheeler   (Seal)
                                        Justice of the Peace

SALE BILL

Account of the Sales of the Personal Property of Thomas Chappell, Late
of the County of Hamilton and State of Indiana, Deceased, at a Public Auction
held at the Late Residence of the Said Deceased, on the 22nd day of September,
A.D. 1838.

Robert Thomason	1 Jack Plane	$	.50
Asa Bales	1 Smooth Plane		1.43
Robert Thomason	1 Smoothing Plane		.87 1/2
Robert Thomason	1 Smoothing Plane		2.00
Asa Bales	1 Set of Match Planes		.50
Asa Bales	1 Rabbit Plane		.43
Asa Bales	1 Reed Plane		.50
Asa Bales	1 Square		.93
Robert Thomason	1 Gauge		.96
Allen Barker	1 Tenant Saw		1.25
Benjamin Chappell	1 Rule		.62
William Wheeler	1 Set of Match Planes		3.12 1/2
Benjamin Wheeler	1 Whip and Umbrella		.06 1/4
Benjamin Chappell	1 Slitting Gauge		.50
John Chappell	1 Saddle and Blanket		8.00
John Chappell	1 Sheep Skin		.75
Benjamin Chappell	1 Pair of Saddle Bags		3.00
Philip Hale	1 Martingill		.37 1/4
Isaac Stubs	1 Bridle		2.25

Benjamin Chappell	1 Box	$	.12 1/2
Frederick Shall	1 Bedstead		3.56
Isaac Stubs	1 Bed Cord		.37
Isaac Stubs	1 Mantle Clock		16.00
Asa Bales	1 Grammer Book		.31 1/4
Benjamin Chappell	1 Book		.25
John Chappell	1 English Reader		.25
Asa Bales	1 Explanatory		.12 1/2
Benjamin Chappell	1 Arthmetic		.12 1/2
Philip Hall	1 Hymn Book		.25
Asa Bales	1 Dissipline Book		.12 1/2
Killiam Hains	1 Question Book		.06 1/4
John Chappell	1 Pocket Book		.25
Benjamin Chappell	1 Beawean		12.00
Benjamin Chappell	1 Set of Windsor Chairs		5.00
Asa Bales	1 Setter		4.00
B. Chappell	1 Slate		.12 1/2
Solomon Wage	1 Lot of Lumber		4.25

Israel Hains, Clerk
September 22, 1838

State of Indiana)
Hamilton County)   The above named Israel Hains, makes oath that the above
is a Just and True Account of the Sale of the Personal
Property of Thomas Chappell, Late of Said County, Deceased, sworn to before Me, a Justice of the Peace of
said County, the 22nd day of September, 1838.

B. Wheeler, (Seal)
Justice of the Peace

NATHAN KELLY'S ESTATE

An Inventory of the Goods, Chattles and Effects of Nathan Kelly, late
of Hamilton County and State of Indiana, deceased, taken by Allen Cole,
Administrator of the Estate of the said Nathan Kelly, deceased, with the
assistance of Zenas Beckwith and Jacob Collip, Appraisors, called and duly
Sworn for that purpose.

7 Head of Sheep	$ 10.00
1 Yoke of 2 year old Oxen	20.00
1 Yoke of 3 year old Swayback	
and Slim Horn Oxen	20.00
1 2 Year Old Red Bull	10.00
1 Small 2 Year Old Red Steer	4.50
8 1 Year Old Small Cows 5 S. 3 H.	40.00
1 Old Red Cow	10.00
1 Black Cow	10.00
1 Red White faced Cow	11.00
1 Brindle Line Back Cow	12.00
1 Spotted Cow	10.00
1 Old Speckeled Cow	10.00

2 Bull Calves	$ 4.00
1 Gray Horse	35.00
1 Old Mare 4 Colts	20.00
1 2 Year Old Bay Horse Colt	22.50
1 2 Year Old Sorel Mare Colt	20.00
3 Sows	6.00
1 Sow and 3 Pigs	3.00
19 Shoats Common Size and 12 Small	13.00
5 Hogs in Pen	8.50
1 G. Stone 1/2 Owned by W. Feerce 1/2 Valued	.75
2 Axes and 1 Mattock	3.50
2 Weeding Hoes	1.00
1 Shovel	.50
1 Iron Wedge	.75
1 Old Cary Plow and Share	1.00
2 Ox Yokes with 3 Mugs & Steeples	3.50
2 Log Chains	3.50
1 Plough Clevis and Stretchers	4.00
1 Set of Double Trees and Clevis	1.50
1 Sled	1.00
1 Wheel Barrow	.25
1 Mans Saddle	3.00
Horse Collar, 1 Set of Chains, 3 traces, 1 Blump and 2 M. Dug Bridle	4.00
2 Shaving Knives, 1 Hammer, 1 Auger, 1 File, 1 Chezzel, 1 File, 1 Sprinchers	1.50
1 Hand Saw	1.25
1 Set of Steel Yards	.75
1 Axe, 1 Horse Shoe	.25
1 Sythe and Ring, 2 Ribs and Heel Wedge	.25
2 Rakes, 1 Pitchfork, 1 Half Bushel, 2 Riddles	.75
3 Old Boxes	.25
1 Curry Comb	.25
1 Large Pot	1.50
1 Sugar Kettle	3.00
1 Oven, 1 Tea Kettle, 1 Stew Kettle, 1 Speder and Cad, 1 Pan, 1 Hook, 1 Copper Kettle	4.00
1 Fire Shovel and Old Hand Irons	.75
1 Dreping Iron	.50
2 Tin Buckets, 1 Wash Pan, 1 Wooden Bucket, 1 Large Pan, 1 Coffee Pot 1 Coffee Boiler	1.87 1/2
2 Tin Pans, 5 Tin Cups, 4 Crocks, 1 Jar, 1 Dish, 1 Wooden Bowl, 3 Crocks, 1 Churn	1.25
1 Cheese Press and Hoops	1.50
4 Old Sickles	.50
1 Old Well Bucket	.50

1 Meat Barrel	$ .37
8 Chairs and 1 Little One	2.00
1 Bucket at Well	.37 1/2
2 Basket, 1 Old Keg	.25
1 Cubboard	1.00
1 Table	2.00
1 Safe	.75
2 Sets of Plates, Cups, Saucers 1 1/2 Sets, 1 Tea Pot, 1 Sugar Bowl	
1 Set of Bowls, 2 Dishes, 2 Set of Knives and Forks, Cream Cup, Satts, 2 Glass Tumblers, 2 Tea Canesters, 6 Bottles, Part One Set of Table Spoons, 1 Set of Tetanted Spoons, 1 Tea Board, 1 Coffee Mill, 1 Small Tray, 1 Wooden Colw ?	6.12 1/2
1 Feather Bed, 1 Under Bed, Beadstead and Cord and 2 Sheets	
1 Quilt and Blanket	15,00
1 Quilt and Blanket	15.00
1 Quilt and Blanket	10.00
1 Trundle Bed	3.00
1 Bedstead and Cord	1.00
1 Spare Bedding, Blankets, Quilts, Sheets, Etc.	10.00
1 Big Wheel	1.00
1 Little Wheel	1.50
1 Lanthern, Flower Barrel, 1 Meal Barrell and Vinegar Keg	.75
1 Bible, Atlas, Map and Other Books	3.50
1 Small Chest	.50
1 Slate	.12 1/2
1 Flase Hackle	1.00
2 Meat Tranghs, 1 Jar, 1 Old Barrel	1.00
1 Part of a Kilno of Bricks	12.50
1 Stack of Oats	15.00
1 Part of Oats	7.50
1 Mow and a Part of Wheat	65.00
1 Stock of Hay, No. 1, South Stack	7.50
1 Stack of Hay, No. 2, North of No. 1	6.50
1 Stack of Hay in Orchard	6.50
1 Lot of Corn and Upland	24.00
1 Lot of Corn in Bottom	41.50
1 Colt	
Whole Amount	$630.12 1/2

Allen Cole, Administrator

Given under Own Hands, this 20th day of October, A.D. 1838.

Jacob Collip)
) Apprs.
Zenas Beckwith)

State of Indiana)
Hamilton County) To Wit: Personally appeared before Me, John Collip, A
                    Justice of the Peace in and for said County Allen Cole,
                    Administrator of the Estate of Nathan Kelly, deceased
                    and Zenas Beckwith and Jacob Collip, one of the Appra-
                    isors of said Estate and being by Me, duly Sworn the
                    said Zenas Beckwith, say that the above Inventory and
                    and Appraisement as Signed by Him is a Just and True
                    Inventory and Valuation of the Goods, Chattles and
                    Effects of the said Nathan Kelly to the best of His
                    Judgment and the said says that the above is a true
                    Inventory of the Personal Estate of the said Nathan
                    Kelly so far as the same has come to His hands to be
                    Administrated, this 12th day of November, A.D. 1838.

                                        John Collip, (Seal)
                                        Justice of the Peace

        The above named Allen Cole and Jacob Collip being duly sworn
by Me, Samuel Dale, a Justice of the Peace of said County, this 13th day
of November A.D. 1838.

                                        Samuel Dale, (Seal)
                                        Justice of the Peace

        Amount of the Property taken at the Appraised Value by the Widdow of
the Late Nathan Kelly, deceased of Hamilton County and State of Indiana,
To Wit:

7 Head of Sheep	$ 10.00
1 Black Cow	10.00
1 Brindle Line Back Cow	12.00
1 Spotted Cow	10.00
1 Gray Horse	35.00
1 Sow and 3 Pigs	3.00
5 Hogs in Pen	8.00
1 Shoat	1.00
1 Half Grindstone	.75
2 Axes and 1 Mattock	3.50
2 Weeding Hoes	1.00
1 Iron Wedge	.75
1 Old Cary Plough	1.00
1 Plough, Clevis and Stretchers	4.00
1 Set of Double Trees and Clevis	1.50
1 Mans Saddle	3.00
1 Set of Stillyards	.75
1 Large Pot	1.50
1 Oven, Tea Kettle, Stew Kettle, pot Hooks, and Spider	4.00
1 Fire Shovel and Old Hand Irons	.75
1 Dressing Iron	.50
2 Tin Buckets, 1 Wash Pan, 1 Wooden Bucket, 1 Tin Pan, Coffee Pot and Quart Pot	1.87
1 Cheese Press and Hoops	1.50

```
2 Tin Pans, 5 Tin Cups, 4 Crocks,     $
  1 Jar, 1 Dish, 1 Wood Bowl, 5
  Crocks, 1 Old Churn                    1.25
1 Meat Barrel                             .37 1/2
8 Chairs and One Little One              2.00
1 Bucket at Well                          .37 1/2
1 Table                                  2.00
1 Stack of Hay                           6.50
1 Part of Stack of Oats                  7.00
1 Sled                                   1.00
2 Old rakes, 1 Pitchfork, 1 Old
  Half Bushels, 2 Laddles                 .75
3 Boxes                                   .25
2 Set of Plates, cups and Saucers, 1
  1/2 Set, 1 Tea Pot, 1 Sugar Barrel
  1 Set of Bowls, 2 Dishes, 1 Set of
  Knives and Forks, Cream Cup, 1 Salt,
  2 Glass Tumblers, 2 Tea Canesters,
  6 Bottles, Part of Set of Tablespoons,
  1 Set of Putar Tea Spoons, Tea Board,
  1 Coffee Mill, 1 Small Tray, 1 Wooden
  Bowl                                   6.12 1/2
1 Feather Bed, Under Bed, Bedstead and
  Cord, 2 Sheets, 6 Towels, 1 Quilt     15.00
1 Do  Do                                15.00
1 Do Do                                 10.00
1 Trindle Bed                             .50
1 Spar Bedding, Blanket, Quilts, Sheets,
  Etsc.                                 10.00
1 Lathern, 1 Plough, Barrel Meal Barrell
  and Vinegar Keg                         .75
1 Bible, Map and other Books            3.50
1 Slate                                   .12 1/2
1 Flax Hackle                           1.00
1 Mow and Part of Wheat                65.00
              Whole Amount        $269.37 1/2
```

The above included One Hundred Dollars, subject to be taken by the Widdow as is allowed by Law. Which leave said Widdow indebted to Said Estate in the Sum of One Hundred and Sixty Nine Dollars and Thirty Seven and 1/2 Cents.

```
                              Jacob Collip   ) Appraisors
                                             )  of Said
                              Zenas Beckwith )   Estate
```

BILL OF SALE

Account of Sales of the Personal Property of Nathan Kelly, Late of Hamilton County and State of Indiana, Deceased at Public Auction held at the Late dwelling House of the said Deceased on the 20th day of October, A.D. 1838.

Peter Princehouse	1 Hovel	$ .36	
Jacob Collip	1 Big Wheel	1.31 1/4	
Allen Cole	1 Well Bucket	.50	
John Mooney	1 Box & Lumber	.43 3/4	
Peter Princehouse	1 Bedstead	1.00	
Suel Willes	1 Wheel Barrow	.25	
Joshua Hamilton	1 Log Chain	2.37 1/2	
Joshua Hamilton	1 Log Chain	3.06 1/4	
Eliza Hutson	1 Sugar Kettle	3.06 1/4	
William Kelly	1 Hammes & Traces	4.62 1/2	
Levi Allman	1 Shaving Knife	.25	
Joshua Hamilton	1 Auger	.25	
Isaac Stephens	1 Shaving Knife	.56 1/4	
Peter Princehouse	1 handsaw	1.50	
Peter Princehouse	1 Safe	1.75	
Hutton Mc Gill	1 Cubboard	1.00	
Eliza Hutson	1 Bridle	.50	
Peter Princehouse	1 Ax Hammer & Sythe	1.00	
Zenas Beckwith	2 Ox Yokes	1.26	
John Cary	1 Yoke of Oxen	25.50	
Peter Princehouse	1 White Face Cow	15.00	
Eliza Hutson	1 Speckle Cow	10.00	
Peter Princehouse	1 Red-White Face Cow	9.00	
Suel Wylis	1 Calf	2.25	
Suel Wyllis	1 Calf	2.12	
Horace Stowell	1 Small Steer	5.26	
Horace Stowell	1 Small Steer	5.62	
Suel Wyllis	1 Brindle Steer	5.62	
Suel Wyllis	1 Steer	6.12	
Horace Stowell	1 Steer	3.50	
Bennana Freel	1 Heiffer	6.00	
Bennana Freel	1 Line Back Heiffer	6.00	
James Dennand	1 Bull	12.00	
William Peck	1 Steer, 2 yrs. Old	6.37	
Horace Stowell	1 Yoke of Oxen	20.00	
Jacob Benjamin	1 Sorrel Colt	28.00	
William Fleetwood	1 Colt Horse	25.06 1/4	
Elza Hutson	1 Mare Horse	12.00	
Zenas Beckwith	1 Stack of Hay at Crib	9.12	
James Dennand	1 Stack at Barn	10.75	
Zenas Beckwith	1 Stack of Oats	18.00	
Elza Hutson	1 Trangh (?)	.76	
Suel Wyllis	1 Barrel	.26	
William Kelly	1 Trangh (?)	.50	
A. Ferguson	1 Lot of Corn	30.50	
Eli Budd	1 First Lot of Bricks 3000	9.43	
Zenas Beckwith	1 2nd Lot of Bricks, 3000	9.12 1/2	
James Dennand	1 3rd Lot of Bricks, 3000	9.43	
William Kelly	1 Lot of Corn in Bottom	30.00	
Edwin G. Ceawal	2 Hogs	6.78	
Horace Stowell	15 Head of Hogs	13.00	
William Kelly	1 Colt	10.00	
	Whole Amount	$389.01	

Test: Jacob Collip
      Clerk of Said Sale

Allen Cole,
    Administrator

State of Indiana)
Hamilton County) The written named, Jacob Collip, makes oath that the
                   within is a Just and True Account of the Sale of the
                   Personal Estate of Nathan Keily, late of Said County,
                   Deceased.
                   Sworn before Me, Samuel Dale, a Justice of the Peace
                   of Said County, the 18th day of November, 1838.

                                        Samuel Dale   (Seal)
                                        Justice of the Peace

ESTATE OF WM. PIGGOTT

An Inventory of the Goods, Chattles and Effects of William Piggott,
Late of Hamilton County, State of Indiana, Deceased. Taken by John Piggott
and Phebe Piggott, Administrators of the Estate of the Said Deceased, with
the assistance of James Fisher and Joseph Sumner, Appraisors, called and
duly qualified for that Purpose:

1 Red Cow and Calf and Bell	$ 16.75	
1 Bay Mare	40.00	
1 Bell	.75	
1 Gray Mare	55.00	
1 Set of Hogs (5)	6.00	
1 Lot of Flax	1.00	
1 Lot of Wheat in the Field	7.00	
1 Lot of Hogs (14)	17.00	
1 Year old Steer	3.00	
1 Rear Shear Plough	2.00	
1 Hoe	.67	
1 Iron Wedge	.62	
1 Pair of Gears	2.50	
1 Reap Hook	.62	1/2
1 Lot of Plunder	1.25	
1 Plough and 2 Clevices	2.00	
1 Tub and Basket	1.00	
4 Tubs and Lids	3.12	1/2
2 Gums, 3 Twbs.	1.75	
1 Bell	.75	
1 Ax	1.50	
1 Mans Saddle	10.00	
1 Rifle Gun and Shot Pouch	10.00	
1 Lot of Wool	2.00	
1 Cradle	.37	
1 Big Pot	1.50	
1 Stew Kettle	1.00	
1 Churn	.75	
1 Oven, Lid and Skillet	2.00	
1 Tea Kettle	1.50	
1 Shobel and Tongs	1.25	

Cubboard Ware in a Srump (?)	$	6.00
1 Razor, Box and Strap		1.43
1 Lot of Ales, Gimlets, Whetstones		.62
1 Pair of Brushes		.25
5 Bottles		.75
1 Lot of Books, 4 in number		.62 1/2
1 Slate		.50
1 Looking Glass		.75
1 Mantle Clock		10.00
1 Beawreath and Cober		9.00
1 Table		1.25
1 Set of Chairs		2.50
1 Coffee Mill		.50
1 Bucket		.50
1 Vials		.20
1 Bed, Bedstead & Bedding & Curtains		20.00
1 Bed, Bedstead, Curtains & Bedding		6.00
1 Flat Iron		.25
1 Chain Halter and Bell		.50
Whole Amount		$256.15

Given under Our Hands this 13th day of July, 1838

James Fisher)
Joseph Sumner) Appraisors

Given under Our Hands this 13th day of July, 1838

John Piggott)
Phebe Piggott) Administrators

State of Indiana)
Hamilton County) Personally appeared before Me, B. Wheeler, a Justice of the Peace in and for said County, John Piggott and Phebe Piggott, Administrators of the Estate of William Piggott, deceased and James Fisher and Joseph Sumner, Appraisors of said Estate and being duly qualified the said James Fisher and Joseph Sumner, says that the above Inventory and Appraisement as signed by them is a Just and True Inventory and Valuation of the Goods, Chattles, and Effects of the said William Piggott, the Rest of them, Judgement, and the said John and Phebe Piggott, says that the above is a true Inventory of the Personal Estate of the said William Piggott, so far as the same has come to their hands to be administrated.

B. Wheeler, J.P. (Seal)

Account of the Sales of the Personal Property of William Piggott, late of the County of Hamilton and State of Indiana, Deceased at Public Auction held at the late dwelling house of the said Deceased on the 9th of August, A. D. 1838:

George Hayworth   1 Meal Tub $ .87

Phebe Piggott	1 Lot of Tubs	$ 1.50
George Hayworth	1 Tub	.37 1/2
Enos Hiatt	1 Barrell of Seeds	.31 1/4
Levi Sumners	3 Gimis (?)	.18 3/4
Pleasant Bond	2 Manls (?)	.37 1/2
Enos Hiatt	1 Lot of Horse Shoes	.18 3/4
Levi Sumners	1 Axe	.38
Phebe Piggott	1 Hoe	.25
George Hayworth	1 Curry Comb	.06 1-4
James Moreow, Sr.	1 Chain	.45
Phebe Piggott	1 Axe	1.00
George Hayworth	1 Sicel	.50
Johnathan Hayworth	1 Wedge	.65
Phebe Piggott	1 Parcel of Gears	2.00
Levi Sumners	1 Bell	.18 3/4
John Piggott	1 Bell	1.05
Phebe Piggott	1 Plough	2.00
John Piggott	1 Plough	2.00
Pleasant Bond	1 Cradle	.18 3/4
John Piggott	1 Slate	1.00
George Hayworth	1 Set of Alls	.31 1/4
Levi Sumners	1 Bar of Lead	.12 1/2
George Hayworth	1 Whetstone	.11
Timothy Sumners	1 Whetstone	.46
Levi Sumners	1 Whetstone	.20
Enoch Jackson	1 Whetstone	.12 1/2
Timothy Sumners	2 Brushees	.16
Peter West	1 Razor and Box	1.57
Enos Hiatt	1 Bottle	.12 1/2
Levi Sumners	1 Bottle	.12 1/2
Pleasant Bond	1 Lot of Something	.18 3/4
Phebe Piggott	1 Lot of Veals	.25
Phebe Piggott	1 Clock	9.00
James Marrow	1 Gun	9.06 1/4
Daniel Piggott	1 Saddle	9.81 1/4
Trustran Davis	3 Hogs	5.12 1/2
Michael Reveal	6 Hogs	4.26
Levi Sumners	5 Hogs	3.31
Stephen Cary	1 Steer	5.44
James Marrow, Sr.	1 Steer	3.25
Phebe Piggott	1 Mare	30.00
James Piggott	1 Mare	41.06 1/4
	Whole Amount	$140.44

Nathan Hockett, Clk. of Sale

State of Indiana)
Hamilton County)   The above named Nathan Hocket, makes affermation that
the above is a Just and True Account of the Sale of the
Personal Estate of William Piggot, Late of said County,
Deceased, affirmed before Me, a Justice of the Peace of
Said County, the 9th day of August, A.D. 1838.

B. Wheeler,   (Seal)
Justice of the Peace

JOSEPH WILLIAMS' ESTATE

An Inventory made out of the Personal Property of Joseph Williams, Late Deceased of Hamilton County by and between J. Lemming and Semore Shutts, this 31st of October, A.D. 1838:

1	Mare	$ 20.00
1	Horse	40.00
1	Sucking Colt	10.00
1	Mare Colt	25.00
1	Mare Colt	15.00
3	Calves	6.00
42	Head of Hogs	90.00
3	Cows	44.00
2	Yearling Steers	9.00
9	Sheep	18.00
1	Waggon	40.00
2	Grub Hoes	1.50
1	Log Chain	2.00
1	Lot of Flax	1.00
1	Lot of Gears	3.00
1	Plough and Doubletree	4.00
50	Bushels of Corn	195.00
12	Bushels of Wheat	12.00
1	Rifle Gun	8.00
1	Mantle Clock	12.00
1	Bed and Bedding	20.00
3	Augers	1.50
15	Geese	7.50
1	Spinning Wheel	2.00
1	Loom and riging	12.00
2	Still Tubs	2.00
3	Kettles	12.00
2	Meat Tubs	1.00
1	Note of Hand, August Lemore Shutts	65.55
	Whole Amount	(Amount Erased)

Rachel Williams)
Judah Lemming)
Semore Shutts)

I hereby certify the appraisors was duly sworn before the undersigned, November 2nd, 1838.

Samuel Dale, (Seal)
Justice of the Peace

JAMES KING'S ESTATE

An Inventory of the Goods, Chattles and Effects of James King, deceased late of Hamilton County and State of Indiana, taken by John Smith, Jr., Administrator of the Estate of the said Deceased with the Assistance of Isaac Coppock and William W. Way, Appraisors called and duly qualified for that purpose.

1 Lot of Flax	$ 1.00	
1 Flat Iron	.12 1/2	
1 Coffee Mill	.50	
1 Turning Lathe and Tools	10.00	
2 Hand Saws and Drawing Knife	33.25	
5 Augers and a Jack Plane	1.50	
1 Chizzlee and 1 Pair of Compasses	1.50	
1 Barrel of Flax Seed	.75	
1 _____ Barrel	.50	
1 Wheel	.75	
1 Lot of Pot Metal	4.00	
1 Big Kettle	1.50	
1 Axe	1.50	
1 Lot of Bedding	3.00	
2 Pairs of Bedsteads	.75	
1 Bed and Bedding	10.00	
6 Chairs	.75	
1 Lot of Cubboard Ware	1.50	
1 Fiddle	2.50	
1 Spotted Heiffer	7.00	
1 Pair of Hames & Shovel	.87	
12 Fowls	1.00	
1 Lot of Corn	5.00	
Making in all	$ 59.34	

Given under Our Hands and Seals this 5th day of January, 1839.

Isaac Coppock   (Seal)
William Way   (Seal)

Given under My hand this 5th day of January, 1839.

John Smith

State of Indiana)
Hamilton County)   To Wit: Personally appeared before Me, Eliza Brock,
a Justice of the Peace in and for said County, John
Smith, Jr., Administrator of the Estate of James King,
Deceased and Isaac Coppick and Wm. W. Way, Appraisors
of Said Estate and being duly qualified the said Isaac
Coppick and William W. Way say that the above Inventory
and Appraisement as signed by them is a Just and True
Inventory and Valuation of the Goods, Chattles and
Effects of the said James King to the best of their
Judgment and the said John Smith, Jr., says that the
above is a true Inventory of the Personal Property of
the said James King, so far as the same has come to his
hands to be administrated.

Eliza Brock, J.P., (Seal)

ISAAC PRATER'S ESTATE

An Inventory of the Goods, Chattles and Effects of Isaac Prater, late of Hamilton County and State of Indiana, Deceased, taken by Peter Casteter Administrator of the Estate of the said deceased, with the assistance of Robert Lowery and Johnathan Mc Carty, Appraisors, called and duly sworned for the purpose.

1 Mantle Clock	$ 12.00	
1 Beawiean	8.00	
1 Cubboard	6.50	
1 Loom	7.00	
1 Bed and Bedding	13.00	
1 Knife, Gun and Shot Pouch	9.00	
1 Set of Waggon Tires and Hubs	1.00	
1 Oven	1.75	
2 Ploughs	1.50	
1 Box of Old Iron	3.50	
1 Lot of Old Iron	1.50	
1 Waggon Tire	.75	
1 Box of Old Iron	.50	
1 Set of Boxes (Waggon)	1.00	
1 Half Bushels	.25	
2 Draw Knives and Iron Wedge	1.00	
2 Axes	1.00	
1 Broad Axe and Hamer	1.50	
1 Lot of Tools	1.50	
1 Set of Augers and Square	2.50	
1 Lot of Tools	3.00	
1 Jointer and Plane	.50	
2 Hand Saws	2.00	
1 Big Wheel	1.00	
1 Little Wheel	2.00	
1 Pair of Britchen	1.00	
1 Cross Cut saw	5.00	
1 Large Kettle and Bales	2.50	
1 Small Kettle and Bales	1.25	
1 Saddle	3.00	
1 Grindstone	1.00	
1 Pair of Doubletrees	1.50	
6 Waggon Hubs	3.00	
1 Lot of Waggon	6.00	
1 Work Bench	1.00	
1 Copper Kettle	3.00	
1 Stew Kettle, Oven and Skillet and Tea Kettle	2.75	
1 Lot of Paints	1.75	
1 Gug and Oil	.62 1/2	
1 Fire Shovel	.37 1/2	
1 Pair of Tooth Drawers	1.00	
1 Sow and 7 Pigs	7.00	
6 Hogs	18.00	
6 Hogs and 2 Pigs	18.75	
1 Cow	11.50	
1 Calf	4.50	
1 Lot of Rent Corn	4.00	
1 Lot of Corn Cut-up	13.00	

```
1 Lot of Corn Cut-up                            $  3.00
1 Lot of Corn on the Stock                         27.25
1 Black Mare, Bell & Bridle                        21.00
1 Black Colt                                       25.00
1 Bay Filley                                       15.00
1 Pair of Horse Gears                               1.25
1 Pair of Horse Gears                                .50
1 Razor and Shaving Box                              .50
1 Churn                                              .50
1 Mattick                                           1.00
1 Waggon Hub                                       1.37 1/2
1 Pon                                                .23
1 Bay Colt                                          3.00
                         Whole Amount       $202.12 1/2
```

Given under Our hands and Seals this 16th day of November, 1838.

Jonathan Mc Carty
Robert Lowery

Notes and Amounts of Isaac Prater, deceased:

```
1 Note on David Whel                             $ 14.50
1 Note on James Warp                                2.50
1 _____ Account on Joseph Prater                  60.00
          John Wilkey;                             18.00
          Isaac Hurlock                             1.50
          Joseph Kendal                            1.12 1/2
          Abner Jones                               4.00
          James Samuel                             1.37 1/2
          George Barns                             1.12 1/2
          Enos Ratliff                              2.75
          John Wheeler                               .50
          Uriah Farlow                              1.00
          Henderson Brown                          14.00
          Feilder Low                              12.00
          Thomas Olvey                             11.50
          Abram Richart                             .62 1/2
          Westly Burget                             3.50
          Peter Casteter                            3.00
          Robert Lowery                             2.83
          John Olvey, Jr.                           1.35
          John Olvey, Sr.                           1.20
                         Whole Amount       $132.40 1/2
```

I do hereby certify that Robert Lowery and Jonathan Mc Carty was by me duly sworn to Appraise the Personal Property of Isaac Prater, deceased, late of said County on the 16th day of November, 1838.

Moses Craig,   (Seal)
Justice of the Peace

An Account of Sales of the Personal Property of Isaac Prater, late of the County of Hamilton and State of Indiana, Deceased at public auction held at the late dwelling house of the said Deceased on the 17th day of November, A.D. 1838.

H. Branan (?)	1 Lot of Old Iron	$ 1.43 3/4
John Mc Carty	1 Box of Iron	.56 1/2
H. Prater	1 Large Box of Old Iron	3.56
H. Brauhans (?)	1 Lot of tools	1.31
John Mc Carty	1 Drawing Knife	.76
George Barns	1 Iron Wedge	.38
H. Prator	1 Drawing Knife	.12 1/2
John H. Butterfield	1 Waggon Boxes	.62 1/2
John B. Wright	1 Foot Adds	1.54
John B. Wright	1 Lot of Chizels	.43
John B. Wright	1 Lot of Tools	.95
John H. Butterfield	1 Lot of Old Tools	.75
John Mc Carty	1 Hand Ax	.85
H. Prater	1 Tougs	.37 1/2
John Mc Carty	1 Ax and Hammer	.89
Reason Lacky	1 Bar of Iron	.75
H. Prater	1 Chopping Axe	1.00
George Barns	1 Old Axe	.44
Robert Lowery	1 Half Bushel	.12 1/2
John H. Butterfield	1 Pair of Brichen	.81
John T. Kineaman	1 Set of Waggon Hubs	2.86
John Mc Carty	2 Sets of Waggon Hubs	.50
John Olvey, Sr.	1 Hand Saw and Auger	1.31
Wm. Macustry	1 Hand Saw	1.50
John T. Kinnaman	1 Frow Square	.50
Henry S. Burcham	1 2 inch Auger	1.00
Henry S. Burcham	2 Augers	.62
Henry S. Burcham	2 Augers	.62
Henry S. Burcham	2 Plainers	.50
Noah Cardvell	1 Cross Cut Saw	6.81
C. B. Whelch	1 Spinning Wheel	2.12 1/2
John B. Wright	1 Churn	.38
Moses Craig	1 Work Bench	1.13
John Mc Carty	1 Pair of Doubletrees	1.25
C. B. Welchel	1 Shovel Plough	1.62
N. Prater	1 Plough	1.62 1/2
R. Lowery	1 Dutch Oven	2.00
John Olvey	1 Man's Saddle	4.34
H. Prater	1 Set of Hubs and Tire	5.06
William Mc Kinsley	1 Iron Kettle	1.76
Samuel Richart	1 Frow	.31
R. Lowery	1 Grubbing Hoe	1.78
John Mc Carty	1 Waggon Hub	.38
James Murrey	1 Brass Kettle	3.25
Jont. Mc Carty	1 Lot of Paint	1.56
H. Prator	1 Lot of Timber	.50
John Burk	1 Set of Shaving Implements	.31
Abram Richart, Sr.	1 Gug of Oil	.40
John Olvey, Sr.	1 Pair of Gears	1.00
Robert Lamberton	1 Tooth Drawers	.31
George Barns	1 Grindstone	1.51
John Mc Carty	1 Rifle and Shot Pouch	12.00

Sally Prater	1 Loom	$	3.00
Sally Prater	1 Clock		8.00
Wm. Mc Kinsley	1 Cow		9.00
Jonathan Mc Carty	1 Calf		3.25
John H. Butterfield	2 Hogs (1st Choice)		5.25
Abram Richhart	2 Hogs (2nd Choice)		4.25
Abram Richhart	4 Hogs (3rd Choice)		3.62 1/2
Thomas Olvey	1 Black Colt		37.25
N. Prater	1 Bay Colt		17.00
Daniel Johnson	1 Lot of Corn		51.00
	Whole Amount		$223.07

Samuel Richhart

State of Indiana)
Hamilton County)   I, do hereby certify that Samuel Richhart was sworn before
Me, the undersigned, this 15th day of December, 1838.

Samuel Dale, (Seal)
Justice of the Peace

THOMAS REVEAL'S ESTATE

An Inventory of the Personal Estate of Thomas Reveal, Late of Hamilton
County, Indiana, deceased. Taken on the 29th day of September, 1838 by
William Stoops, Administrator, with the assistance of Stephen Cary and
Emory Powell, two respectable Freeholders, who were duly sworn as Appraisors.

Articles Appraised

North Field of Corn	$60.00
South Field of Corn	45.00
North Stack of Wheat	10.00
Middle Stack of Wheat	20.00
1 Gray Horse	55.00
1 Bay Horse	50.00
1 Young Bay Mare	35.00
1 Sorrel Colt	25.00
1 Bay Mare	20.00
1 Large Spotted Cow with White Face	16.00
1 Red Cow with white Face	11.00
1 Old Red Cow	6.00
1 Red and White Heiffer	8.00
1 Brindle Cow with White Face	12.00
2 Bull Calves	4.00
1 White Heiffer Calf	2.00
1 Red Heiffer Calf	1.75
1 Waggon	18.00
5 Sheep	7.50
1 Buck Sheep	.75
4 Burrows Choice	7.00
7 Head of Stock Hogs	12.00
1 Hog in Pen	1.25
4 Hogs in Pen	7.50

29 Geese	$ 2.50	
1 Two Horse Plough	3.50	
1 Hogs Head and Wheat	1.50	
1 Set of Pump Tools and Box	12.00	
1 Hand Saw	1.00	
1 Broad Axe	1.50	
1 Large Drawing Knife	.50	
1 Lot ot Tools	2.00	
1 Sythe and Irons	.25	
1 Barrel and Half Bushel	.37	1/2
1 Cary Plough Irons	1.50	
1 Log Chain	1.37	1/2
1 Shovel Plough	1.25	
1 Pair of Double Trees	1.12	1/2
1 Lot of Old Chains	.62	
1 Collar and Gears	2.50	
1 Bridle, 3 Pairs of Hams and Brichen	3.00	
1 Bell	.50	
2 Clevises and Stritchers	1.00	
1 Horse Shoe and Piece of Iron	1.00	
Halter Chain, Steeple and Hook	.50	
1 Hone and Singletree	.18	3/4
1 Frow and Iron Wedge	1.25	
2 Sickles	.62	1/2
1 Large Kettle and Bales	3.25	
1 Ten Gallon Kettle & Bales	2.25	
1 Eight Gallon Kettle & Bales	2.00	
1 Well Bucket	.50	
1 Loom and Lacklins	10.00	
1 Man's Saddle	1.00	
1 Side Saddle	1.50	
1 Man Saddle and Sheep Skin	11.00	
1 Hand Saw and Auger	1.25	
1 Axe	1.25	
1 Axe	1.50	
1 Barrel	.25	
2 Barrel and 1 Gun	.37	
1 Grinwheel and Chain Frame	.62	1/2
1 Grindstone and Tar Can	.25	
Soap and Barrel	.75	
1 Meal Serve	.37	
1 Large Oven and Lid	.50	
1 Riding Bridle	.37	1/2
1 Small Oven and Lid	1.00	
1 Tea Kettle	.50	
1 Pot and Bales	.75	
1 Flat Iron and Hammer	.37	1/2
1 Pot Trammel	1.00	
1 Rifle Gun and Shot Pouch	1.50	
1 Beawrean and Toilet	5.00	
1 Cubboard	6.00	
1 Cubbard Ware	2.00	
1 Fall Leaf Table	3.00	
1 Tin Bucket	.25	

1 Coffee Pot	$	.12 1/2
1 Looking Glass		.50
1 Quilt and 2 Coverlids		10.00
2 Pair of Beadsteads and Cords		1.50
1 Bed and Bed Clothes		7.00
1 Bed and Clothing		5.00
1 Bed and Clothing		3.00
1 Quilt and Sheet		1.50
1 Piece of Leather		1.00
1 Pair of Cotton Cards		.25
1 Basket and Craps		1.00
1 Pair of Sheep Shears		.25
1 Sugar Can		.50
1 Coffee Mill		.37 1/2
1 Fire Shovel		.06 1/4
1 Pair of Shlyards		1.25
1 Stack of Hay		4.50
5 Chairs		1.50
1 Grindstone		.12 1/2

Whole Amount	$508.56 1/4
Widdows Amount	100.00
	$ 608.56 1/4

State of Indiana)
Hamilton County) Personally appeared before Me, Samuel Dale, a Justice of the Peace in and for Said County, Stephen Cary and Emory Powell, Appraisors of the Personal Estate of Thomas Reveal, Deceased and being by Me, duly sworn the said Stephen Cary and Emory Powell, the within Inventory and Appraisement as signed by them is Good and True Inventory and Valuation of the Chattles and Effects of Thomas Reveal to the best of their Judgment, this 16th day of October, A.D. 1838.

Samuel Dale, (Seal)
Justice of the Peace

SALE BILL

James Marrow, Sr,	1 Shovel Plough	$	.50
Jonathan Chance	1 Cow Bell		.25
Michael Reveal	1 Pair of Doubletrees		.62 1/2
Peter Strait	1 Set of Breast Chains		.38
Jonathan Hayworth	1 Lot of Old Iron		1.02
Jesse Reese	1 Halter Chain		.31 1/4
Jonathan Hayworth	1 Pair of Gears		2.21
Nathan Fisher	2 Lots of Gears		1.37 1/2
James Marrow, Jr.	2 Clevices, 1 Stretcher		.75
Stephen Cary	2 Cickles		.37 1/2
Garret Wall	1 Dinner Pot		.62
Emory Powell	1 Meal Tub		.25
Jonathan Hayworth	1 Blind Halter		.18 3/4
James Morrow, Jr.	1 Log Chain		1.44
Edward Bray	1 Iron Wedge		.69

74

Mathew Kirkendall	1 Frow	$	.50
James Morrow, Sr.	1 Chopping Axe		.75
James Morrow, Jr.	2 Chopping Axe		1.46
Michael Reveal	1 Saddle		.62
Michael Reveal	1 Side Saddle		.37 1/2
James Morrow	1 Robe or Sheep Skin		.77
Jesse Reese	1 Rifle Gun		1.16
Emory Powell	1 Bull Plough		.50
John Scott	1 Barcels & Gum		.25
Martin Davis	1 Loom and Apparatus		2.62
Martin Davis	1 Set of ___ Spolls		2.13
Rains	1 Skillet and Bales		3.00
Daniel Applegate	2 Bull Calves		4.31 1/4
Daniel Applegate	1 Red Heiffer		2.00
Seth Beason	10 Head of Geese		3.31
Wm. Strickland	1 Old Red Cow		8.00
Samuel Monroe	1 Pided Heiffer		7.59
Thomas Reveal	1 Brindle Cow		12.43 3/4
Stephen Cary	1 White Spotted Cow		16.27
Thomas Sally	13 Head of Stock Hogs		13.00
Jonathan Hayworth	2 Horse Waggon		19.12 1/2
Moses Reveal	1 Sorrel Mare		30.00
Thomas Reveal	1 Brown Horse		45.00
Samuel Monroe	1 Gray Horse		48.31
Ebenezar Hurlock	1 Sorrel Colt		21.00
Mathew Kirkendall	1 Lot of Corn		31.96 1/4
Thomas Reveal	2 Lot of Corn		21.01 1/4
Thomas Reveal	3 Hogs		6.06 1/4
James Rains	1 Bareshear Plough		2.00
Moses Reveal	1 Set of Pump Tools		10.00
Henry Marshall	1 But of Wheat Stack		6.56 1/4
To The Widow	1 2nd Stack of Wheat		8.00
Thomas Reveal	1 3rd Stack of Wheat		15.06 1/4
Mathew Kirkendall	1 Sythe		.35
Jonathan Chance	1 Iron Square		.25
Moses Reveal	1 Broad Axe		1.50
Emory Powell	1 Hand Saw		1.06 1/4
Seth Beason	1 Jack Plane		.32
Jonathan Chance	1 Drawing Knife		.31
Moses Reveal	1 2 Inch Chizel		.31 1/4
Stephen Cary	1 2 Inch Chizel		.06 1/4
Wm. Stoops	1 Small Drawing Knife		.18 3/4
Stephen Cary	2 Augers		.31 3/4
Emory Powell	3 Quarter Augers		1.50
Moses Reveal	1 Hammer		.17
Emory Powell	1 Tub and Wheat		1.50
Stephen Cary	1 Briddle and Barrel		.12
Stephen Cary	1 Half Bushel		.18 3/4
Stephen Cary	1 Lot of Leather		.75
Stephen Cary	1 Tar Bucket & Grindstone		.12 1/2
Thomas Reveal	2 Augers and Hand Saw		.43 3/4
Emory Powell	1 Sugar Tub		.37 1/2
Allen Barker	1 Well Bucket		.12 1/2
Emory Powell	1 Basket and implements		.62 1/2

Robert Tailor	1 Pair of Sullyards	$ 1.08
Thomas Reveal	1 Curry Comb	.06 1/4
Elizabeth Reveal	1 Crack Reel	.31 1/4
Stephen Cary	1 Basket and Hoe	.06 1/4
To the Widow	1 Old Bay Mare	16.00
Ditto	3 Head of Sheep	7.75
Ditto	1 Buck Sheep	.75
Ditto	10 Gallon Kettle	2.25
Ditto	Soap and Barrel	.75
Ditto	Meal Serve	.37
Ditto	Small Oven and Lid	1.00
Ditto	1 Tea Kettle	.50
Ditto	1 Flat Iron and Hammer	.37
Ditto	1 Pot Trammel	1.00
Ditto	1 Cubboard	6.00
Ditto	1 Cubboard Ware	2.00
Ditto	Fall Leaf Table	3.00
Ditto	2 Inch Bucket	.25
Ditto	1 Coffee Pot	.12
To the Widow	1 Looking Glass	.50
Ditto	3 Quilts and Coverlid	10.00
Ditto	2 Pair of Bedsteads	1.50
Ditto	2 Bedsteads and Cords	7.00
Ditto	1 Bed and Bedding	5.00
Ditto	1 Bed and Bedding	5.00
Ditto	1 Bed and Bedding	1.50
Ditto	1 Bed and Bedding	.23
Ditto	1 Quilt and Sheet	.37 1/2
Ditto	1 Pair of Cotton Cards	.06 1/4
Ditto	1 Coffee Mill	4.50
Ditto	1 Fire Shovel	1.50
Ditto	1 Stack of Hay	
Ditto	5 Chairs	
		$459.58 3/4

The Amount of Property sold after the Widdow had taken Her 100 Dollars at Appraisement.

Thomas G. M. Salley,
Clerk

State of Indiana)
Hamilton County) Personally appeared Thomas G. M. Sally, who being by Me duly Sworn says the within Sale Bill is correct to the best of his Judgment sworn to and Subscribed to in the presence of Me, the undersigned.

Samuel Dale, J.P. (Seal)

WILLIAM LACY'S ESTATE

An Inventory of the Goods, Chattles and Effects of William Lacy, late of Hamilton County and State of Indiana, Deceased, taken by Thomas Lamham and Charles F. White, Administrators of the Estate of the said Deceased, with the Assistance of John Bell and John Stoops, Appraisors, called and duly sworn for that purpose:

1 Pair of Stylyards	$ 3.00	
1 Lot of Tin Ware	2.50	
1 Lot of Potters Ware	.37	1/2
1 Tray, Bones & Gond (?)	.50	
1 Lot of Cubboard Ware	2.25	
1 Lot of Spoons	.75	
2 Bottles	1.00	
1 Lot of Cubboard Ware	4.62	
1 Forkes	1.25	
1 Cubboard Ware	.87	
1 Lot of Razors, Strap and Box	1.12	
1 Smoothing Iron	.50	
1 Smoothing Iron	.25	
1 Wrasp, Candlestick and Hammer	.75	
1 Lot of Books	1.00	
1 Looking Glass	.50	
1 Stramer and Rolling Pin	.25	
1 Churn	.50	
1 Tea Kettle and Pan	1.25	
1 Pair of Dog Irons	3.00	
1 Shovel	.75	
1 Oven, Lid and Hooks	1.25	
1 Sugar Kettle	3.00	
1 Lot of Yarn	5.25	
2 Trunks	1.00	
1 Gun	15.00	
1 Shovel Plough	3.00	
1 Dryed Hide	1.00	
1 Barrel	1.00	
4 Head of Sheep	10.00	
1 Black and White Cow	16.00	
1 Bridle Cow	15.00	
1 Brown Heiffer	6.00	
4 Red Calves	10.00	
1 Black and White Calf	2.50	
1 Horse	10.00	
4 Fat Hogs	17.00	
19 Head of Stock Hogs	31.00	
1 Feed Croft	.25	
1 Lot of Flax	2.00	
1 Weeden Hoe	.50	
1 Wash Tub	.50	
1 Wash Tub	.50	
1 Side Saddle	17.00	
2 Barrels	.39	
1 Mowing Sythe	2.00	
1 Cradle Sythe	3.50	
1 Cutting Knife and Box	1.25	
1 Sickle	.50	
1 Pitchfork	.25	
1 Pitchfork	.37	
1 Blind Bridle	.62	1/2

1 Black and White Cow	$ 17.00
1 _____ Straps	4.00
1 Fiftt Chain	3.00
1 _____	.39
1 Inch Auger	.50
1 Inch and Half Auger	1.50
1 Riding Bridle	12.50
3 Acres of Wheat	15.00
3 Acres of Wheat	12.00
1 Lot of Corn	37.00
1 Lot of Gears	2.00
1 Shovel	.25
1 Waggone Sheet	5.00
1 Blanket	2.25
1 Pair of Horse Hams	.25
1 Lot of Course Flour	1.00
1 Iron Wedge	.75
1 Rocking Chair	1.50
1 Bed, Bedding and Sheet	20.00
1 Bed, Bedding and Sheet	15.00
1 Bed, Bedding and Sheet	15.00
1 Cubboard	8.00
2 Tables & Cloth	6.00
1 Bag	.75
1 Serve	.50
1 Blind Bridle	2.50
2 Bee Stands	5.00
1 Lot of Gears	3.50
1 Lot of Iron	4.50
1 Lot of Barrels	2.87
1 Lot of Soap	1.00
1 Loom	12.00
1 Coffee Mill	.25
1 C. Chamber	.25
1 Pair of Stretchers and Singletrees	2.00
1 Axe	2.00
1 Wind Mill	8.00
1 Plough	6.00
1 Lot of Geese	1.75
1 Outs 25 cts per Dog Slauf ?	
1 Lot of Wheat 75 cts per Bushel	
1 Lot of Hay $600 per ton	
1 Halter Chain	.75

Given under Our Hands this 11th day of January, 1839.

John Beal
John Stoops

An Account of Notes:

An Account of James Samuel	$ 9.00
An Account of John Kirkendall	2.00

```
An Account of  Thomas J. Sharp       $   8.00
An    Do       James Sharp               .50
An    Do       Thomas L. Tharp          3.00
An    Do       _____ Lanham           3.56 1/4
An    Do       B. L. Dunning            2.00
An    DO       Robert Stuart            1.00
An    Do       John Lacy                2.50
An    Do       John Lacy               28.00
An    Do       John Lacy               11.12
An    Do       John Lacy                1.00
An    Do       Thomas J. Tharp          5.00
An    Do       William Reddick          1.50
An    Do       Vincent Tharp            3.50
```

State of Indiana)
Hamilton County)   Personally appeared before Me, Eliza Brock, a Justice
                    of the Peace in and for said County, Thomas Lanham and
                    Charles F. White, Administrators of the Estate of
                    William Lacy, Deceased and John Beal and John Stoops
                    says that the above Inventory and Appraisement as signed
                    by them is a Just and True Inventory and Valuation of
                    the Goods Chattles and Effects of the said William
                    Lacy to the best of their Judgment and the said Thomas
                    Lanham and Charles F. White says that the above is a
                    true Inventory of the Personal Estate of the said
                    William Lacy, so far as the same has come to their
                    hands to be Administrated.

                    Given under my hand and Seal this 12th day of January,
                    A.D. 1839.   =

                                        Elija Brock, (Seal)
                                        Justice of the Peace

SALE BILL

    Account of the Sale of the Personal Property of William Lacy, Late of
the County of Hamilton and State of Indiana, Deceased at a Public Auction
held at the Late dwelling House of the Said Deceased on the 5th day of January
A.D. 1839.

```
Reuben Stinson     1 Tin Bucket                    $   .18 3/4
Elizabeth Lacy     1 Pan                               .25
John F. Greening   1 Bucket and Wash Pan              .37 1/2
James Ridgway      1 Tray and Cup                     .18 3/4
Leonard Medsker    2 Crocks                           .18 3/4
Leonard Medsker    2 Crocks                           .25
Alexander Irwin    2 Crocks                           .18 3/4
Leonard Medsker    1 Lot of Tin Ware                  .25
John F. Greening   1 Pair of Sheep Shears
                     and Tin Ware                     .37 1/4
Thomas Lanham      1 Pair of Candle Moles
                     and Tin Ware                     .25
John Lacy          1 Pair of Stillyards              3.81 1/2
```

John F. Greening	1 Lot of Sundries	$	.12 1/2
William Slater	1 Pitcher and Tea Pot		.50
William Slater	3 Plates		.38
Leonard Medsker	4 Plates		.39
Reuben Stinson	4 Plates		.25
Reuben Stinson	1 Lot of Queensware		.25
William Slater	1 Gouge Plate		.75
Robert Stuart	1 Lot of Sundries		.25
Reuben Stinson	1 Lot of Teaspoons		.18 3/4
Thomas Bradley	1 Lot of Sundries		1.00
John Scott	1 Lot of Books & Medisons		.50
Elizabeth Lacy	1 Tea Kettle		.25
Robert Stuart	1 Churn		.62 1/2
John Stoops	1 Pair of Hand Irons		2.75
John Lacy	2 Fire Shovels		1.31 1/4
Elizabeth Lacy	1 Wash Tub		.62 1/2
Russel Burroughs	1 Oven and Lid		.70
James Morrow, Sr.	1 Stew Kettle		.76
Henry Medsker	1 Large Kettle		2.00
Leonard Medsker	1 Skillet and Lid		.63
Abram Roose	1 Pot		1.06 1/4
John Scott	1 Sevre and Slate		.31 1/4
Thomas Lanham	1 Gun		11.37 1/2
Russel Burroughs	3 Chairs		1.50
Russel Burroughs	3 Chairs		1.50
John Lacy	1 Bed and Bedding		13.00
Allison Burget	1 Cubboard		10.25
John Scott	1 Bag and Meal		.81 1/4
L. Fallis	1 Bee Stand		3.75
John Stoops	1 Bee Stand		3.81 1/4
Humphrey Irwin	1 Collar and Hams		1.00
John Scott	1 Collar and Backband		.81 1/4
John Irwin	1 Collar and Hames, Bridle		.50
Abram Boose	3 Chizzles and 1 Square		.81 1/4
Russel Burroughs	1 Set of Harrow Teeth		1.62
James Marrow, Sr.	1 Lot of Sundries		1.12 1/2
John Bell	1 Lot of Chains		.64
George Kirkendall	2 Halter, Chains & Collars		1.18
Hiram Bradley	1 Barrel & Flour		1.37
Hiram Bradley	1 Barrel & Meat		.50
John Davis	1 Barrel		.25
Hiram Bradley	1 Loom		7.12 1/2
Hiram Bradley	1 Coffee Mill		.25
John Irwin	1 Axe		1.00
John Stoops	1 Barrel		.06 1/4
S. Fallis	1 Pair of Stretchers		1.00
S. Fallis	1 Pair of Singletrees		1.75
Humphrey Irwin	1 Plough		6.50
John Lacy	1 Wind Mill		2.25
Samuel Recter	1 Blind Bridle		2.00
Charles F. White	18 Doz. Oats at 25 per doz.		4.50
S. Fallis	1 Lot of Hay		12.12 1/2
John F. Greening	1 Lot of Hay		6.62
S. Fallis	28 Bushels of Wheat		28.50

John Scott	10 Bushels of Wheat	$ 10.20
Elizabeth Lacy	10 Bushels of Wheat	6.25
Robert Stuart	1 Shovel Plough	3.00
Humphrey Irwin	1 Singletree	.43 3/4
Elizabeth Lacy	1 Cow	16.00
John Lacy	1 Cow	14.00
John Stoops	1 Brown Heiffer	6.25
John Lacy	2 Calves	6.25
S. Fallis	3 Calves	6.25
Samuel Pryor	1 Horse	5.75
Hiram Bradley	1 Sow	6.31 1/2
Samuel Rector	3 Hogs	4.18 3/4
Hiram Bradley	1 Sow	3.06 1/4
Hiram Bradley	1 Sow	1.12 1/2
Hiram Bradley	1 Sow	2.12
John Stoops	1 Sow	3.00
David Mc Kinney	1 Sow	3.25
Jonas Bradfield	1 Sow	4.37
Samuel Rector	1 Sow	1.18 3/4
David Mc Kinney	1 Sow	1.12 1/2
Jonas Bradfield	1 Sow	1.12 1/2
Jonas Bradfield	1 Sow	.68 3/4
Hiram Bradley	1 Hog	1.31 1/4
Hiram Bradley	1 Sow	.06 1/4
William Strickland	1 Lot of Flax	.81 1/4
John Irwin	1 Sythe & Cradle	2.37 1/2
John Davis	1 Hoe	.40
Asa Bales	1 Pitchfork	.20
John Lacy	1/2 Pitchfork	.25
Charles F. White	1 Sickle	.12 1/2
John Lacy	1/2 Pitchfork & Knife	1.00
Geo. W. Kirkendall	1 Pair of Hip Straps	1.25
John Lacy	1 Feed Trough	.18 3/4
Geo. W. Kirkendall	2 Pair of Hip Straps	3.00
John Stoops	1 Pair of Gears	1.62 1/2
John F. Greening	1 Waggon Sheet	1.37 1/2
Samuel Rector	6 Quarter Augers	.75
Charles F. White	1 Grass Sythe	2.18 3/4
Samuel Rector	1 Fifth Chain	2.18 3/4
Elija Brock	1 Bridle	1.25
Allison Burgett	3 Acres of Wheat	9.93 1/4
David Dawson	3 Acres of Wheat	6.00
Robert Stewart	1 Lot of Corn	52.50
John Lacy	1 Pair of Horse Flemes	.26
Peter Wise	1 Chizle	.18 3/4
Abram Thomas	1 Pan	.50
John Lacy	6 Shoats	3.00
John Lacy	1 Lot of Shaving Utencils	1.18 3/4

Jacob Mull, Clerk

I do hereby certify that Jacob Mull was duly sworn by Me, that the above Sale Bill of the Goods, Chattles and Effects of William Lacy, Deceased is Just and True according to the best of his knowledge.

Given under My hand this 12th day of January, A.D. 1839.

Elija Brock, (Seal)
Justice of the Peace

JOSEPH WILLISON'S ESTATE

An Account of the Sales of Personal Property of Joseph Willison Estate, Late of Hamilton County and State of Indiana, deceased at a Public Auction held at the late dwelling house of the said Deceased on the 17th day of April, 1838.

SALE BILL

Joseph Nicholas	1 Collar	$	.87 1/2
B. Cole	1 Vinegar Keg		.31
James A. Bryan	1 Pork Barrel		.50
Joseph Nicholas	1 Barrel		.37 1/2
A. B. Cole	1 Box		.27
James S. Ross	1 Curry Comb		.06 1/4
Joseph Nicholas	1 Chopping Axe		.56
Perry Colborn	1 Bedstead		3.00
Samuel Dale	1 Clock		.44
John Huchen	1 Serve		.87
James S. Ross	1 Pot		.68
David G. Gates	1 Spider and Lid		1.00
James S. Ross	1 Lot of Blacksmith Tools		38.00
Samuel Baty	1 Barrel of Salt		8.00
James S. Ross	4 Planks		.62 1/2
James S. Ross	1 Axe		.62
Jonathan Fox	1 Hand Axe		.62
Perry Cobbourn	1 Keg, White Lead		.62
James S. Ross	1 Sythe		.12 1/2
David Gates	1 Sugar Kettle		3.00
Samuel Baty	1 Lot of Old Iron		2.00
John Mc Kee	1 Black Colt		13.00
Samuel Baty	1 Sorrel Colt		8.00
W. B. Potter	1 Bay Mare		42.00

Test: Joseph Nicholas,
Clerk of Said Sale

State of Indiana)
Hamilton County) To Wit: The above named Joseph Nicholas, makes oath
that the above is a Just and True Account of the Sale
of the Personal Estate of Joseph Willison, late of
said County, Deceased sworn to before Me, a Justice of
the Peace of said County, August 15th, 1838.

Samuel Dale, (Seal)
Justice of the Peace

The following is a list of the Personal Property of Goods, Chattles property to be appraised, belonging to the Estate of Joseph Willison,

Deceased, late of Hamilton County and State of Indiana.

1 Bay Mare	$ 30.00	
1 Black Mare Colt	12.00	
1 Sorrel Mare Colt	8.00	
1 Red Cow	13.00	
1 Red, 2 year old Heiffer	10.00	
1 Speckled Yearling Calf	3.50	
1 White Cow	15.00	
1 Set of Blacksmith Tools	45.00	
1 Barrel of Salt	9.00	
1 Box of Old Irons	2.00	
4 Axes	3.00	
1 Keg of White Lead		
(Pretty Full)	2.12 1/2	
1 Sign	1.50	
1 Hoe	.37 1/2	
1 Sow and 4 Shoats	5.00	
1 Bedstead, Shugar Tree	5.00	
1 Clock (Wall Sweeper)	1.00	
1 Kegg	.37 1/2	
1 Big Wheel (Widdow)	1.50	
1 Basket (Widow)	.50	
1 Wash Tub & Wash Board (Widow)	.50	
1 Pair of And Irons (Widow)	2.00	
4 Bed Quilts (Widow)	2.00	
1 Box Phials (Widow)	.25	
1 Rat Trap (Widow)	.25	
1 Small Oven (Widow)	.25	
1 Horse Collar	1.00	
1 Back Law	.50	
1 Barrel	1.00	
5 Barrels	2.25	
1 Writing Desk (Not Sold)	.50	
2 Crocks	.25	
1 Clock	20.00	
2 Large Kettles	3.75	
1 Stove and Pipe	16.00	
1 Brass Kettle	2.00	
1 Spider	.50	
1 Oven and Hooks	.50	
1 Pan and Tea kettle	.62 1/2	
1 Rifle Gun	8.00	
1 Table and Oil Cloth	2.00	
1 Writing Desk	2.00	
1 Chest	2.00	
1 Stand	1.00	
1 Small Chest	.25	
1 Looking Glass	.75	
5 Chairs	1.62 1/2	
2 Smoothing Irons	1.25	
1 Set of Cupboard Ware	6.00	
1 Testament	.50	
1 History of the United States		
and Maps	.75	

1 Bedstead, Bed and Bedding	$ 20.00	
1 Trunelle, Bed and Bedstead	5.00	
1 Sive	.75	
1 Lot of Planks	.50	

State of Indiana)
Hamilton County) Personally appeared before Me, Samuel Dale, a Justice of the Peace in and for said County, Samuel Baty and Samuel Monroe and say upon their oaths that the above and foregoing contains a correct Appraisement of the Personal Property propper to be Appraised belonging to the Estate of Joseph Willison, deceased so far as has come to their knowledge.

Samuel Monroe
Samuel Beaty

I hereby certify the above Appraisors was duly sworn before me, the undersigned., this 13th day of March A.D. 1838.

Samuel Dale, (Seal)
Justice of the Peace

ELISHA OLVEY'S ESTATE

Appraisement of the Property of Elisha Olvey:

1 Mantle Clock	$ 15.00	
1 Bed and Bedding	15.00	
Washing Clothes	7.00	
1 Vest	2.00	
1 Bible	.50	
1 Pocket Book	.37	1/2
2 Books	.75	
1 Razor and Shaving Box	.75	
1 Pair of Shoes and some tow Thread	.25	
1 Oven and Frying Pan	2.00	
Dresser Ware	2.00	
1 Meat Tub	.37	1/2
1 Pencil	.25	
1 Bucket	.25	
4 Hoes and Tubs	.75	
2 Chairs	.50	
Powder Horn, Shears and Purse	.50	

State of Indiana)
Hamilton County) I, John T. Kinnaman do hereby certify that Isaac Prator and Peter Castoller were qualified before Me to well and truly Appraise the Personal Property of Elisha Olvey, late of Hamilton County, Indiana, Deceased, 25th of April, 1838

John T. Kinnaman, (Seal)
Justice of the Peace

Account of Sales of the Personal Property of Elisha Olvey, late of
Hamilton County and State of Indiana, Deceased at a Public Auction held
at the Late Dwelling House of John Olvey, April 28th day, 1838.

Isaac Prater	1 Pan	$	.18 3/4
Elijah Manship	1 Caske		.50
Elijah Manship	1 Washing Tub		.25
Lucius Dayton	1 Tub		.25
Elijah Manship	1 Basket		.12 1/2
Elijah Manship	1 Fat Tub		.70
Elijah Manship	1 Hoe		.37 1/2
Lucius Dayton	1 Powder Horn & Purse		.31 1/4
Thomas Olvey	1 Pair of Shoes		.12 1/2
Thomas Olvey	1 Bottle		.12 1/2
Elijah Manship	1 Knives, Forks, Tins, Spoons, Coffee Pot		1.00
Thomas Olvey	1 Slate		.25
Elijah Manship	Tea Ware		.37 1/2
Elijah Manship	1 Razor		.14
Lucius Dayton	1 Oven		.50
Thomas Olvey	1 Frying Pan		.25
Thomas Olvey	1 Clock		
Lucius Dayton	1 Wiset		
Thomas Olvey	1 Pocket Book		.37 1/2
		$	5.83 1/2

Attest: Elijah Manship, Clk.

State of Indiana)
Hamilton County)   The above named Elijah Manship, makes oath that the
above is a Just and True account of the Personal Estate
of Elisha Olvey, Late of said County, Deceased.
Sworn to before me, a Justice of the Peace of said
County on the 21st day of March, 1839.

Moses Craig, (Seal)
Justice of the Peace

JAMES KING'S ESTATE

An Inventory of the Goods, Chattles and Effects of James King, Deceased,
late of Hamilton County and State of Indiana, taken by John Smith, Junior,
Administrator of the Estate of the said Deceased with the assistance of Isaac
Coppock and William W. Way, Appraisors called and duly qualified for that
purpose.

1 Lot of Flax	$ 1.00
1 Flat Iron	.12 1/2
1 Coffee Mill	.50
1 Turning Lathe & Tools	10.00
2 Hand saws and Drawing knife	3.25
5 Augers and 1 Jack Plain	1.50
1 Chisel and 1 Pair of Compass	.50

```
1 Barrel of Flax Seed          $    .75
1 Lite Barrel                       .50
1 Wheel                             .75
1 Lot of Pot Mettle               4.00
1 Big Kettle                      1.50
1 Axe                             1.50
1 Lot of Bedding                  3.00
2 Pair of Bedsteads                 .75
1 Bed and Bedding                10.00
6 Chairs                            .75
1 Lot of Cupboard Ware            1.50
1 Fiddle                          2.50
1 Spotted Heiffer                 7.00
1 Pair of Harness and Shovel
    Plough                          .87 1/2
1 Dozen of Fowls                  1.00
1 Lot of Corn                     5.18
              Making in all   $ 58.41
```

Given under Our Hands this 5th day of January, A.D. 1839.

Isaac Coppock
Wm. W. Way

Given under My Hand this 5th day of January, A.D. 1839.

John Smith, Junior

State of Indiana)
Hamilton County) To Wit:

Personally appeared before Me, Elijah Brock, a Justice of the Peace in and for said County, John Smith, Junior Administrator of the Estate of James King, Deceased and Isaac Coppock and Wm. W. Way, say that the above Inventory and Appraisement as signed by them is a Just and True Inventory and valuation of the Goods, Chattles, and Effects of the said James King to the best of their judgment and the said John Smith, Junior says that the above is a True Inventory of the Personal Estate of the said James King, so far as the same has come to His hands to be Administrated.

Elijah Brock, (Seal)
Justice of the Peace

A Sale Bill of the Personal Estate of James King, Deceased, sold on February 14th, A.D. 1839.

Samuel Smith	1 Axe	$ 2.43 3/4
Joseph Smith	1 Tenant Saw	1.12 1/2
Joseph Smith	1 Hand Saw	2.00
Samuel Smith	1 Inch Auger	.56 1/4
John Smith	1 Quarter Auger	.25
Samuel Baxter	1 Half Inch Auger	.25

Joseph Smith	1 5/8 Inch Auger	$	.50
Joseph Smith	1 3/16 Inch Auger		.37 1/3
Joseph Smith	1 Drawing Knife		1.00
Joseph Smith	1 Plane		.12 1/2
William W. Way	1 Pr. of Compasses		.12 1/2
Samuel Smith	1 Pr. of Hames		1.06 1/4
Joseph Smith	1 1/4 Inch Chisel		.25
Joseph Smith	1 Turning Lathe & Tools		6.00
William A. Smith	1 Shovel Plough		.18 3/4
Abraham Smith	1 Barrel		1.25
John Smith	1 Oven		.12 1/2
Mary King	1 10 Gallon Kettle		2.43 3/4
Abraham Smith	1 Stew Kettle		.93 3/4
Joseph Smith	1 Pr..of Nippers		.06 1/4
Abraham Smith	1 Fire Shovel		.68 3/4
Samuel Smith	1 Coffee Mill		1.00
William A. Smith	1 Smoothing Iron		.31 1/4
Joseph Smith	1 Lot of Flax		1.06 1/4
Mary King	1 Lot of Corn, 18 3/4 per Bushel		1.00
Mary King	1 Bucket and Pigger		.56 1/4
Mary King	1 Skellet		.25
John Smith	1 Barrel and Flax Seed		5.00
Mary King	1 Heifer		8.00
Mary King	1 Bedding		10.00
Mary King	1 Lot of Cupboard Ware		1.50
John Stafford	1 Lot of Chairs		1.00
		$	.

(Note: Amount Not Given)

I, hereby certify that William Huffman was duly Sworn that the above Bill of Sale was Just and True according to the best of his Judgement, by Me, this the 25th day of February, 1839.

                                        Elijah Brock,   (Seal)
                                        Justice of the Peace

HENRY JONES' ESTATE

An Inventory of the Goods and Chattles and Effects of Henry Jones, late of Hamilton County and State of Indiana, deceased, taken by Sally Jones, the Wife of the Deceased, the Administrator of the Estate of the said Deceased, with the assistance of Josiah Conkling and Edward Hawl, Appraisors, called and duly sworn by Me, E. Redmon, J.P., for that purpose.

1 Bay Mare	$ 40.00
1 Red and White Cow and Bell	10.00
1 Red Heiffer	5.00
1 Calf with a White Face	2.50
1 Lot of Corn and Fodder in the Shock	5.00
1 Lot of Corn in the Heap	4.00
1 Matoc	1.00
2 Axes	1.50

1 Pair of Horse Gears	$ 2.00
1 Single Tree and Clevice	.50
1 Single Tree and Stretcher	1.50
1 Bell and Colar	.50
1 Hoe	.50
1 Lot of Sheep	1.50
1 Tea Kettle and Skellet	1.00
2 Washing Tubs	1.00
2 Bridles	.50
1 Mans Saddle	.50
1 Hammer	.50
1 Meat Tub and Barrel	1.50
1 Chest	.25
1 Lot of Beding	
1 Looking Glass	.25
2 Tin Trunks	.25
1 Razor and Strap & 1 Pocket Book	1.00
2 Beds and Bedsteads	14.00
1 Loom and Riggings	3.00
1 Lot of Cupboard Ware	4.00
1 Bucket and Churn	.50
1 Family Bible	1.50
1 Sifter	.37 1/2
1 Iron Wedge	.75
1 Spinning Wheel	1.00
1 Big Wheel	1.00
1 Lot of Chairs	.00
1 Big Kettle	3.00
1 Lot of Pot Mettle	5.00
1 Shovel Plough	1.25
1 Half of a Cross Cut Saw	2.00

Josiah Conkling)
Edward Hall   ) Appraisors

Noblesville, November 30th, 1839

An Inventory of the Goods and Chattles and Effects of Henry Jones,
Late of Hamilton County and State of Indiana, Deceased, taken by Sally
His wife of the said Deceased, the Administrator of the Estate of the
said Deceased with assistance of Josiah Conkling and William Kesterson

1 Lot of Hogs	$ 22.00

Josiah Conkling)
William Kesterson) Appraisors

State of Indiana)
Hamilton County)   The above named William Kesterson came this day before
Me and was duly sworn to the above Appraisement.

Given under My Hand and Seal this 9th day of May, 1839.

Ellis Evans, J.P., (Seal)

A Late Bill of the Personal Property belonging to the estate of Henry Jones, late of Hamilton County, Indiana, Deceased, sold on the 30th day of November, 1839.

James M. Thompson	1 Pr. of Stretchers	$ 2.12 1/2
John Stinson	1/2 of a Crosscut Saw	2.12 1/2
James Bishop	1 Matoc	1.50
Sally Jones	1 Mare	10.00
		$15.74 1/2

Samuel J. Pickerill
Clerk of Sale

State of Indiana)
Hamilton County) SS The above named Samuel J. Pickerill, came personally before Me and made Oath that the above is a True Bill of Sale contained in the above Bill.

Given under My Hand and Seal, this 9th day of May, 1839.

Ellis Evans, J.P., (Seal)

ELEAZAR HOCKETT'S ESTATE

An Inventory and Appraisement Bill of the Goods, Chattles Rights, Credits, Monies and Effects which were of Eleazar Hockett, late of Hamilton County, Indiana, deceased, taken by Nathan Hockett, Administrator of said Deceased with the assistance of John Piggott and Edward Bray, two respectable freeholders of the neighborhood, as Appraisors on the 29th day of October, A.D. 1838.

Articles Appraised

1 Plough	$ 2.50
3 Chairs	1.50
1 Pair of Tongs	.50
1 Stew Kettle	1.50
1 Skellet and Lid	1.12 1/2
1 Bucket	.62 1/2
1 Churn	1.12 1/2
1 Sugar Kettle	2.00
1 Lot of Plunder	1.25
1 Hoe	.75
1 Meat Tub	1.50
1 Coffee Mill	.50
1 Table	4.00
1 Bedstead	5.00
1 Tea Kettle	1.25
1 Mantle Clock	12.00
1 Pair of And Irons	1.25
1 Lot of Books	10.50
1 Bureau	12.00
1 Bed and Bedstead and Bedding	30.00
3 Chairs	1.50
1 Cow	15.00

1 Heifer	$ 5.00	
Bottles and Table Cloths	.75	
1 Lot of Cupboard Ware	7.00	
1 Cradle	.50	
3 Crocks	.25	
1 Wash Tub	.75	
1 Pair of Gears	2.25	
1 Candlestick	.12 1/2	
1 Lard Tub	1.00	
1 Heifer Calf	2.50	
1 Lot of Hay	5.00	
1 Lot of Hogs	13.00	
1 Mare	40.00	
Corn per Bushel	.37 1/2	
1 Flat Iron	.50	
1 Bucket	.82 1/2	
1 Lot of Sawed Logs		
1 Axe	1.50	
1 Pan	.37 1/2	
2 Hogs	10.00	

Given under Our Hands, this 1st day of the 11th Month, 1838.

John Piggot and
Edward Bray
Appraisors

State of Indiana)
Hamilton County) To Wit:
Personally appeared before Me, B. Wheeler, a Justice of
of the Peace in and for said County, Nathan Hockett,
Administrator of the Estate of Eleazar Hockett, deceased
and Edward Bray and John Piggot, Appraisors of said
Estate and being duly qualified the said Edward Bray
and John Piggot says that the above Inventory and
Valuation of the Goods, Chattles and Effects of the
said Eleazar Hockett is the best of their Judgement
and the Nathan Hockett says that the above is a True
Inventory of the Personal Estate of the said Eleazar
Hockett, so far as the same has come to hsi hands to
be Administrated.
B. Wheeler, J. P., (Seal)

An Inventory of the Goods, Chattles and Effects of Eleazar Hockett,
late of Hamilton County and State of Indiana, deceased, taken by Nathan C.
Bails, Administrator Debonis non of the Estate of the late Deceased with
the assistance of James Reace and Samuel Sumner, Appraisors and duly
qualified to that purpose.

6 Saw Logs	$ 2.00	
4 Saw Logs	2.00	

Given under Our Hands this 4th day of the 3rd Month, A.D. 1839.

One Hundred Dollars on an Acknowledgement from the Estate of Nathan Hockett.

$100.00

State of Indiana)
Hamilton County) To Wit:

Personally appeared before Me, Benjamin Wheeler, a Justice of the Peace in and for said County, Nathan C. Beals, Administrator Debonas nun of the Estate of Eleazar Hockett, Deceased and James Reace and Samuel Sumner, Appraisors of said Estate and being duly affirmed the said James Reace and Samuel Sumner say that the foregoing Inventory and Valuation of the Goods and Chattles and Effects of the said Eleazar Hockett to the best of their Judgement and Nathan C. Beals says that the within is True Inventory of the Personal Estate of the said Eleazar Hockett so far as the same has come to his hands to be administered.

B. Wheeler, (Seal)
Justice of the Peace

A SALE BILL

Account of sales of the Personal Property of Eleazar Hockett, late of said County of Hamilton and State of Indiana, Deceased at a Public Auction held at the late Dwelling House of the said Deceased on the first day of November, A.D. 1838.

Joseph Powel	1 Lot of Kegs	$	.12 1/2
Nathan Fisher	1 Jug and Jar		.33 1/2
John Nickson	1 Churn		1.43 3/4
Edward Bray	1 Bucket		.81 1/4
John Baily	1 Frying Pan		.50
John Baily	1 Skellet		1.33 1/3
Nathan Fisher	1 Stew Kettle		1.62 1/2
Richard Rich	1 Tea Kettle		1.06 1/4
Jacob Shaul	1 Kettle		2.25
James Morrow	1 Hoe		1.00
Edward Bray	1 Axe		1.93
Benjamin Wheeler	1 Pair of Tongs		.68
Joseph Powel	1 Meat Tub		1.50
James Morrow	2 Chairs		1.43 3/4
James Morrow	1 Chair		.69
Levi Sumner	1 Coffee Mill		.87 1/2
Jacob Shaul	1 High Post Beadstead		5.50
Enos Hiatt	1 Bottle		.06 1/4
Jacob Shaul	1 Table		3.50
Enos Hiatt	1 Mantle Clock		11.50
Jacob Shaul	1 Cary Plough		4.50
Edward Bray	1 Pr. Harness & Chains		2.22
John Nickson	1 Cow		20.00

John Nickson	1 Heifer	$ 7.50	
John Nickson	1 Calf	4.00	
Jacob Shaul	1 Mare	40.00	
Enos Hiatt	Cup & Saucers, Spoons	1.00	
James Morrow	1 Set of Plates	.77	
Jesse Piggot	1 Sugar Bowl	.50	
John Nickson	1 Tea Pot	.64	
Enos Hiatt	Teacups & Saucers	.35	
Joseph Powel	Bowls	.37 1/2	
John Nickson	Plates	.33	
James Morrow, Jr.	1 Tea Pot	.30	
Enos Hiatt	Pans	.20	
Enos Hiatt	Knifes and Forks	1.50	
Joseph Powel	1 Tin Pan	.20	
John Baily	1 Large Tin Pan	.40	
John Baily	Tins	.30	
John Nickson	1 Coffee Pot	.37 1/2	
Nathan Hockett	1 Tin Jar	.75	
Joseph Sumner	1 Smoothing Iron	.87	
Richard Rich	1 Tin Bucket	.50	
James Morrow	1 Book	.31 1/4	
Richard Rich	1 Introduction Book	.14	
Nathan Hockett	1 Bible	.50	
Enos Hiatt	2 Books	.62 1/2	
Nathan Hockett	2 Books	5.00	
Enos Hiatt	1 Dictionary	2.25	
Richard Rich	1 Sow	4.25	
Edward Bray	2 Hogs	4.93	
Richard Rich	3 Hogs	8.37 1/2	
Henry	25 Bushels .40 cts per Bushel	10.00	
William Clampet	25 Bushels .40 cts per Bushel	10.00	
John Baily	25 Bushels .42 cts per Bushel	10.50	
George Hayworth	25 Bushels .43.3/4 per Bushel	10.93 3/4	
Ezekiah P. Harold	25 Bushels .43 3/4 per Bushel	10.93 3/4	
Benjamin Sturdivan	25 Bushels .44 per Bushel	11.00	
Levi Hayworth	25 Bushels .43 cts per Bushel	6.45	
Levi Hayworth	1 Lot of Corn .43 3/4		
Nathan Hockett	1 Pen of Hay	5.00	
John Nickson	1 Calf	2.50	
John Nickson	1 Calf	3.25	
John Nickson	1 Lot of Clover Seed	.68	
Nathan Hockett	1 Washing Tub	.71	
Nathan Hockett	1 Pr. of Hand Irons	1.27	
Nathan Hockett	1 Crock	.18 3/4	
Joseph Powel	2 Crocks	.12 1/2	
Henry B. Wheeler	1 Shovel	.18 3/4	

Test.: Joel Reace, Clerk of said Sale

Nathan Hockett, Administrator

State of Indiana)
Hamilton County) To Wit:
       The above named, Joel Reace, makes affirmation that the
       above is a Just and True Account of the Sale of the Per-

sonal Estate of Eleazar Hockett, Late of said County, deceased, qualified to before Me, a Justice of the Peace of said County, the first day of November, 1838.

B. Wheeler,   (Seal)
Justice of the Peace

NATHAN HOCKETT'S ESTATE

An Inventory of the Goods, Chattles and Effects of Nathan Hockett, Late of Hamilton County and State of Indiana, deceased, taken by Nathan C. Beals, Administrator of the Estate of the said Deceased, with the assistance of James Reace and Samuel Sumner, Appraisors and duly qualified to that purpose.

1 Colt	$ 16.00
1 Black & White Cow & Calf	14.00
1 Red Cow	10.00
1 Bell	.75
2 White Heifers	11.00
4 Head of Sheep	6.00
1 Sow and 5 Pigs	2.00
4 Shoats	3.00
1 Lot of Corn in Crib	6.00
1 Grindstone	1.50
1 Tub of Lard	4.00
2 Tubs of Salted Meat	20.00
1 Pickle Tub	.75
1 Meat Tub	.50
1 Barrel and Some Salt	1.62 1/2
1 Whiskey Barrel	.25
1 Man's Saddle	7.00
1 Pair Drawing Chains	1.00
1 Pair of Hand Irons	1.00
2 Handsaws	2.00
1 Foot Addze	1.00
2 Augers	1.00
1 Bench Hook	.75
2 Tennor Saws & 2 Key Saws	3.00
1 1/2 Dozen Farmers Chisels	3.00
4 Mortising Chisels	2.50
2 Gouges & 4 Duck Bill Chisels	1.00
2 Turning Gouges & 2 Chisels	1.00
1 Brace with 3 Dozen Bits	4.00
1 Frannal Plane	1.00
1 Set of Small Match Plane	1.00
1 Sash Plane	1.25
1 Set of Table Planes	1.00
1 Rabit, 1 Cove & Bead, 1 Red Plane	.50
2 Bead Planes	.37 1/2
1 Set of Bench Planes	3.75
2 Large Cove Planes	1.25
2 Squares and Inglis Rule	2.00
1 Plane Bit and Scraper	.56 1/4

1 Old Brace & 4 Old Bits	$	.75
1 Oval Plane Bit		.25
1 Hand Axe, 3 gages and Spoke Thave		1.00
1 Rat Trap		.75
1 Vinegar Keg		.50
1 Log Chain		4.00
4 Split Bottom Chairs		1.50
1 Mantle Clock		8.00
1 Cupboard		7.00
Cupboard Ware		2.00
1 Table and 3 Tin Buckets		2.50
1 Lot of Pot Ware		3.00
1 Bureau		6.00
Half One Big Wheel		1.00
1 Bed, Bedding and Bedstead		13.00
1 Bed, Bedding and Bedstead		7.00
1 Stock Lock		.25
1 Washing Tub and Large Pot		2.00
2 Rifle Guns		14.00
2 Spades and Shovels		.75
1 Crosscut Saw		6.00
1 Pair of Compasses		.12 1/2
1 Lot of Corn in Mill		4.00
1 Lot of Wheat		7.00
1 Lot of Clover Seeds		1.00
1 Lot of Ruff Feal		4.00
1 Matock		1.75
Half of Joseph Baker's Doctor Book		1.00
1 Band and some Old Scrapes of Iron		2.00
1 Old Saw Mill Saw		3.00
2 Axes		2.75
8 Blew Ash Logs		4.00
2 Poplar Logs and the Ballance of the Tree		3.25
4 Poplar Saw Logs		1.75
1 Lot of Books		9.00
1 Introduction to Algebra		.75
Summers Surveying		2.50
1 Lot of Ploting Instruments		2.50
1 Iron Lathe, part of a set of Silver Ln itte Tools		5.00
Some Brass Clock Wheels		.75
1 Frying Pan		.50
Saw Set		.75
2 Farmers Chisels, 2 Plane Bits		.50
1 Tooth Plane Bit		.37 1/2
15 Old Foils		.75
1 Land Vise		1.50
1 Iron Wedge		.62 1/2
1 Old Bench and Screw		.50
2 and 1/2 Bushels of Corn		.93 3/4

```
        13 Poplar Saw Logs           $  6.00
         1 Poplar Log
         4 Saw Logs                      1.25
           Part of a Hay Stack          1.00
         1 Lot of Plank and
           1 the Skids                   2.50
       270 Feet of 1 Inch Plank         1.68 3/4
       130 Feet of 3/4 Inch Plank        .80 1/2
       175 Feet of 3/8 Inch Plank        .65
                                       ----------
                                      $ 39.83
                                      $ 82.75
```

Given under Our Hands, this 2nd day of March, A.D. 1839.

Thomas Reace)
Samuel Sumner) Apprs.

Book Accounts

```
     1 Note of Hand on Thomas Hockett
            Due 29th of Feb., 1839  $12.00
                     Emery Powel      2.73
                James Morrow, Jr.    12.06 1/4
                   Stephen Carey     16.64 1/4
                   Samuel Sumner      6.56
                     Eli Murray       7.27 1/2
                    James Hoover      35.52
                   Marten Sumner      4.31 1/4
                  John Cottingham     7.50
                                    ----------
                                   $101.80 1/4
          Robert Taylor (Debt Full)  17.14
     1 Note on James Brown for        3.00
       (Interest on the Same)         1.25
     1 The Signor of this Note is
         not known to Me
        John Nickson                  4.65
        Philo Smith                  10.25
        Benjamin Chappel             25.03 1/4
        Mathew Kirkendall            20.00
        Paul Wood                     6.37 1-4
        Riley Moon                    2.20
                                    ----------
                                   $ 72.82 1/4
```

```
        Total Amount  $ 17.14 1/2
                      $487.74 3/4
                     -----------
                      $504.89 1/4
```

An Account of Sales of the Personal Property of Nathan Hockett, late of the County of Hamilton and State of Indiana, Deceased at a Public Auction held at the late Dwelling House of the Deceased on the 2nd day of March, A.D. 1839.

```
        Nathan Fisher         1 Steel Trap          $  .40
```

Edward Bray	1 Lot of Files	$ .40	
Samuel Sumner	1 Vise	1.65	
James Morrow	1 Anville & Chisel	.44	
Nathan C. Beals	1 Lot of Tools	.63	
Nathan Fisher	1 1 Inch Auger	.43	
George Hayworth	1 1 1/2 Inch Auger	.66	
George Hayworth	2 Plains	1.86	
James Morrow	1 Plain	.87 1/2	
Nathan C. Beals	3 Plains and 1 Chisel	.37 1/2	
Enos Hiatt	1 Tenant Saw	.37 1/2	
Levi Sumner	1 Tenant Saw	.50	
Levi Sumner	1 Smoothing Plain	.50	
Levi Sumner	1 Set of Match Plains	.56 1/4	
Nathan Fisher	2 Table Plains	.45	
Nathan C. Beals	1 Cove and Lead Plain	.25	
Nathan C. Beals	1 Bench Hook	.75	
Nathan C. Beals	1 Sash Plain	.25	
Enos Hiatt	1 Pannel Plough	.90	
Nathan C. Beals	1 Plain	.25	
George Hayworth	1 Drawing Knife	.62 1/2	
Nathan C. Beals	1 Plain	.25	
Levi Sumner	1 Chisel	.50	
George Hayworth	1 Chisel	.51	
James Morrow	1 Chisel	.50	
Enos Hiatt	1 Plain	.31 1/2	
		$ 15.20 1/2	
Samuel Sumner	1 Chisel	.31 1/4	
Nathan C. Beals	1 Plain	.25	
Nathan C. Beals	1 Plain	.15	
Nathan C. Beals	1 Plain	.13	
Nathan C. Beals	1 Chisel	.25	
Enos Hiatt	1 Square	1.43	
Levi Sumner	1 Square	.65	
Trustan Davis	1 English Rule	.37 1/2	
Samuel Sumner	1 Turning Chisel & Gauges	1.86 1/4	
Nathan C. Beals	1 Drawing Knife	.12 1/2	
James Morrow	1 Spoke Shave	.14	
George Hayworth	1 Saw	.13	
Trustan Davis	1 Saw Set	.34	
Nathan C. Beals	1 Saw	.06 1/4	
James Reace	1 Compass	.14	
Levi Sumner	2 Chisels	.13	
Levi Sumner	2 Chisels	.11	
Enos Hiatt	1 Screwdriver	.19	
Nathan C. Beals	2 Chisels	.20	
Levi Sumner	2 Chisels	.15	
Nathan Fisher	2 Chisels	.12 1/2	
Nathan C. Beals	2 Plain Bits	.06 1/4	
Samuel Sumner	1 Plain Bit	.12 1/2	
James Reace	2 Chisels	.18 3/4	
Nathan C. Beals	1 Handsaw File	.06 1/4	
Nathan C. Beals	2 Gauges and Chisels	.18 3/4	
Zebulon Overman	1 File & 2 Chisels	.12 1/2	
Edward Bray	2 Chisels	.20	

Levi Hayworth	2 Chisels	$	.19
Edward Bray	1 File and Chisel		.05
Levi Hayworth	1 Rasp		.25
Nathan C. Beals	1 Plain Bit		.37 1/2
		$	8.17 3/4
Enos Hiatt	1 Screw		.56 1/4
John Bray	1 Gauge		.06 1/4
James Morrow	1 Guage		.06 1/4
Nathan C. Beals	1 Plain Handle Pattern Scraper and Look		.06 1/4
Timothy Sumner	1 Brace Stock		.12 1/2
Levi Sumner	1 Brace & 3 Doz. Bits.		3.25
Levi Sumner	1 Pair of Foot Addizer and Square		.87 1/2
Nathan C. Beals	1/2 of a Book		.50
Edward Bray	1 Book		1.35
Nathan Fisher	2 Books		1.68
Edward Bray	1 Book		.87 1/2
Nathan C. Beals	1 Book		1.00
Enos Hiatt	1 Book, Scales & Dividers		2.50
Enos Hiatt	1 Book		.56 1/4
Nathan C. Beals	1 Book		.75
Daniel Fishers	1 Book		.12 1/2
John Hayworth	2 1/2 Bushels of Corn		1.22 1/2
Joseph Tolston	1 Bushel of Corn		4.62 1/2
Timothy Sumner	1 Rifle Gun		8.81 1/4
Daniel Fisher	1 Rifle Gun		2.31 1/4
Truston Davis	1 Crosscut Saw		5.13
Elizabeth Hockett	Corn in the Crib		5.00
John Hayworth	1 Table		2.50
Elizabeth Hockett	1 Mantle Clock		8.00
Elizabeth Hockett	1 Cupboard Ware		2.00
Elizabeth Hockett	1 Bureau		6.00
Elizabeth Hockett	1 Cupboard		6.00
Jonathan Hayworth	1 Grindstone		2.62 1/2
Elizabeth Hockett	Hay		1.00
Enos Hiatt	Hay		5.03
Nathan Fisher	Drawing Chains		.41 1/2
James Morrow	1 Log Chain		3.62 1/2
		$	79.09
James Fisher	Hand Irons		.93 3/4
Benjamin Wheeler	1 Pair of Sillyards		1.06 1/4
James Reace	1 Hand Saw		1.51
Nathan Fisher	1 Hand Saw		1.07 1/2
Elizabeth Hockett	2 Chisels & 3 1/4 Augers		.37 1/2
Joseph Powel	1 Fire Shovel		.50
Elizabeth Hockett	1 Sugar Kettle		2.00
Jonathan Hayworth	1 Salt Barrel		.06 1/4
Jonathan Hayworth	51 lbs of Salt .03 per lb		1.53
Elisabeth Hockett	1 Pickle Tub		.50
Nathan Fisher	1 Barrel		.75
Elisabeth Hockett	1 Vinegar Kag		.37 1/2
Martin Sumner	1 Spade		.37 1/2
Jacob Shaul	1 Mans Saddle		7.50
Levi Pennington	1 Hand Axe		.45

Elisabeth Hockett	1 Pot and Oven	$ 1.50
Jonathan Hayworth	1 Skellet & Lid	1.00
Jacob Shaul	1 Pot	.62 1/2
Elisabeth Hockett	1 Frying Pan	.37 1/2
Elisabeth Hockett	1 Cow	8.00
Jacob Shaul	2 Chairs	1.25
Levi Hayworth	2 Chairs	1.18 3/4
Elisabeth Hockett	1 Half of Big Wheel	1.00
Elisabeth Hockett	2 Pot Hack	.25
Benjamin Wheeler	1 Iron Wedge	.50
Elisabeth Hockett	1 Axe	1.00
Elisabeth Hockett	2 30 Saw Logs	15.00
Jacob Shaul	1 Meat Tub	1.00
Jacob Shaul	1 Washing Tub	.75
James Morrow	1 Bench & Screw	.75
James Morrow	Scraps of Iron	.37 1/2
James Morrow	1 Band of Iron	1.12 1/2
Enos Hiatt	1 Mill Saw	2.12 1/2
		$ 56.42 3/4
Joseph Bishop	1 Matock	.12 1/2
Joanthan Hayworth	1 Spade	.25
Riley Moor	1 Axe	.81 1/4
John Nixson	9 Bushels of Clover Seed at .12 1/2 per Bushel	1.12 1/2
Charles Vestel	575 Feet Plank at .79 cts. per Hundred	4.54
Enos Hiatt	430 Feet Plank at .80 Cts. per Hundred	3.44
Elisabeth Hockett	1 Tin Bucket	.50
Jonathan Hayworth	1 Tin Bucket	.18 3/4
Enos Hiatt	1 Tin Bucket	.21
Nathan Fisher	1 Set of Knives and Forks	1.68 3/4
James Morrow	1 Candle Stick	.19
Jacob Shaul	1 Matoc	1.62 1/2
		$ 14.69 3/4

Daniel Fisher, Clerk of said Sale

Total Amount is $173.59 1/4

Nathan C. Beals, Administrator

State of Indiana)
Hamilton County) To Wit:
The above named, Daniel Fisher, makes oath that the above
is a Just and True Account of the Sale of the Personal
Estate of Nathan Hockett, late of said County, Deceased,
qualified to before Me, a Justice of the Peace of said
County, the fourth day of March, A.D. 1839.

B. Wheeler,   (Seal)
Justice of the Peace

JOB TOLBERT'S ESTATE

An Inventory of the Goods, Chattles and Effects of Job Tolbert, late of

Hamilton County, and State of Indiana, deceased, taken by Isaac Baldwin and Mordecai Moore, Administrators of the Estate of said Deceased, with the assistance of John White and Zenas Carey, Appraisors, chosen for that purpose.

1 Sythe and Hangings	$ .50	
2 Sythe and 1 Hangings	1.25	
5 Sickles	1.50	
3 Old Barrels	.25	
1 Real	.25	
5 Augers	2.00	
3 Iron Pitchforks, .25 cts each	.75	
1 Churn and Sundries	2.00	
4 Mortising Chisels	1.50	
1 Brace and ten Bits	1.00	
5 Awls and 1 Punch	.12 1/2	
3 Thumb gages and Iron Square	.50	
1 Steel Trap	.25	
1 Turners Gaugh, clevis, coulter	.25	
1 Dressed Dear Skin	.75	
1 Cast Plough Mole and 2 Shares	.50	
3 Iron Wedges & Some Scraps of Iron	2.75	
1 Lot of Harness Cathers	2.50	
1 Fore Plain Pack and Smoother	1.25	
4 lbs of Nails and Box	.50	
1 Crosscut Saw	5.00	
1 Pair of Stillyards	.50	
1 Wool Wheel	2.00	
1 Cant Hook	.75	
6 Chopping Axes	5.00	
2 Washing Tubs, Half Bushel & Drawing Knife	1.50	
1 Man's Saddle	4.00	
1 New Saddle	14.00	
4 Mill Picks & Some Cast Iron		($53.12 1/2)
4 Mill Picks & Some Lath Irons	1.75	
1 Bridle and Martingales	1.25	
2 Pieces of Sash	.37 1/2	
1 Grindstone	5.00	
1 Lot of Horse Colars, 2 Pairs of Trace Chains and other old Gearing	3.50	
1 Cutting Knife and Box	1.00	
1 Lot of Wheat, .75 cts per Bushel	3.75	
1 Lot of Hay, .25 cts per hundred	2.00	
1 Lot of Oats, .12 1/2 cts a Dozen	1.50	
1 Lot of Corn, .37 1/2 per Bushel	7.50	
1 Bay Horse	60.00	
1 Bay Horse Younger	45.00	
1 Pair of Stretchers	1.00	
1 Clevis Bolt & Bolt & Ring & Log Chain	2.00	
1 Plough	4.00	
1 Waggon	20.00	
1 Fallow Harrow	3.00	

4 Hogs	$ 6.00
1 Sythe and Cradle	2.50
1 Hogshead and 2 Salt Barrels	.56 1/4
1 Iron Bound Barrel & Cucumbers Pickled	1.00
1 Wood Bound Barrel & Cucumbers Pickled	..75
1 Barrel and Scraps of Meat	.50
1 Barrel of Pickled Pork	7.00
1 Tar Bucket and Tar	.50
1 Kettle of Soap and Ladle	.75
1 Trough Bucket and Soap	.75
1 Lot of Bacon	7.00
1 Broad Axe $2.50 and 1 2 Inch Auger $.75	3.25
1 Red and White Pided Cow	15.00
1 Brown Cow with a White Faced and Calf	20.00
1 Red Cow	20.00
1 Red Durham Bull	25.00
1 Yearling Heifer	3.50
	$276.68 3/4
1 Yearling Bull	2.00
1 Dark Red Cow and Calf	15.00
1 2 Year old Heifer with a White Face	7.00
1 Red Cow with a White Face	15.00
2 10 Gallon & 1 Twelve Gallon Kettle at 2.00 & 4.50	6.50
1 Log Sled	.50
1 Set of Carriage Harness	2.00
A Part of a Set of Smith Tools	25.00
1 Shovel Plough	1.25
1 Bay Mare	30.00
1 Red Heifer	12.00
2 Small Kettles, $1.50 Each	3.00
1 Shovel Plough	1.25
1 Pair Trace chains, Twisted Links	1.25
2 Singletrees	.37 1/2
1 Pair of Trace Chains, Strait Links	1.00
2 Kettles at $2.00 and .50 Cts.	2.50
1 Stand	3.00
1 Chest	1.50
3 Slates, at .25 cts each	.75
1 Close Press	12.00
1 Barrel and Sugar	4.00
1 Large Crock and Sugar	2.50
1 Bed & Bedding, Bedstead & Cord	10.00
1 Bed & Bedding, Bedstead & Cord	15.00
1 Trunnel Bed and Bedding	3.00
1 Bedstead & Cord, 2 Feathers Beds and Bedding for One	12.00

```
2 Pieces of Linen                    $  1.50
1 Umbrella, a Lot of Bottles
            and Shetts                  1.50
2 Rough Boxes                            .25
1 Calico Bed Quilt $1.50 and
      other Beding Clothers $3.00       4.50
    Single Sleyed Curtin $.25 and 2
      Factory Sheets $.75 and one
      Check Sheet $.25                  1.25
    Bed Ticking $1.75; 1 Pair Rose
      Blankets $3.00; 1 Bedquilt $1     4.75
2 Check Counterpairs $1.00; one
      Cotton Sheat $.50                  1.50
1 Flax and Cotton Theat $.50 and
      on Check Sheet $.25                 .75
                                  $205.37 1/2
1 Sheat                               .37 1/2
    Barkley Works in 3 Volumns $4.00
      and One Family Bible $.50         4.50
1 Lot of Books of Sundry Rinds         3.00
1 Oil Table Spread                      .75
11 Chairs                              2.75
1 Breakfast Table                      2.00
1 Keg $.25; One Small Coffee Pot
      $.12 1/2 and Two Tin Pans and
      one Dipper $.50                   .87 1/2
1 Tin Bucket and One Large Tin
      $.37 1/2 and 4 Wooden Ladler
            $.25                        .62 1/2
4 Earthern Pans $.31 1/4; Earthen
      Crocks (4) $.50; One Jug
            $.12 1/2                    .93 3/4
1 New Coffee Pot $.37 1/2; One Old
      Coffee Pot $.06 1/4; One Sausage
      Stuffer $.25                      .68 3/4
4 Chipand Teacanisters and 2 Pepper
                        Boxes           .50
1 Pron Ladle; 1 Flesh Fork Roler
      Pin and Bumpit                    .37 1/2
2 Brass Candlesticks $.25; 1 Funel
      Spice Mill and Coffee Box
            $.62 1/2                    .87 1/2
1 Lot of Cupboard Ware                 4.00
1 Strainer Knife Box, Knives and
                        Forks          1.50
2 Smoothing Irons $.75; Shovel
                  and Tongs $.75       1.50
1 Crain and Hanings $1.00; and
                  Irons $.25           1.25
1 Small Dresser $1.00 and Miclch
                  Cupboard $.25        1.25
1 Bedstead, Bed and Bedding           10.00
1 Trunel Bedstead, Bed and Bedding     5.00
1 Meal Chest $.25; 1 Meal Sive
      $.37 1/2; Bread Bowl $.12 1/2     .75
```

```
1 Barrel and Dried Fruit            $    .50
1 Brass Kettle $.25; 2 Stew
      Kettles and Lids $.50              .75
1 Oven Bale and Lid $1.00 and
      One Tea Kettle $1.50               2.50
1 Skellet and Lid $.62 1/2 and
      One Round Bottom Skellet
            $.37 1/2                     1.00
1 Spade $.75; 1 Lard Tub and Lard
      $1.00 and One Do $2.50             4.25
1 Sasuage Trough $.06 1/4; One
      Ladle $.06 1/4; Candle Mole
            $.25                         .37 1/2
1 Reflector $.12 1-2; One Pair of
      Warfler Irons $.25                 .37 1/2
1 Piece of Galow $.25; 5 Milch Pans
            $.25                         .50
1 Cabbage Cutter and Pan Handle
      $.25; 2 Weeding Hoes $.37 1/2      .62 1/2
1 Sorrel Horse                         35.00
1 Sorrel Horse, Dark Main and Tail 60.00
1 Pair of Four Gears $2.00; One Pr.
      Hind Gears $2.75                   4.75
1 Pair Bands                             .25
2 Sheets of Iron                       5.50
1 Lot of Lumber $4.50; One Sythe
      and Hangings $1.50                 6.00
1 Matock $1.25; 1 Basket $.25 and
      1 Smaller Basket $.12 1/2          1.62 1/2
1 Half Barrel of Salt $3.75; One
      Chest $4.00                        7.75
1 Watch                               10.00
1 Mantle Clock                         6.00
1 Rifle Gun                           10.00
1 Flas Wheel                           2.00
```

Property at the Mill

```
1 Pair of Sand Creek Burrs          100.00
  Wheat by the Bushel                 1.00
1 Set of Mill Irons, viz Mill
      Spindle & Gudgeons etc.         41.00
1 Hand Saw and other articles         1.50
1 Lot of Rounds and Cogs              3.00
1 Mill Screw                          5.00
1 Grul Hoe and Shovel $.75 and
      A Lot of Sawed Timber $13.41    14.16
1 Lot of Hewed Timber                10.00
```

Given under Our Hands, 4th Mo., 26th, 1839.

John White)
            } Apprs.
Zenas Carey)

```
1 Note on George Custer         $   13.14
1 Note on Elijah Tolbert          150.00
1 Note on Elijah Tolbert, due
            January 15th, 1841     400.00
1 Note on Alexander Pugh           10.00
1 Note on Benjamin Fyet, ass-
      igned over by Alex. Pugh     15.00
1 Note on Elijah Talbert           50.00
1 Note on John Barker               7.00
1 Note on Robert Earl              27.00
1 Receipt on Alexander Mock
      for note on Ezra W. Osborn
      for $100.00 with a Credit of
      $83.00                       17.00
1 Receipt on Thomas Tolbert for
      3 Due bills of $625.00 each
      making in all             $ 1875.00
      One Due 1st Mo, 1st, 1840
      One Due 1st Mo, 1st, 1841
      One Due 1st Mo, 1st, 1842

      Making in All             $ 3477.23 3/4
```

Given under Our Hands the 4th Month, 26th day, 1839.

```
                          Isaac Baldwin  )
                                         ) Admrs.
                          Mordecai More  )
```

State of Indiana)
Hamilton County) To Wit:
      Personally appeared before Me, Benjamin Wheeler, A Justice of the Peace of said County, Isaac Baldwin and Mordecai More, Administrators of the Estate of Job Tolbert, Deceased and John White and Zenas Carey, Appraiseors of said Estate and being duly qualified the said John White and Zenas Carey say that the above Inventory and Appraiseement as assigned by them is a Just and True Inventory and Valuation of the Goods, Chattles and Effects of Job Tolbert to the best of their Judgement.
      And the said Isaac Baldwin and Mordecai More says that the above is a True Inventory of the Personal Estate of the said Job Tolbert, so far as the same has come in their hands to be administered.

                    B. Wheeler, J.P. (Seal)

     An Account of Sales of the Personal Property of Job Tolbert, late of Hamilton County and State of Indiana, deceased at a Public Auction held at the late Dwelling House of the said Deceased on the 26th day of the 4th Month (April), A.D. 1839.

```
      Jesse Reace                          $   .
      Wm. Osborn, Ser.      1 Sickle           .25
```

Thomas Clayton	1 Sythe	$ .78	
William Osborn)	1 Pitch Fork	.26	
and)			
Jesse Reace)	1 Pitch Fork	.25	
Benjamin Wagaman	1 Churn	1.67	
Paul Wood	1 Mortising Chisel	.70	
The Widow	1 Mortising Chisel	.56	
The Widow	1 Mortising Chisel	.25	
George Bowman	1 Corner Chisel	.25	
James A. Groves	1 Brace and Bits	1.25	
Mordecai More	1 Lot of Awls	.12 1/2	
Aaron Lindley	3 Thumb Gauges	.15	
William Osborn	1 Iron Square	.58	
Robert Townlinson	1 Shut Grass	.20	
Thomas Tolbert	1 Lathe Iron	1.12 1/2	
The Widow	1 Iron Wedge	.51	
Aaron Lindley	1 Iron Wedge	.38	
Aaron Lindley	Fenders	1.15	
The Widow	1 Iron Wedge	.37	
Andrew Jackson	Back Band	.56 1/4	
Thomas Clayton	Back Band	.65	
John Piece	Briech Bands	1.26	
John Piece	1 Lot of Leather	.79	
Zac. Rease	1 Lot of Leather	.70	
David Baldwin	1 Lot of Leather	.75	
Jacob Vanderslice	1 Lot of Leather	.76	
Zachariah Rease	1 Lot of Leather	.37 1/2	
Aaron Lindley	1 Plain	.83	
Aaron Lindley	1 Fore Plain	.93	
		$ 18.22 3/4	
Jonas Bradfield	1 Crosscut Saw	5.07	
Levi T. Penington	1 Drawing Knife	.43 3/4	
Levi T. Penington	1 Broad Axe	3.00	
The Widow	1 Saddle	14.00	
Daniel Antrim	6 Light Sash	.37 1/2	
Daniel Antrim	4 Light Sash	.14	
The Widow	1 Two Inch Auger	.62	
Asa Bales	1 Sheet of Iron	1.37 1/2	
Asa Bales	1 Sheet of Iron	1.50	
John W. Hacker	1 Refector	.50	
James Raines	1 Set of Smith Tools	27.50	
Asa Peacock	1 Sugar Kettle	1.25	
Abel Roberts	1 Sugar Kettle	2.81	
The Widow	1 Grub Hoe	.12 1/2	
Joseph Bishop	1 Shovel	.38	
Benjamin Chappel	1 Shovel	.63	
Elijah Tolbert	1 Froe	1.00	
Isaac Rich	1 Axe	.37 1/2	
Jacob Vanderslice	1 Axe	1.06 1/4	
The Widow	1 Axe	.25	
The Widow	1 Axe	.75	
The Widow	1 Axe	.75	
Paul Wood	1 Book	1.06 1/4	
Daniel Antrim	1 Book of Martars	2.43 3/4	

David Baldwin	1 Book " History of the United States"	$ 1.37 1/2
Asa Bales	1 Lot of Books	1.06 1/4
Job Smith	1 Waggon	30.00
James Antrim	1 Axe	.43 3/4
Zachariah Reace	1 Axe	.76
Isaac Haines	1 Set of Harness	5.00
Widow	Gearing	4.06 1/4
Nehemiah Payne	1 Pair of Chains	2.37 1/2
Jonas Bradfield	1 Collar	.50
Robert Stout	1 Set of Breeching	1.38
Edward Bray	1 Harness & Chains	2.31
		$117.04
Nehemiah Payne	1 Line Leather	.21
Jonathan Colborn	2 Collars	.25
Edward Bray	1 Collar	.25
Jacob Vanderslice	1 Bridle	.19
Ira Thendal	1 Bridle	.20
Benjamin Wagaman	1 Bridle	.06 1/4
Nehemiah Payne	1 Bridle	.21
Daniel Antrim	1 Red and White Cow	19.00
Elijah Brock	1 Sorrel Horse	31.75
Asa Bales	1 Durham Bull	71.00
Jesse Rease	1 Bull Calf	24.00
Jacob Vanderslice	1 Spotted Bull Calf	3.66
Jacob Vanderslice	1 Red Heifer	4.75
Lot Beason	1 Heifer	8.00
Jesse Rease	1 White face Cow	20.25
The Widow	1 Horse	62.50
Jesse Tolbert	1 Bay Horse	51.00
Joseph Tolbert	1 Bay Horse	60.00
Jesse Tolbert	1 Rifle Gun	10.00
Joseph Tolbert	1 Watch	8.56
Job Smith	1 Mantle Clock	13.00
The Widow	1 Flax Wheel	2.62
Isaac Baldwin	1 Lot of Lumber	2.50
The Widow	2 Singletrees	.62 1/2
		$394.56

```
$394.56
 117.04
  18.22 3/4
$529.82 3/4
```

Test: Evan B. Clayton, Clerk

Isaac Baldwin)
) Administrators
Mordecai More)

State of Indiana)
Hamilton County) To Wit:
        The above named Evan B. Clayton makes affirmation that the
        above is a Just and True Account of the Sales of the Per-

sonal Property of Job Tolbert, late of said County, deceased.

Affirmed before me, a Justice of the Peace of said County, the 26th day of the 4th Month, 1839.

B. Wheeler, J.P.

NATHAN MANSHIP ESTATE

State of Indiana)
Hamilton County) I do hereby certify that Abraham Hilms and John C. Kinnaman were duly qualifyed before Me, the undersigned to appraise all the Goods and Chattles of Nathan Manship, late of Fall Creek Township, Hamilton County, Indiana, deceased as handed to us by the administrator for appraisement.

Given under My hand and seal, this 19th day of July, 1839.

John T. Kinnaman, (Seal)
Justice of the Peace

An Inventory of the Goods, Chattles and Effects of Nathan Manship, late of Hamilton County and State of Indiana, deceased, taken by Elias Morgan, Administrator of the Estate of the said Deceased with the assistance of John C. Kinnaman and Abraham Helms, Appraisors called and duly sworn for that purpose.

1 Sorrel Horse	$ 55.00
1 Bay Horse	30.00
1 Gray Horse	30.00
1 Carriage and Harness	50.00
1 Waggon and 2 Pair of Gears	42.00
1 Pair of Gears	3.00
1 Still	35.00
2 Ploughs	6.00
1 Axe	1.50
1 Axe	1.50
1 Mantle Clock	12.00
1 Beaureau	3.00
2 Beds and Bedding	25.00
2 Saddles	10.00
3 Boxes	1.50
Kitchen Ware	11.37 1/2
Kitchen Ware	3.12 1/2
3 Beds	2.25
1 Lot of Raw Cotton	2.00
1 Saw and Foot and Adze	1.25
Chains and Sundries	1.50
1 Note on Peter Castator	50.00
1 Note on John Mc Gee	10.00
1 Note on Dick Hodgin	10.56 1/4
1 Note on Dick Hodgin	167.81 1/4

Accounts of Sales of the Personal Property of Nathan Manship, late of the County of Hamilton and State of Indiana, Deceased at a Public Auction held at the late Dwelling House of the said Deceased on the 20th day of July, A.D. 1839.

Pendleton Wright	1 Shovel Plough Shear	$ 2.40
Elizabeth Manship	1 Skillet	.19
Thomas Creekmore	1 Wedge & Gun Barrel	2.37
Elijah Manship	1 Lot of Pewter Plates	2.87 1/2
John Burk	1 Oven & Lid	1.75
John Manship	1 Reed	1.07
John Manship	1 Reed	.25
Pendleton Wright	1 Reed	.75
John Manship	1 Axe	1.80
Thomas Ledmun	1 Stand	.37 1/2
Elijah Manship	1 Pair of Doubletrees	1.40
John Manship	1 Hand Saw	1.00
John Manship	1 Foot Addze	1.00
John Manship	1 Still	40.00
John Rickhart	1 Bay Horse	20.00
Benjamin Murer	1 Gray Horse	25.25
Linzy Manship	1 Carriage & Harness	40.12 1/2
Wm. Kinnaman	1 Large Waggon	25.62 1/2
George Austin	1 Horse Collar	.12 1/2
Benjamin Murrer	1 Pair of Gears	2.06 1/4
John Manship	1 Collar	1.50
Thomas Creekmore	1 Collar	1.75
Elijah Manship	1 Pr. of Harness and Trees	1.50
Elizabeth Manship	1 Sorrel Horse	50.00
Samuel Heffer	1 Sythe and Cradle	1.75
		$226.85

July the 20th, A.D. 1839
Test: Moses Craig, Clerk of said Sale   Elias Morgan,
                                                          Administrator

SAMUEL LENUN, JR. ESTATE

Praise Bill, May 22, 1839

Inventory Appraisement Bill of the Personal Property belonging to the Estate of Samuel Lenon, Junior, Deceased.

1 Lot of Hogs (19 Head)	$ 39.00
1 Brown Cow	15.00
1 White Cow	12.00
1 Red Heifer	8.00
1 Pided Heifer	5.00
1 Dun Heiffer	4.00
1 Hoe	.75
1 Plough	8.00
1 Log Chain	4.00
1 Mare	65.00
1 Axe	1.50

1 Bridle	$ 1.50
1 Srafel Bridle	.75
1 Set of Gears	3.00
2 Clevises	1.25
1 Shovel Plough and 1 Clevis	3.00
1 Iron Wedge	1.00
1 Saddle	10.00
1 Bedstead and Cord	1.00
1 Churn	1.00
1 Crock and Lard	.50
2 Barrels	.62 1/2
2 Bushels of Potatoes	1.50
1 Lot of Meat and Soap	2.00
1 Lot of Chair Frames	1.87 1/2
1 Lot of Bed Clothes	20.00
1 Lot of Pillar Cases and Sheets	6.00
2 Towels	.50
1 Lot of Crocks	.50
1 Lot of Tin Ware	1.25
1 Lot of Cupboard Ware	3.00
1 Lot of Sundries	2.00
1 Smoothing Irons, Trivit & Hooks	1.25
1 Fire Shovel and Hammer	1.25
1 Lot of Castings	2.75
1 Lot of Knives, Forks and Spoons	1.12 1/2
1 Pitcher and 3 Plates	.12 1/2
1 Looking Glass	1.00
1 Set of Window Curtains	.25
1 Slate	.37 1/2
1 Bed, Bedstead and Bedding	17.50
1 Piece of Leather	.37.1/2
1 Beaureau	13.00
1 Lot of Sugar at $.10 cts per lb.	5.00
2 Sugar Kettles	5.00
1 Pair of Pinchers	.62 1/2
2 Mauls and Ropes	.50
2 Meal Bags	1.25
1 Sheep	2.25

We the Appraisors of the Estate of Samuel Lenor, Deceased, do certify that the above is a True Copy of the Appraisement.

Samuel Lenor
Jonathan Bratton

JOB TOLBERT'S ESTATE

An additional Inventory of the Goods, Chattles and Effects of Job Tolbert, late of Hamilton County, Deceased. Taken by Isaac Baldwin and Mordecai More, Administrators of the Estate of said Deceased on the 30th day of December, A.D. 1840. (To Wit)

John Hunt	Account of	$ 2.00
James Brown	1 Note	20.00

James Hoover	1 Note	$ 10.00
Henry Frazer	1 Note	1.00
Tolbert & Wright	1 Note Due on the 17th of January, 1840	1.50
Stubbs & Stubbs	1 Note Due same Date	3.28 1/2
Tolbert & Stubbs	1 Note	2.06 1/4
Wright & Tolbert	1 Note	3.12 1/2
Stubbs & Stubbs	1 Note	1.12 1/2
George Custer	1 Note	1.00
Enos Pray	1 Note	2.12 1/2
	Making in All	$ 47.12 1/2

Given under our hands the day and year above written.

State of Indiana)
Hamilton County) To Wit

        Personally appeared before Me, Benjamin Wheeler, a Justice of the Peace in and for said County, Isaac Baldwin and Mordecai More, Administrators of the Estate of Job Tolbert, Deceased and being duly affirmed says that the above is a Just and True Additional Inventory of the Personal Property (Estate) of said Deceased, so far as has come into their Hands to be administered.

                             Benjamin Wheeler (Seal)
                             Justice of the Peace

HENRY FOLAND'S WILL

    The Last Will and Testament of Henry Foland of Hamilton County, Indiana made the 15th day of July, A.D. 1834.

    Item First: I hereby give and bequeath to my Son, John, One Dollar to be paid to him by my Executor at My death.

    Item 2nd.: I hereby give, divise and bequeath to Betsey Freel all the rest and residue of my personal property of whatso ever name and nature also to her, I hereby give divise and bequeath all the Real Estate to which I may hold on Equitable or Legal Title and may own or possess at the time of My death, indencting (?) Such as shall acquire or may hereafter acquire by Her to be enjoyed so long as She may remain unmarried after My Death and so long as she may survive Me and at her intermarriage or death then all such property and its increase and all such real estate shall go to and vest in the children of the said Betsey, that have been or may be born during my life or within nine months thereafter and by them to be enjoyed in equal parts absolutely and in fee simply forever.

    Item Third: I hereby constitute and appoint my friend and neighbor Elias Hoddy of said County the executor of this my Last Will, desiring him to see it strictly carried into effect

    In Testimony whereof I have hereunto set My hand and seal the day and year first above written. In presence of Calvin Fletcher and Daniel D. Pratt.

                               Henry Foland, (SEAL)

The foregoing Will and Testament attered by intesting between the third and fourth line of Second Page, the words have been or and between the fourth and fifth lines of same page the words except her eldest Son Elisha and re-published in our presence.

In Witness of which We have hereunto subscribed our names as Witnesses thereto in the presence of the said Henry Foland at his request on this 9th day of August in the Year Eighteen hundred and thirty Eight.

Ovid Butler
Calvin Fletcher

State of Indiana)
Hamilton County) Be it Remembered that on the 18th day of April, 1839, personally appeared before Me the undersigned the Clerk of the Hamilton County Probate Court in the State aforesaid Calvin Fletcher of lawful age, one of the subscribing Witnesses and the foregoing will and the foregoing alteration and republication of the said Will of Henry Foland, deceased, who after being duly sworn upon his Oath says that the foregoing instruament and the atteration and republication thereof was made signed, sealed and declared by the within named Henry Foland to be his Last Will and Testament and that He this defendant and Daniel D. Pratt in the first instance and this defendant and Ovid Butler in the second instance were called on at the respecting dates third of by the said Testator Henry Foland, as witnesses third of and that as such witnesses this defendant and the others have named did subscribe and sign their names thereto as Witness in the presence of the Testator, Henry Foland and in the presence of each other at the respective dates thereof and further that He has defendant deponent believes that the said Testator Henry Foland and the time of making the said foregoing Will and the alteration of the same was of perfect mind and memory at the execution thereof and further saith not.

Sworn and subscribed the day and year first above written.

Calvin Fletcher

Given under my hand the day and date above written.

Jno. G. Burns, Clerk

A Inventory of the Goods, Chattles and Effects of Henry Foland, late of Hamilton County and State of Indiana, deceased, taken by Jonathan Carey, Executor of the Estate of said Deceased, with the assistance of James Hughey and Robert P. Heddy, Appraisors called and duly sworn for that purpose.

1 Cross Cut Saw	$ 4.50
1 Mantle Clock	12.00
1 Lot of Cupboard Ware	5.00

1 Wool Wheel	$ 1.50	
9 Chairs at $.37 1/2 Cts. Each	3.37 1/2	
1 Gun	6.00	
1 Lot of Books	5.00	
1 Coffee Mill	.25	
1 Table	1.00	
1 Tin Bucket	.62 1/2	
1 Churn	.50	
1 Iron	.75	
1 Cradle	.87 1/2	
1 Lot of Shaving Implements	3.75	
2 Beds at $15.00 Each	30.00	
1 Great Coat	10.00	
1 Chest	1.00	
1 Looking Glass	.25	
1 Inkstand	.12 1/2	
1 Pair of Martingales	1.25	
1 Saddle	2.00	
1 Bridle	.37 1/2	
1 Pair of Streetyards	1.00	
1 Lot of Old Waggon Irons	3.00	
1 Old Gun	.75	
1 Lot of Tanner Tools	8.00	
1 Set of Grain Measures	1.25	
1 Lot of Small Castings	5.75	
3 Kettles	12.90	$122.80 1/2
1 Pair of Sheep Shears	.37 1/2	
1 Iron Wedge	.75	
1 Axe	1.50	
1 Tub and Wash Board	.75	
1 Garden Hoe	.50	
5 Crocks	.75	
1/2 Barrel of Soap	2.00	
1 Tub of Pickle Pork, supposed to be 350 lbs.	28.00	
1 Barrel and Salt	1.25	
100 Lbs. of Bacon	8.00	
1 Can and Lard	2.00	
2 Meal Bags at $.75 cts. each	1.50	
1 Roan Mare	40.00	
1 Iron Gray Mare	35.00	
12 Hogs	27.00	
1 Log Chain	1.25	
2 Four Year Old Steers	28.00	
1 Brindle Cow	15.00	
1 Two year Old Heifer	6.00	
2 One Year old Heifer	7.00	
1 Wash Tub and Hoops	.37 1/2	
1 Doubletress	.62 3/4	
1 Lot of Corn, Supposed to be 400 Bushels at $.37 1/2 cts each	150.00	
1 Lot of Corn, Supposed to be 125 Bushels at $.37 1/2 cts each	56.35	
1 Bullet Ladle	.12 1/2	

```
1 Pair of Shoe Brushes          $   .13 3/4
1 Pocket Book                       .25
1 Rubber                            .25
1 Side Upper Leather               3.00
1 Pair of Boots                    2.50
1 Spring Lancet                     .37 1/2
1 Set of Tooth Keys                 .75
1 Hatchet                           .37 1/2
                                 $534.43
```

Given under our hands, this 17th day of May, A.D. 1839.

James Hughey)
R. P. Hoddy) Appraisors

Also I have added to the above amount the following notes of Hand belonging to said Estate/

```
          John Carey          Note              $ 15.50
          John Carey          Interest             .46
          George H. Millers   Note               12.50
          John Osborn )
          Joseph Dyre )       Note (Balance on)   1.50
          R. P. Hoddy         Note                4.28
          Benjamin Savage     Note                7.55
          Benjamin Savage     Interest             .38
          Sylvestius
             Bartholemew      Note                5.00
          Sylvestius
             Bartholemew      Interest             .37
          J. A. Graves        Note (Balance on)   1.52
                                                $ 49.06
                                                 534.43
          John Thomas         Note               16.98
                              Making in All     $600.47
```

Given under My hand, this 12th day of August, A.D. 1839.

Jonathan Carey, Executor

State of Indiana)
Hamilton County)   To Wit:

      Personally appeared before Me, John Colip, a Justice of the Peace in and for said County, Jonathan Carey, Administrator of the Estate of Henry Foland, deceased and James Hughey, R. P. Hoddy, Appraisors of said Estate and being duly Sworn the said James Hughey and R. P. Hoddy, says that the above Inventory and Appraisement assigned by them is a Just and True Inventory and Valuation of the goods and Chattles and effects of the said Henry Foland to the best of their Judgement and the said Jonathan Carey says that the above is a True Inventory of the Personal Property Estate of the said Henry Foland so far as the same has come to his hands to be administered.

An Inventory of the Sale of the Goods, Chattles and Effects of Henry Foland, late of Hamilton County and State of Indiana, deceased sold by Jonathan Carey, Administrator of the Estate of said Deceased - May 17th, 1839.

Jonathan Carey	1 Lot of Pamphlets	$ .62
Charles Whitehead	1 German Book	.26
William Kirkpatrick	1 Musick Book	.31 1/4
Soloman Wise	1 German Book	.12 1/2
Jacob Colip	1 German Bible	.12 1/2
Soloman Wise	1 Geography	.56 1/4
Jacob Foland	1 Set of Tooth Kegs	.37 1/2
Jonathan Carey	1 Spring Lancet	.12 1/2
Jacob Colip	1 Hatchet	.37 1/2
Amos Gough	1 Pair of Boots	7.50
John Osborn	1 Razor and Box	.75
William Freel	1 Pair of Martingales	.81 1/4
John Mooney	1 Old Gun	7.25
C. W. Freel	1 Lot of Old Iron	2.18 3/4
Jas. Hughey	1 Lot of Tanners Tools	7.37 1/2
Patrick Shiel	1 Heiffer	6.06 1/4
Patrick Shiel	1 Heiffer	6.57 1/2
Ira Kingsbury	2 Steers	43.00
John Mooney	1 Doubletree	1.37 1/2
James Hughey	1 Roan Mare	37.25
James Larew	1 Gray Mare	40.00
John Mooney	1 Log Chain	2.06 1/4
John Osborn	20 Bushels of Corn	11.40
C. W. Freel	20 Bushels of Corn	10.40
William Dick	20 Bushels of Corn	10.60
Sampson Castor	20 Bushels of Corn	10.60
Jacob Mock	20 Bushels of Corn	10.60
Benjamin Castor	20 Bushels of Corn	11.20
		$227.46 1/4
Jacob Mater	20 Bushels of Corn	10.60
Amos Gough	20 Bushels of Corn	10.40
J. L. Tyson	20 Bushels of Corn	10.40
Wm. Murphey	20 Bushels of Corn	10.60
John Murphey	20 Bushels of corn	10.60
Levi Wheatly	20 Bushels of Corn	10.60
Levi Wheatly	20 Bushels of Corn	10.60
J. W. Cochran	20 Bushels of Corn	10.60
Daniel Wilshire	4 Bushels of Corn	2.12
Jonathan Carey	1 Crosscut Saw	4.50
	Total	$318.48 1/4

State of Indiana)
Hamilton County)   Personally appeared before Me, the Undersigned, a Justice of the Peace within and for the County and State aforesaid, James Hughey and after being duly Sworn deposeth and saith that the within is a full and true account of the Sale of the Goods, Chattles belonging to the Estate of the said

Henry Foland as Sold by said Administrator of said Estate
on the said 17th day of May, 1839 and That He the said
James Hughey acted as Clerk at said Sale James Hughey.

Sworn to and Subscribed before Me, this 22nd day of October,
A.D. 1839.

William Wykoff, (Seal)
Justice of the Peace

BETSY FREEL'S ESTATE

An Inventory of the Goods, Chattles and Effects of Elizabeth Freel,
late of Hamilton County and State of Indiana, deceased, taken by Jonathan
Carey, Administrator of the Estate of said Deceased, with the assistance
of R. P. Hoddy and Daniel Hare, Appraisors called and duly Sworn for that
purpose, December 28th, 1839.

1 Lot of Cupboard Ware	$ 7.50
1 Trunk	2.00
1 Chest and Cradle	1.00
4 Beds, Bedsteads and Bedding	34.07
1 Clock and Glass	8.51
1 Lot of Castings	4.75
1 Brass Kettle	3.00
2 Sadirons	.75
1 Drawing Knife and chisel	1.50
1 Sive	.50
1 Bell	.37
3 lbs. of Flax	.75
2 Bags	1.00
1 Lot of Books	1.87 1/2
1 Razor and Glass	1.50
1 Gun	1.00
1 Knife Box and Knives	.50
1 Gag and Barrel	.50
2 Casks	.25
1 Bedstead	1.00
1 Table	.50
1 Over Coat	6.00
1 Lot of Chairs	2.25
1 Lot of Irons	.50
1 Crib of Corn, 250 Bushels	
at $.20 cts	50.00
1 Mare and Colt	30.00
	$161.99 1/2
3 Kettles	10.50
3 Measures	1.00
1 Old Saddle	1.00
1 Wash Board	.18
1 Wash Tub	.37
1 Stew Kettle	1.25
1 Skellet	.75

```
           1 Lot of Crockery                    $   .25
           1 Pair of Spectacles                     .06 1/4
           1 Boal                                    .06 1/4
           1 Calf                                  1.75
           1 Cow                                  10.00
           1 Heiffar                              10.00
          13 Hogs                                 17.25
           1 Lot of Corn 750 Bushels
               at $.18 3/4 per Bushel            137.50
           1 Bed Tick                               .37 1/2
          12 Ducks                                 1.50
          15 Bushels of Oats                       9.00
           2 Pocket Books                           .25
           1 Loom                                   2.00
           1 Iron Wedge                            1.00
           1 Swingletree                            .81 1/4
                                                $206.85
                                                 161.99
                                                $378.84 1/2
```

Given under Our Hands, this 30th day of June, 1840.

Daniel Hare)
R. P. Hoddy) Apprs.

One Account by Book, Account against Samuel M. Smith for House Rent.

```
                                     $  6.00
                       In All        $384.84 1/2
```

Given under My hand, this 30th day of June, 1840.

Jonathan Carey, Administrator

State of Indiana)
Hamilton County) To Wit:
                 Personally appeared before Me, John Colip, a Justice of the Peace of said County, Jonathan Carey, Administrator of the Estate of Elisabeth Freel, deceased and R. P. Hoddy and Daniel Hare, Appraisors of said Estate and being duly Sworn the said R. P. Hoddy and Daniel Hare says that the above Inventory and Appraisement assigned by them is a Just and True Inventory and Valuation of the Goods, Chattles and Effects of said Elizabeth Freel to the best of their Judgement and the said Jonathan Carey, says that the above is a True Inventory of the Personal Estate of the said Elizabeth Freel so far as the same has come to his hands to be administered.

Given under my hand this 30th day of June, 1840.

John Colip, (Seal)
Justice of the Peace

A Sale Bill of the Goods and Chattles and Effects of Elizabeth Freel, deceased, sold by Jonathan Carey, Administrator of said Deceased on Tuesday the 31st day of December, 1839 with the amount of each article sold for annexed to the purchaser name.

Jacob Crull	1 Lot of Tin Ware	$ .81	1/4
Nicholas Zett	1 Lot of Sundries	1.00	
Charles Whitehead	1 Set of Plates	.37	1/2
Adam Gardner	1 Tea Canister	.25	
Samuel M. Smith	1 Lot of Sundries	.56	1/4
William Freel	1 Teapot	.31	1/4
Levi Osborn	1 Set of Plates	.68	1/4
Wm. Humphreys	1 Set of Tea Plates	.12	1/2
Archibald Ferguson	1 Cream Pitcher	.50	
Adam Gardner	Cups and Saucers	.06	1/4
Rebecca Osborn	1 Set of Plates	.68	
John S. Criswell	1 Trunk	1.37	1/2
Purnell Fleetwood	1 Chest	.25	
Jonathan Carey, Jr.	1 Cradle	.37	1/2
Daniel Harrold	1 Shaving Knife	.75	
Nicholas Zett	1 Bedstead and Cord	1.00	
Purnell Fleetwood	1 Quilt	.81	1/4
John Mc Kee	1 Bed and Sheet	1.25	
John Mc Kee	1 Under Bed	.25	
Purnell Fleetwood	1 Sheet and Pillar Case	.37	1/2
Samuel M. Smith	1 Bed	4.18	3/4
Rachel Osborn	1 Quilt	.68	3/4
Purnell Fleetwood	1 Quilt	.50	
Purnell Fleetwood	1 Bed Spread	.62	1/2
Purnell Fleetwood	2 Pillows	.68	3/4
Adam Gardner	2 Straw Ticks	.06	1/4
John Leonard	1 Quilt	2.00	
Joshua Hamilton	1 Cover Lid	1.75	
Joshua Hamilton	1 Cover Lid	2.00	
John Leonard	1 Quilt	.87	1/2
Wm. Humphrey	2 Pillow Slips	.06	1/4
Wm. Fleetwood	1 Quilt	.50	
Elizabeth Freel	2 Pillows	..50	
Joseph Carns	1 Bed and Sheet	6.25	
Willis Mathewson	1 Bed	6.18	3/4
Joseph Carns	2 Pillows	1.00	
Wm. S. Wallace	1 Cover Lid	3.25	
Charles Whitehead	2 Table Cloths and Sheets	1.81	1/4
Joseph Corns, Sr.	1 Quilt	2.87	1/2
Rachel Osborn	1 Bedstead	.25	
Samuel M. Smith	1 Bedstead	1.68	3/4
W. Fleetwood	1 Mantle Clock	9.75	
Purnell Fleetwood	1 Looking Glass	.12	1/2
Robert Hoddy	1 Skellet	.68	3/4
Barnhart Kinders	1 Skellet	.50	
Elizabeth Freel	1 Frying Pan	1.00	
William Fleetwood	1 Tea Kettle	1.00	
John Osborn	1 Oven Lid and Hooks	1.37	1/2
Sary Smith	1 Stew Kettle and Lid	.75	
William Freel	1 Flat Iron	.43	3/4

Rebecca Osborn	1 Flat Iron	$	.50
Ranson C. Smith	Sundries		.31 1/2
Ebzy Hudson	1 Meal Sive		.43 3/4
Ebzy Hudson	1 Cow Bell		.56 1/4
Cornelius More	1 Bunch of Flax		.62 1/2
Elizabeth Freel	1 Brass Kettle		2.75
George Alias	1 Bag		.50
Ebzy Hudson	1 Meal Bag		.56 1/4
Arch Ferguson	1 Large Bowl		.62 1/2
William Freel	1 Bible		.75
John Osborn	1 Razor, Glass & Box		1.00
Arch Ferguson	1 Lot of Books		.50
Thomas Leonard	1 Walker's Dictionary		.75
Charlotte Freel	1 Sistom of Writing		.25
Wm. Humphries	1 Rifle Gun		3.06 1/4
Ranson Smith	Sundries		.81 1/4
John Mc Kee	1 Tin Bucket		.43 3/4
Levi Osborn	1 Bowl		.06 1/4
John Leonard	1 Coffee Pot		.06 1/4
Rebecca Osborn	Sundries		.12 1/2
Coonrod Mospach	1 Pair of Scissors		.18 3/4
Joshua Hamilton	1 Pair of Specks		.06 1/4
Jonathan Carey	1 Barrel		.56 1/4
Nicholas Zett	1 Lot of Barrels		.18 3/4
Jonathan Carey	1 Lard Tub		.31 1/4
William Fleetwood	1 table		1.31 1/4
Charles Whitehead	1 Overcoat		6.31 1/4
Arch Ferguson	1 Set of Chairs		2.18 3/4
Charles Freel, Sr.	1 Lot of Chairs		2.00
Daniel Harrold	1 Wool Wheel		1.00
Daniel Harrold	1 Hand Irons		.37 1/2
Charles Freel, Sr.	1 Lot of Crocks		.18 3/4
Acker Cox	1 Lot of Crocks		.18 3/4
Allen Goodpasture	1 Spade		.31 1/4
Amos Gough	1 Pair of Steelyards		1.00
Patrick Shield	1 Lot of Corn 50 Bus. 27 cts.		13.50
William Deal	50 Bushels of Corn at 29 cts.		14.50
Nathaniel Norwood	50 Bushels of Corn at 32 cts.		16.00
Thomas Casterson	50 Bushels of Corn at 33 1/4 cts.		15.62 1/2
Zachariah West	1 Mare		23.29
Henry Kemp	1 Colt		10.00
Coonrod Mospach	1 Sugar Kettle		3.93 3/4
Wm. Holloway	1 Sugar Kettle		5.00
Ranson Smith	1 Sugar Kettle		5.00
John Colip	1/2 Bushel Peck & 1/2 Peck		1.18 3/4
Allen Goodpasture	1 Saddle and Bridle		.93 3/4
Arch. Ferguson	1 Wash Tub and Board		1.93 3/4
Joseph Wright	1 Stew Kettle		1.12 1/2
Allen Goodpasture	1 Wedge		1.00
Allen Goodpasture	1 Singletree		.81 1/4
John Leonard	1 Barrel		.25
Daniel Lester	1 Loom		2.00
Joseph Corns	1 Calf		2.00
Frederick Foland	1 Cow		21.00

Arch. Ferguson	4 Hogs (1st Choice)	$ 6.68 3/4
Josiah West	4 Hogs (2nd Choice)	2.62 1/2
Josiah West	4 Hogs (3rd Choice)	2.12 1/2
Caleb W. Sparger	50 Bushels of Corn at 31 1/2 cts per Bushel	15.75
Caleb W. Sparger	50 Bushels of Corn at 31 1/4 cts per Bushel	15.62 1/2
Charles Freel	50 Bushels of Corn at 31 1/4 cts per Bushel	15.62 1/2
Willis Mathewson	50 Bushels of Corn at 30 cts per Bushel	15.00
James Dennend	50 Bushels of Corn at 30 Cts per Bushels	15.00
James Freel	50 Bushels of Corn at 29 1/2 cts per Bushels	14.75
Jacob Colip	50 Bushels of Corn at 30 cts per Bushel	15.00
Henry Orth	50 Bushels of Corn at 30 cts per Bushel	15.00
Caleb W. Sparger	50 Bushels of Corn at 30 1/2 cts per Bushel	15.25
Christian Shell	50 Bushels of Corn at 29 cts per Bushel	14.50
Ira Kingsbury	50 Bushels of Corn at 28 cts per Bushel	14.00
Mathias Brittainham	50 Bushels of Corn at 30 cts per Bushel	15.00
Ebzy Hudson	50 Bushels of Corn at 30 1/4 cts per Bushel	15.12 1/2
James West	84 1/2 Bushels of Corn at 31 1/2 cts per Bushel	26.61 1/2
Daniel Lester	12 Ducks	1.25
Charles W. Freel	45 Bushels of Oats at 19 cts per Bushel	8.55
Jonathan Carey, Sr.	2 Pocket Books	.37 1/2
William Peck	1 Sow and Pigs	3.18 3/4
Jane Osborn	1 Heiffer	12.75
		$468.40 3/4

Test: Joshua Cottingham
    Clerk of said Sale   Jonathan Carey, Administrator

State of Indiana)
Hamilton County) The above named, Joshua Cottingham, makes oath that the
    above is a Just and True Account of the Sale of the Per-
    sonal Estate of Betsey Freel, late of said County, deceased.

    Sworn before Me, a Justice of the Peace of said County the
    30th day of June, A.D. 1840.

                                        John Colip (Seal)
                                        Justice of the Peace

THEOBALD MATER'S ESTATE

An Inventory of the Goods, Chattles and Effects of Theobald Mater, late of Hamilton County and State of Indiana, deceased, taken by George Kloepper, Administrator of the Estate of said Deceased and Jacob Meater, the surviving partner with the assistance of James Mc Neal and Robert Criswell, called and duly Sworn for that purpose.

3 Hand Saws	$ 1.25
1 Lot of Old Chains	1.50
1 Pair of Breast Chains	1.00
1 Chopping Axe	1.25
2 Old Axes	2.00
1 Split Axe and Socket Wedges	2.00
1 Split Axe and Socket Wedges	1.00
2 Iron Wedges	1.50
1 Hand Axe, Pinchers and Chissels	1.50
1 Dung fork and 2 Hay Forks	1.00
1 Pair of Sasage Choppers	1.50
1 Drawing Knife and 4 Augers	1.50
2 Plains and 1 Square	2.00
1 Dougherty & Sive	1.00
1 Log Chain	4.00
1 Doubletree and Singletree	2.00
1 Shovel Plough	3.00
1 Sythe and Hangings	1.00
2 Barrels	.75
1 Horse Collar	2.00
3 Pairs of Haims	1.75
3 Bridles and Check Lines	4.00
2 Pair of Traces and Back Band	4.00
2 Pair of Bridging	8.00
3 Sickles	.50
1 Saddle	10.00
1 Riding Bridle	1.50
1 Old Saddle	1.00
1 Side Saddle	15.00
1 Side Saddle	14.00
1 Cow	10.00
1 Red and White Cow	15.00
1 Brindle Cow	11.00
1 Blade Cow	12.00
1 Yearling Heifer	3.00
1 Calf	1.00
1 Mare and Colt	25.00
1 Mare	50.00
1 Yearling Colt	15.00
1 Yearling Colt	15.00
1 Lot of Pot Metal	9.50
1 Mattock	1.00
1 Cradle and Sythe	3.00
Half Bushel, Wash Board and Basket	.50
2 Tarr Cans and Bell	1.00

2	Spades	$ .25
2	Iron Kettles	5.00
2	Tubs	1.00
12	Crocks	.75
1	Plough	4.00
1	Harrow	4.00
1	Sled	.37 1/2
1	Grindstone	2.50
2	Pewter & Soup Ladles	3.00
1	Dozen of Pewter Plates	6.00
1	Lot of Dressen Furniture	6.00
1	Mantle Clock	10.00
1	Brass Clock	12.00
1	Silver Clock	10.00
2	Beds and Bedding	20.00
1	Oil Cloth	1.50
11	Frame Pictures	3.50
3	Under Beds	2.00
1	Tin Horn and Anvill	.50
3	Wairzer Chairs	1.50
4	Frame Chairs	1.00
1	Tramil	1.00
1	Pair of Hand Irons	1.00
1	Pair of Flat Irons	1.00
2	Tables and Oil Cloths	5.00
1	Rifle Gun and Pouch	10.00
1	Churn	1.00
1	Fat Stand and 2 Buckets	1.00
1	Spinning Wheel	.50
1	Corn Hoe and Dung Fork	1.00
1	Reel	.50
1	Waggon Trough	.50
1	Pair of Scails and Sircingle	1.00
10	Hogs	20.00
10	Hogs	10.00
3	Bags	.75
1	Bed and Bedding	20.00
1	Bed and Bedding	15.00
1	Slate	.25
1	Lot of Wheat in the Ground	5.00
9	Acres of Corn in the Ground	18.00
2	Acres of Oats in the Ground	3.00
	Amount of Whole	$475.87 1/2

Given under Our Hands, this 30th day of May, A.D. 1840.

Robert Criswell)
) Apprs.
James Mc Neal)

An Inventory of the Notes and Accounts of Theobald Mater, late of Hamilton County and State of Indiana, deceased, taken by George Kloepper, administrator and Jacob Mater the Surviving Partner:

A. Busher	Note (Balance on) Dated July 1, 1840	$ 10.00	
Martin Oberlies	Note (Balance on) Due Nov. 2, 1838	10.25	
Michael Shield	Note (Balance on) Due May 17, 1840	115.00	
The Canal	One Order for their Money	16.27	
		$157.52	

George Kloepper, Administrator

An Account of the Sales of the Personal Property of Theobald Mater, late of Hamilton County and State of Indiana, sold at Public Auction, held at the late Dwelling House of the Deceased on the 3rd day of June, A.D. 1840.

George Kloepper	1 Hand Saw	$ .12 1/2	
Henry Bardoner	1 Hand Saw	.12 1/2	
Jacob Bartholemew	1 Hand Saw	.87 1/2	
George Kloepper	1 Lock Chain	.31 1/2	
Nicholas Zett	1 Pr. of Breast Chains	1.00	
Nicholas Zett	1 Lot of Old Chains	1.12 1/2	
Jacob Mater	1 Chopping Axe	1.00	
Jacob Mater	1 Chopping Axe	1.50	
John Nepsee (?)	1 Chopping Axe	1.18 3/4	
William Dick	1 Split Axe and Wedges	2.25	
Nicholas Zett	1 Split Axe	1.00	
Jacob Mater	1 Pr. of Iron Wedges	1.31 1/2	
Nicholas Zett	1 Pr. of Pinchers and Chissels	.81 1/2	
James Mc Neal	2 Iron Forks	.75	
Jacob Mater	1 Pr. of Sausage Choppers	1.75	
William Dick	1 Drawing Knife and 2 Chissels	1.00	
George Kloepper	1 Dung Fork	.50	
Jacob Bartholemew	1 Auger	.37 1/2	
John Nysel	1 Inch Auger	.50	
Enos Beard	1 6 Quarter Auger	.62 1/2	
Jacob Mater	1 6 Quarter Auger	.75	
Jacob Mater	1 Hand Axe	1.00	
Nicholas Zett	1 Square	.56 1/4	
Barnhart Kinder	1 Jack and Fore Plains	2.00	
Jacob Mater	1 Doubletree	2.50	
Jacob Mater	1 Log Chain	5.12 1/2	
Jacob Mater	1 Shovel Plough	3.75	
Volentine Keck	1 Sythe and Snead	1.00	
Jacob Mater	1 Meat Barrel	.75	
Jacob Mater	1 Horse Collar	.87 1/2	
Adam Gardner	1 Pair of Haims	.62 1/2	
Jacob Mater	1 Pair of Haims	.87 1/2	
Jacob Mater	1 Blind Bridle	.87 1/2	
Jacob Mater	1 Riding Bridle	.37 1/2	
Jacob Mater	1 Set of Horse Gears	2.43	
Adam Gardner	Chains and Back Band	1.75	

Jacob Mater	1 Leather Line	$ .25	
Jacob Mater	1 Pr. Check Lines	2.00	
Adam Gardner	1 Bland Bridle	1.00	
Alphius Roberts	2 Prs. Breetching	7.00	
Volentine Keck	1 Sickle	.25	
Enos Beard	1 Sickle	.50	
John Nessel	1 Sickle	.75	
Jacob Mater	1 Mans Saddle	11.00	
Jacob Mater	1 Bridle	1.50	
Nicholas Zett	1 Seersingle	.31 1/4	
George Kloepper	1 Old Saddle	1.31 1/4	
Jacob Mater	1 Side Saddle	14.00	
Ellin Mater	1 Side Saddle	14.00	
Enos Beard	1 Sow (1st Choice)	2.75	
George Kloepper	1 Sow (3rd Choice)	1.62 1/2	
George Kloepper	1 Sow (2nd Choice)	2.25	
Jacob Mater	7 Hogs	17.15 3/4	
William Dick	8 Shoats	8.06 1/4	
Ellin Mater	1 Cow	11.00	
Barnard Kinder	1 Black Cow	14.00	
Volentine Keck	1 Red Cow	13.00	
Jacob Tucker	1 Year Old Heifer	4.50	
George Kloepper	1 Calf	2.00	
Adam Gardner	1 Mare and Colt	27.50	
Jacob Mater	1 Mare	56.00	
John Mushbaugh	1 Year old Colt	25.00	
Coonrod Mushpaw	1 Year Old Colt	22.00	
Henry Bardoner	1 Frying Pan	.43 3/4	
Jacob Mater	1 Frying Pan	.50	
Jacob Mater	1 Pot	.31 1/2	
Jacob Mater	1 Tin Kettle	.25	
Volentine Keck	1 Iron Kettle	.50	
Jacob Mater	1 Iron Kettle	.62 1/2	
Jacob Mater	1 Iron Kettle	.12 1/2	
Jacob Mater	1 Pot	.81 1/4	
Jacob Mater	1 Wash Basin	.12 1/2	
Jacob Bartholemew	1 Frying Pan	1.50	
Volentine Keck	1 Pair of Seals	.37 1/2	
Jacob Mater	1 Oven and Lid	.81 1/4	
Jacob Mater	1 Oven and Lid	.56 3/4	
Barnhart Kinder	1 Lard Stand and Bucket	.68 3/4	
Jacob Mater	1 Grubbing Hoe	1.00	
Barnharr Kinder	1 Sugar Kettle	4.50	
Jacob Mater	1 Small Kettle	.62 1/2	
James Mc Neal	1 Sythe and Cradle	4.00	
Jacob Mater	1 Half Bushel	.37 1/2	
John Miller	1 Tar Can	.18 3/4	
Enos Beard	1 Tar Can	.12 1/2	
Jacob Mater	1 Spade	.18 3/4	
Jacob Mater	1 Sifter	.62 1/2	
Jacob Mater	1 Tub	1.00	
Jacob Mater	1 Tub	.62 1/2	
Jacob Mater	1 Wash Board	.31 1/4	
Enos Beard	1 Lot of Crocks	.37 1/2	

Jacob Mater	1 Doughtrough	$ .56 1/4	
Jacob Mater	1 Plough	5.12 1/2	
Nicholas Zett	1 Harrow	5.75	
Enos Beard	1 Log Sled	.25	
Jacob Mater	1 Grindstone	3.00	
Enos Beard	1 Soup Ladle	.50	
Jacob Mater	1 Pewter Dish	.87 1/2	
Jacob Mater	6 Pewter Plates	1.62 1/2	
Jacob Mater	6 Pewter Plates	2.12 1/2	
Jacob Mater	1 Pewter Dish	1.37 1/2	
John Miller	6 Plates	.75	
Jacob Bartholemew	4 Plates	.37 1/2	
Jacob Mater	2 Plates	.25	
John Mushbaugh	4 Cups and Saucers	.25	
Jacob Mater	1 Set of Cups & Saucers	.43 3/4	
John Nessel	2 Iron Ladles	.68 3/4	
Enos Beard	1 Iron Ladle	.12 1/2	
Jacob Mater	1 Coffee Mill	.31 1/4	
Jacob Mater	1 Coffee Mill	.50	
Jacob Mater	1 Lot of Sundries	.87 1/2	
Jacob Mater	2 Iron Pans	.75	
Jacob Mater	3 Iron Pans	.18 3/4	
Jacob Mater	Candle Moulds & Bason	.56 1/4	
Jacob Mater	3 Tin Buckets	1.31 1/4	
Jacob Mater	1 Lot of Books	10.00	
Jacob Mater	1 Mantle Clock	8.00	
Jacob Mater	1 Silver Watch	9.50	
Martin Beard	1 Brass Clock	17.00	
Nicholas Zett	1 Oil Cloth	1.56 1/2	
Nicholas Zett	1 Bureau Cover	.56 1/2	
John Moppius	1 Bed and Bedding	13.50	
Austin Bushing	1 Bed and Bedding	12.75	
Nicholas Zett	2 Frame Pictures	.87	
Volentine Keck	2 Frame Pictures	.62 1/2	
Henry Badoner	2 Frame Pictures	.43 3/4	
Jacob Bartholemew	2 Frame Pictures	.61	
Jacob Mater	2 Frame Pictures	1.00	
Henry Badoner	2 Frame Pictures	.43 3/4	
Volentine Keck	2 Frame Pictures	.31 1/4	
Jacob Mater	1 Umbrellas	1.00	
Jacob Mater	1 Umbrella	.31 1/4	
Coonrod Mushbaugh	1 Tin Horn	.50	
Jacob Mater	1 Dung Hook	.25	
Jacob Mater	3 Windsor Chairs	2.00	
Jacob Mater	3 Frame Chairs	.62 1/2	
Jacob Mater	1 Trammel	1.00	
Jacob Mater	1 Pair of Hand Irons	1.00	
Jacob Mater	1 Pair of Flat Irons	.93 3/4	
Jacob Mater	1 Table	2.00	
Jacob Mater	1 Table	3.25	
Philip Mushbaugh	1 Bell	1.12 1/2	
William St. Clair	1 Rifle Gun and Pouch	11.00	
Jacob Mater	1 Slate	.25	

Attest: " Given under my hand this 3rd day of June, 1840, Robert Criswell, Clerk of Sale", State of Indiana, Hamilton County)VS.
The above named Robert Criswell, makes oath that the above
is a Just and True Inventory of the Sale of the Personal
Estate of Theobald Mater, late of said County, deceased and
Jacob Mater, the Surviving partner of said County, Sworn before me, a Justice of the Peace of said County, this 9th day
of June, 1840.

Allen Cole (Seal)
Justice of the Peace

NICHOLAS KECK'S ESTATE

An Inventory of the Goods, Effects and Chattles of Nicholas Keck, late
of Hamilton County and State of Indiana, deceased, taken by George Kloepper,
Administrator, Peter Achenbach, Administrator with the assistance of Robert
Criswell and James Mc Neal, called and duly sworn for that purpose.

1 Splitting Axe and Wedges	$ 1.50
1 Sythe & Whetstone, hammer and Anviel	2.00
1 Axe	1.00
1 Bake Kettle	1.00
1 Spider	1.00
1 Log Chain	4.00
1 Cross Cut Saw	4.50
1 Mattock	1.00
6 Chairs	5.00
1 Table	3.50
1 Bed and Bedding	15.00
1 Bed and Bedding	13.00
1 Chest and Table Linen	7.00
2 Baskets	.75
1 Clock	12.00
1 Lot of Books	4.00
1 Lot of Cradle Bedding	3.00
3 Bags	1.50
1 Slate and Looking Glass	.50
1 Cupboard with its Contents	15.00
1 Lot of Kitchen Furniture	6.00
1 Plough	11.00
1 Harrow	4.00
1 Sled	.50
1 Trammel	.75
1 Churn	1.00
4 Tubs and Spade	4.00
1 Barrel and Salt	3.00
1 Meat Tub and Lard Can	2.00
1 Grindstone	1.50
1 Corn Hoe	.50
1 Hand Axe	.75
1 Lot of Corn, 30 Bushels at 20 Cts.	6.00
6 Hogs	6.00
1 Saddle and Bridle	7.00

```
1 Blind Bridle and Horse Gears          $  4.00
1 Hay Fork                                  1.00
1 Horse                                    20.00
1 Lot of Hay                                3.00
1 Lot of Wheat, 20 Bushels at
                          40 cts.           8.00
1 White Cow and Bell                       10.00
1 Year Old Calf                             4.00
1 Cow and Calf                             14.00
4 Acres of Grass on the Ground             8.00
1 Lot of Corn on the Ground               10.00
1 Curry Comb and 2 Pine Boxes               .50
1 Piece of Upper Leather                    1.00
                          Amount        $233.65
```

Given under Our Hands, this 7th day of June, A.D. 1840.

> Robert Criswell
> James Mc Neal.,
> Appraisors

State of Indiana)
Hamilton County) Personally appeared before Me, Allen Cole, a Justice of the Peace and was duly Sworn to appraise the Goods, Chattles and Effects of the Estate of Nicholas Keck, Deceased, according to law and the best of their abilities.

May 22, 1840   Allen Cole, (Seal)
                                          Justice of the Peace

An Inventory of the Notes and Accounts of Nicholas Keck, late of Hamilton County and State of Indiana, deceased, taken by George Kloepper and Peter Achenbach, Administrators, June 9th, 1840.

```
1 Note on Simon Conner, Due 1st of March, 1841      $150.00
  The Balance of a Note on Gilbert Kemp, interest
  calculated at 6 percent to March the 16th, 1840    127.86
1 Note on Volentine Keck, due October 1, 1836        100.00
1 Note on Alphius Roberts, due June 3, 1839           13.00
1 Note on Michael Hough, due Feb. 3, 1839             24.00
1 Note on Account on Widow, Susan Morris, due
  October 1st, 1838                                   10.00
1 Note on D. Welshhorns, due January 2, 1839          10.00
1 Note on D. Welshhorns, on Interest from April
  21st, 1838                                          18.00
Account on Michael Hough                               5.62 1/2
William Deal, Borrowed in 1838, no day mentioned       5.00
Augustus Busher, Borrowed , no date mentioned          3.00
Daniel Welshhons, Borrowed, no date mentioned         21.25
Adam Gardner, Borrowed, no date mentioned              6.65
John Nessel, Borrowed, no date mentioned               5.00
Jacob Mater, Borrowed, no date mentioned               9.80
Michael Hough, Borrowed 55 Pounds of Salt
John Crull, Dr.                                        3.00
```

Note on Henry Garsho, due, October 1, 1840 $200.00
                                        Amount $712.18 1/2

George Kloepper,
                                Administrator

Account of Sales of the Personal Property of Nicholas Keck, Deceased,
late of Hamilton County and State of Indiana, Sold at Public Auction held
at the late Dwelling House of the said Deceased on the 3rd. Day of June,
1840.

John Miller	1 Split Axe and Wedges	$ 1.75
John Nessel	1 Sythe and Whetstone	1.37 1/2
Nicholas Zett	1 Hammer and Anvil	1.00
Volentine Keck	1 Log Chain	5.00
Volentine Keck	1 Cross Cut Saw	4.12 1/2
John Miller	1 Grubbing Hoe	.75
George Kloepper	1 Bake Kettle	1.06 1/4
Volentine Keck	1 Plough	1.25
Volentine Keck	1 Harrow	3.00
Volentine Keck	1 Sled	.50
James Karr	1 Saddle	10.37 1/2
Jacob Murry	1 Bridle	.75
Christorpher Steyman	1 Set of Horse Gears	3.12 1/2
Andrew Carpenter	1 Blind Bridle	1.56 1/4
Andrew Carpenter	1 Leather Line	.31 1/4
Volentine Keck	1 Horse	22.00
George Kloepper	1 Box and Curry Comb	.18 3/4
Peter Achenbach	1 Box	.18 3/4
Peter Achenbach	1 Grindstone	2.50
N. Zett	1 Hand Ax	1.18 3/4
Andrew Carpenter	5 Bushel Wheat 50 cts.	2.50
James Mc Neal	5 Bushel Wheat 56 1/4 cts.	2.81 1/4
Caleb Sparger	6 1/4 Bushel Wheat 56 1/4 cts.	3.50
Daniel Welshkons	10 Bushel Corn 29 cts	2.90
Caleb Sparger	10 Bushel Corn 28 1/2 cts.	2.85
John Nessel	10 Bushel Corn 27 1/2 cts.	2.70
D. Welshkons	1 Piece of Leather	1.00
		$ 88.01 3/4

Attest: Robert Criswell

Given under my hand this 6th day of June, A.D. 1840/

State of Indiana)
Hamilton County)   The Above named Robert Criswell, makes oath that the above
                    is a Just and True account of the Sale of the Personal
                    Estate of Nicholas Keck, late of said County, deceased,
                    Sworn before Me, a Justice of the Peace of said County,
                    the 9th day of June, A.D. 1840.

Allen Cole, (Seal)
Justice of the Peace

An Additional Account of Sales of the Personal Property of Nicholas Keck, late of Hamilton County and State of Indiana, deceased. Taken by George Kloepper and Peter Achenbach, Administrators sold at Public Auction, January 18th, 1841.

Enos Beard	1 Ton of Hay	$ 6.00
Enos Beard	1 Ton of Hay	6.00
Nicholas Zett	500 Lbs. of Hay at 3.00 a Hundred	1.80
Nancy Keck	10 Bushels of Corn at $.20 Cts. each	2.00
Henry Leonard	10 Bushels of Corn at $.21 cts. each	2.10
Nancy Keck	10 Bushels of Corn at $.21 cts each	2.10
Nancy Keck	10 Bushels of Corn at $.25 cts each	2.50
Hildebrandt	16 Bushels of Corn at $.20 cts each	3.20
G. Kloepper	2 Bushels of Buckwheat at .40 cts each	.80
G. Kloepper	2 Bushels of Buckwheat at .41 cts each	.82
Henry Leonard	2 Bushels of Buckwheat at .50 cts each	1.00
Enos Beard	2 Bushels of Buckwheat at..50 cts each	1.00
Henry Leonard	2 Bushels of Buckwheat at .45 cts each	.90
Enos Beard	2 Bushels of Buckwheat at .50 cts each	1.00
Nancy Keck	3/4 Bushel of Buckwheat at .37 1/2	.56 1/4
		$ 31.78 1/4

George Kloepper, Administrator

LEONARD ELLER'S ESTATE

An Inventory of the Goods, Chattles and Effects of Leonard Eller, late of Hamilton County and State of Indiana, deceased. Taken by David Wilkinson, Administrator of the Estate of the Said Deceased, with the assistance of Amasa Bond and Michael Wise, Appraisors, called and duly Sworn for that purpose.

1 Gray Mare	$ 45.00
1 Lot of Sawmill Irons	12.50
1 Bedstead, Bed and Bedding	15.00
1 Rifle Gun	4.00
1 Dutch Oven	1.00
1 Watch	1.00
1 Box	.25
1 Trunk Box	.37 1/2
1 Pair of Saddle Bags	.25

Given under our hands this 21st of November, 1839.

Amasa Bond)
) Appraisors
M. Wise   )

State of Indiana)
Hamilton County) Personally appeared before Me, Samuel Campbell, a Justice
of the Peace in and for said County, David Wilkinson,
Administrator of the Estate of Leonard Eller, deceased
and Amasa Bond and Michael Wise, Appraisors of said Estate
and being duly Sworn, the said Amasa Bond and Michael Wise
says that the above Inventory and Appraisement assigned
by them is a Just and True Inventory and Valuation of the
Goods, Chattles and Effects of the said Leonard Eller to
the best of their Judgement and the said David Wilkinson
says that the above is a True Inventory of the Personal
Estate of the said Leonard Eller, so far as has come to
his hands to be administered.

Given under my hand, this 25th day of November, 1839.

Samuel Campbell
Justice of the Peace

1 Note On	Jacob Eller	$ 14.00
	Interest on the same	7.90
1 Note On	Jacob Eller	170.00
	Interest on the Same	29.57
1 Note On	Jacob Eller	118.50
	Interest on the Same	64.18
1 Receipt	Jacob Eller	20.00
1 Note On	Jacob Eller	33.00
	Interest on the Same	18.36
1 Note On	Mary Flanigan	20.00
	Interest on the Same	13.06 1/4
1 Note on	James North	18.18 3/4
	Interest on the Same	10.09 1/2
1 Note on	James North	10.00
	Interest on the Same	1.00
1 Note on	Mary North	20.00
	Interest on the Same	2.00
1 Note on	Mary North	10.00
	Interest	2.40
1 Receipt	Mary Flannagon	37.00
1 Note on	James North	15.00
	Interest	2.62
1 Note On	Mary North	18.00
	Interest	.27
1 Note On	John Eller	20.00
	Interest	14.68 1/2
1 Note on	John Eller	25.00
	Interest	14.49
1 Note on	John Eller	18.75
	Interest	11.07

1 Note on	Sarah Eller	$ 5.62 1/2
	Interest	2.75
1 Receipt	John Eller	2.50
1 Receipt	John Eller	20.00
1 Note on	Joseph Eller	50.00
	Interest	24.75
1 Note on	Joseph Eller	40.00
	Interest	29.92
1 Note on	Joseph Eller	15.00
	Interest	6.60
1 Receipt	Joseph Eller	20.00
1 Receipt	Adam Eller	20.00
1 Note on	David Eller	20.00
	Interest	7.58
1 Note on	David Eller	10.00
	Interest	.75
1 Note on	Samuel North	7.00
	Interest	1.75
1 Note on	David Eller	15.00
	Interest	.56 1/4
		$1007.12

David Wilkinson, Admr.

1 Note on	Thomas Cooper	63.50
	Interest	4.75
1 Note on	Alexander Mock	150.00
	Interest	3.33
1 Note on	Aaron Osborn	12.00
	Interest	.50
1 Note on	Joshua Reddick	100.00
	Interest	2.50
1 Note on	Deford George	62.50
	Interest	4.28 1/2
1 Note on	William Dickerson	50.00
	Interest	2.05
1 Note on	William Dickerson	42.00
	Interest	4.08
1 Note on	Peter Smith	110.00
	Interest	37.24
1 Note on	James Ellis	50.00
	Interest	3.20
1 Note on	Bethel J. Duning	70.00
	Interest	5.25
1 Note on	Ezekiah Mills	25.20
	Interest	2.59
1 Note on	John S. Richardson	100.00
	Interest	6.95
1 Note on	John S. Richardson	12.50
	Interest	.86 3/4
1 Note on	Madison Urell	18.00
	Interest	1.08
1 Note on	Elisha Reddick	100.00
	Interest	7.93

1 Note on	Elisha Reddick	$ 79.88
	Interest	6.20
1 Note on	Bethel J. Duning	100.00
	Interest	7.50
1 Note on	George Owen	48.00
	Interest	17.48
1 Note on	William Rice	47.00
	Interest	8.68
1 Note on	Robert Kimberlin	17.21
	Interest	.86
1 Note on	Peter Flanagon	16.66
	Interest	.45
1 Note on	Leonard Flanagon	50.00
	Interest	9.49
1 Note on	Peter Flanagon	55.00
	Interest	11.11
1 Note on	Jonathan Parrons	22.12
	Interest	6.55
1 Note on	Absalum Eller	30.00
	Interest	3.94
1 Note on	John Flanagon	8.00
	Interest	.54
1 Note on	John Eller	20.00
	Interest	4.00
1 Note on	E. B. & Peter Flanagon	5.00
	Interest	1.20
1 Note on	James Flanagon	16.25
	Interest	8.52
1 Note on	Thomas Dodson, Due April 1, 1841	300.00
1 Note on	Thomas Dodson Due April 1, 1841	300.00
1 Note on	Thomas Dodson Due April 1, 1842	300.00
1 Note on	Thomas Dodson Due April 1, 1843	300.00
1 Note on	Ephraim Hoover	112.50
	Interest	1.40 1/2
1 Note on	Ephraim Hoover Due June 3, 1840	112.50
1 Mortague on	Jonathan Goley Due the 18th day of July, 1840 to the amount of When Due	360.00
	The Money on Hand	255.62 1/2
Amount Due	From Adam Eller, dec'd.	286.00
		$3981.92

December 21, 1839   Wm. Strickland, Clerk

                                        David Wilkinson, Administrator

" I hereby certify that William Stricklin was duly sworn by Me, the
undersigned, a Justice of the Peace, this 30th day of December, 1839."

Account of Sales of the Personal Property of Leonard Eller, late of the County of Hamilton and State of Indiana, deceased at a Public Auction held at the late Dwelling House of the said Deceased, on the 21st day of December, A.D. 1839.

Absalum Eller	1 Rifle Gun	$ 2.00
Absalum Eller	1 Watch	1.60
Joseph Eller	1 Oven & Lid	.50
Joseph Eller	1 Bedstead, Bed & Bedding	6.00
Joseph Eller	1 Trunk	.25
Joseph Eller	1 Box	.87 1/2
William Stricklin	1 Pair of Saddle Bags	.37 1/2
Joseph Eller	1 Set of Sawmill Tools	8.37 1/2
Alexander North	1 Gray Mare	34.00
		$ 54.07 1/2

December 21st, 1839   William Stricklin, Clerk

                                       David Wilkinson, Administrator

"I hereby certify that William Stricklin was duly sworn by me, the undersigned, a Justice of the Peace, this 30th day of December, 1839.

                                       Samuel Dale, (Seal)
                                       Justice of the peace

Additional Inventory of Notes on E. Brock $ 35.00

JOHN ALLMAN'S ESTATE CONTINUED

Inventory of the Goods, Chattles and Effects of John Allman, late of Hamilton County and State of Indiana, deceased. Taken by James H. Cochran, Administrator of the Estate of the said Deceased, with the assistance of Zenas Beckwith and Robert P. Hoddy, Appraisors, called on and duly Sworn for that Purpose.

1 French Bedstead, 2 Straw Ticks, 1 Feather Bed, 1 Sheet and 1 Quilt	$ 10.00
1 Common Bedstead, Straw Ticks and 2 Feather Beds	10.00
2 Sheets	1.00
1 Table	1.00
1 Little Wheel	2.00
1 Mantle Clock	12.00
1 Looking Glass	.87 1/2
1 Old Chest	.25
1 Cupboard	.75
1 Tin Bucket and Coffee Pot	.87 1/2
1 Lot of Cupboard Ware	1.00
1 Pewter Dish	.25
7 Chairs	2.00

```
1 Equil Mority Fetchers Books          $
            4 Volumes.                    2.00
1 Hymn Book                                .25
1 Univ. Salvation                          .25
1 Barrel and Pickle Pork                  2.00
1 Old Coffee Mill                          .06 1/4
1 Sive                                     .37 1/2
1 Man Saddle                              9.00
1 Bridle                                   .12 1/2
1 Collar, haims and 1 Set of Traces       2.50
1 Doubletree and Singletree               1.25
1 Plough, Clevis and Singletree           2.00
1 Flax Brake                               .25
1 Axe                                     2.00
1 Axe                                     2.00
1 Old Axe                                  .25
2 Hay Forks                                .37 1/2
1 Kettle                                  3.00
1 Pot                                      .25
1 Spider & Lid                            1.00
1 Skellet                                  .25
1 Dutch Oven                               .12 1/2
1 Tea Kettle                               .25
1 Tub and Half Bushel                      .25
1 Pair of Haims                            .25
1 Lot of Horse Shoes                       .37 1/2
1 Square, Chisel and Shaving Knife        1.00
1 Blind Bridle                             .37 1/2
1 Lot of Old Irons                         .25
1 Loom, 2 Reeds Quill Wheel & Etc.        3.00
1 Yoke of Oxen                           30.00
1 Cow and Calf                            8.00
3 Sows and Five Pigs                      7.50
1 Bay Mare                               30.00
1 Two Year Old Colt                      20.00
1 Old Log Chain                           2.00
1 Little Bedstead                          .50
1 Stack of Wheat                          7.00
1 Wheat Fan                              16.00
1 Flax Brake                               .50
                                        --------
                                       $198.56
```

Given under our hands, this 7th day of February, 1840.

Zenas Beckwith
R. P. Hoddy

```
William Pecks    Balance on Note    $ 18.62
Amos Gough       Balance on Note      19.82
John Colip       Account               1.00
                                     --------
                 Making in All      $237.98
```

Given under My hand, this 7th day of February, 1840.

                                    his
                         James H.   X   Cochran
                                    mark

132

State of Indiana)
Hamilton County) Personally appeared before Me, John Colip, a Justice of
the Peace in and for said County, James H. Cochran, Ad-
ministrator of the Estate of John Allman, deceased and
Zenas Beckwith and Robert P. Hoddy, Appraisors of said
Estate and being by Me, duly Sworn the said Zenas Beck-
With and Robert P. Hoddy says that the above Inventory
and Appraisement assigned by them is a Just and True
Inventory and Valuation of the Goods, Chattles and Effects
of the said John Allman, deceased to the best of their
Judgement and the said James H. Cochran says that the above
is a True Inventory of the Personal Estate of the said
John Allman deceased, so far as the same has come to his
hands to be Administered, February 7th, 1840.

John Colip, (Seal)
Justice of the Peace.

Property taken by the Widow to Wit:

1 French Bedstead, 2 Strawticks, 1 Feather Bed, 2 Sheets and 1 Quilt	$ 10.00
1 Common Bedstead, 1 Strawticks, 2 Feather Beds, 1 Sheet and 2 Quilts	10.00
1 Table	1.00
2 Sheets	1.00
1 Little Wheel	2.00
1 Looking Glass	.87 1/2
1 Cupboard	.75
1 Tin Bucket and Coffee Pot	.87 1/2
1 Cupboard Ware	1.00
1 Pewter Dish	.25
7 Chairs	2.00
1 Hymn Book	.25
1 Barrel and Pickle Pork	2.00
1 Old Coffee Mill	.06 1/4
1 Sive	.37 1/2
1 Bridle	.12 1/2
1 Plough, Clevis and Singletree	2.00
1 Axe	2.00
1 Kettle	3.00
1 Pot	.25
1 Spider and Lid	1.00
1 Dutch Oven	.12 1/2
1 Tea Kettle	.25
1 Tub and Half Bushel	.25
1 Loom, 2 Reeds Quill and Wheel Etc	3.00
1 Cow and Calf	8.00
3 Sows and 5 Pigs	7.50
1 Old Log Chain	2.00
1 Stack of Wheat	7.00
Making in All	$ 68.93

Invoice of the Goods, Chattles and Effects of John Allman, deceased,

Sold by James H. Cochran, Administrator of said Estate on the 8th day of February, 1840.

Jesse Justice, Jr.	1 Lot of Horse Shoes	$. .25	
E. Holliway	1 Shaving Knife	.50	
C. Moore	1 Square	.31	1/4
Jesse Justice	1 Chisel	.19	
Jesse Justice	1 Lot of Old Irons	.14	
Jesse Justice	1 Pair of Haims	.31	1/4
John Newby	1 Bridle	.75	
Jacob T. Tyson	Haims and Traces	1.06	1/4
P. George	1 Collar	1.50	
Samuel Fleetwood	1 Singletree & Doubletree	.75	
Eli Goin	1 Skellet	.25	
Jacob Colip	2 Hay Forks	.31	1/4
George Peck	1 Lid	.18	3/4
P. George	1 Axe	1.87	1/2
J. S. Tyson	1 Axe	.26	
C. Whitehead	1 Flax Brake	.35	
J. S. Tyson	1 Little Bedstead	.37	1/2
Jonathan Carey	1 Equil Moutz Flechers	2.00	
Alphius Fore	1 Book	.25	
William Allman	1 Man's Saddle	10.00	
P. George	1 Chest	.12	1/2
Zenas Beckwith	1 Mantle Clock	10.00	
Adam Rutter	1 Yoke of Oxen	30.00	
James Hughey	1 Mare	24.00	
Jonathan Allman	1 Two Year Old Colt	12.50	
Henry Deaver	1 Wheat Fan	14.00	
Henry Deaver	1 Flax Brake	.83	

Making in All $113.09

Signed Jacob Colip, Clerk of Appraisors of Sale

State of Indiana)
Hamilton County)   May 9th, 1840
Personally appeared before me, Allen Cole, a Justice of the Peace in and for said County, Jacob Colip, who being duly Sworn upon his Oath deposeth and saith that the foregoing is a true copy of the appraisement and sale of the Goods, Chattles and Effects of the said John Allman, deceased. Kept by Him as acting Clerk at the Appraising and selling of the goods, Chattles and effects by James H. Cochran, Administrator of said Estate aforesaid as set forth in the foregoing Schedule to the best of his knowledge.

Allen Cole,   (Seal)
Justice of the Peace

John Montgomery's Estate to the Estate of John Allman, deceased, To the Amount of $5.00 for borrowed Money, February 8th, 1841.

James Cochran, Admir.

Mr. Simon Cochran, Bought of Mahin and Ritchie 8 Yards of Linsey for
John Allman at 81 1/4 cts. $ 6.50
Noblesville, December 7th, 1839

Noblesville, August 1st, 1839.
         Simon Cochran, Dr. to Allman, John   1 Horse $50.00

         Cr. By Pork   5.00
             By Lime   3.00
             By Ballance on Account   5.87 1/2

LEMUEL DARROW'S ESTATE

Inventory of the Personal Estate of Lemuel Darrow, late of Hamilton
County, Indiana, deceased, March the 17th, A.D. 1840.

1 Bed and Bedding	$ 20.00
1 Bed and Bedding	20.00
1 Bed and Bedding	14.00
3 Table Cloths and 2 Towels	3.00
1 Looking Glass	.50
3 Chests and Trunk	3.50
1 Sugar Tub and Lard Keg	.75
1 Man's Razor, leather Box, Pair of Steelyards and 5 Hooks	2.50
1 Lot of Dressen Ware and Reflector	9.00
1 Skellet, Tea Kettle and iron Pot	1.75
1 Coffee Mill, 2 Flat Irons and One Shovel	2.00
2 Sugar Kettles	6.00
1 Pair of Hand Bellows, Hammer and Square, Compass	1.25
1 Earthen Jug and Crock	.31 1/4
1 Wash Tub	.37 1/2
2 Axes, 2 Plows, Clevis, 1 Ring and Stelple (?)	7.00
2 Meat Barrels	1.25
6 Head of Sheep	12.00
1 Lot of Meat	13.00
2 Cows and Yearling Calf	26.00
7 Head of Hogs	5.50
	$149.18 3/4

Given under Our hands, this 17th day of March, 1840.

                                        James Shaw   )
) Apprs.
                                        Hugh Johnson)

A list of Notes outstanding in favor of the Estate of Lemuel Darrow,
late of Hamilton County, Indiana, deceased, March the 17th, 1840.

         1 Note of Hand on Wm. Peck and James Hughey for $ 70.00

1 Note of Hand on Hugh John for $ 37.16
                                            $107.16

Given under my hand, this 17th day of March, A.D. 1840.

                                     James Beeson, Admr.

State of Indiana)
Hamilton County) Personally appeared before Me, John Colip, a Justice of the
                  Peace in and for said County, James Beeson, Administrator
                  of the Estate of Lemuel Darrow, deceased and James Shaw
                  and Hugh Johnson, Appraisors of said Estate and being duly
                  Sworn the said James Shaw and Hugh Johnson says that the
                  above Inventory and Appraisement assigned by them is a
                  Just and True Inventory and Valuation of the Goods,
                  Chattles and Effects of the said Lemuel Darrow to the
                  best of their Judgement and the said James Beeson says
                  that the above is a True Inventory of the Personal Estate
                  of the said Lemuel Darrow so far as the same has come to
                  his hands to be administered.

                                     John Colip   (Seal)
                                     Justice of the Peace

COONROD FEARCE'S ESTATE

   An Inventory of the Goods, Chattles and Effects of Coonrod Fearce, late
of Hamilton County and State of Indiana, deceased, taken by Christopher Fearce
Administrator of the Estate of the said Deceased, with the assistance of
Joshua Cottingham and Allen Cole, Appraisors, called and duly Sworn for that
purpose,

1 Bed and Bedstead and Coverlids (8)	$ 25.00
1 Bed and Bedstead and 6 Coverlids (X)	20.00
1 Bed and Bedstead and 8 Coverlids (X)	12.00
1 Clock (X)	10.00
1 Little Beaureaugh (X)	15.00
1 Looking Glass (X)	.62
1 Chest (X)	1.00
1 Chest	.50
1 Trunk (X)	.75
1 Table	1.50
9 Chairs (X)	4.50
1 Churn	.50
1 Tin Pan, Canister, Set of Plates, 1/2 Set of Cups and Sucers (X)	1.25
1 Lot of Cupboard Ware	1.75
1 Pair of Flat Irons	.62 1/2
1 Tea Kettle, Tramel, Shovel, Hand Irons	1.75
1 Set of Knives and Forks Box	1.00
1 Pair of Steelyards, Coffee Mill & Horn	.75
1 Lot of Cupboard Ware	2.50
4 Old Axes	3.00
1 Box of Plunder	3.00

```
         2 Hoes, 1 Mattock, 1 Chain, 1 Wedge        $  3.38
         2 Half Bushels                                 .75
           Harness & Bridles, 1 Set of Bridles (X)     6.00
         1 Lot of Wheat                                 4.00
         2 Boxes                                         .50
         1 Tub and Kettle and Tar Bucket               1.90
         1 Lot of Baskets                              1.00
         3 Sythes and Hangings                         2.25
         2 Old Saddles                                 5.00
         1 Dung Fork and Shovel                        2.00
         2 Sive and Wheels                             4.00
         1 Lot of Old Barrels & 1 Not Mall             1.25
         1 Bag of Flour (X)                            3.75
         2 Bags                                         .50
         1 Lot of Meat (X)                             9.00
         1 Lot of Barrels                              9.75
         1 Lot of Potatoes and 2 Bee Gums              3.25
         1 Lot of Corn                                25.00
         1 Waggon                                     20.00
         1 Field of Wheat on the Ground               15.00
         2 Ploughs and Singletree                      7.50
        11 Acres of Meadows                           25.00
         1 Lot of Poultry                              5.00
         6 Hogs                                       22.50
         1 Stack of Wheat                              8.50
           Hay                                         3.00
         1 Wheat Fan                                  10.00
           Forks, Rakes and Flails                     .50
         1 Gray Colt                                  18.00
         1 Sorrel Colt                                20.00
         1 Bay Colt                                   12.00
         1 Gray Mare (X)                              60.00
         1 Bay Mare                                   40.00
         1 Cow                                        12.00
         1 Cow and Bell (X)                           14.00
         5 Yearling Calves                            16.00
         6 Sheep (4 Sheep (X))                        25.00
           of a Harrow                                 1.00
           of a Grindstone                             .75
                             Making in All         $510.50
```

(X) The Widow has taken all that is Crossed.   Joshua Cottingham)
                                                    Allen Cole   ) Apprs.

        Given under my hand this 25th day of April, 1840.

                                           Christopher J. Fearce
                                                 Administrator

        The Widow has taken One Hundred and fourteen dollars $114.00

State of Indiana)
Hamilton County) Personally appeared before Me, William Wykoff, a Justice of
                   the Peace in and for said County, Christopher J. Fearce,

Administrator of the Estate of Coonrod Fearce, deceased
and Allen Cole, Joshua Cottingham, Appraisors of said
Estate and being duly Sworn the said Allen Cole and Joshua
Cottingham says that the Inventory and Appraisement,
assigned by them is a Just and True Valuation of the Goods
Chattles and Effects of the said Coonrod Fearce, deceased
to the best of their Judgement and the said Christopher
Fearce says that the above is a True Inventory of the
Personal Estate of the said, Coonrod Fearce, so far as the
same has come to his hands to be administered.

Justices Fee's 25   William Wykoff   (Seal)
                                           Justice of the Peace

    Invoice of the Goods, Chattles and Effects of Coonrod Fearce, deceased
sold by Christopher J. Fearce, Administrator of said Estate, Sold on the
13 th day of May, 1840.

Jane Fearce	1 Bed and Bedding	$ 10.00
Ira Kingsbury	1 Chest	1.00
Ira Kingsbury	1 Table	1.00
Daniel Harrold	2 Chairs (1st Lot)	.70
William Fearce	2 Chairs (2nd Lot)	.81 1/2
Henry Ferguson	3 Chairs (3rd Lot)	.75
Thomas Murphy	2 Windsor Chairs	.37 1/2
John Mc Kee	1 Churn	.68 1/2
Andrew Kickson	2 Crocks	.12 1/2
Chris Fearce	2 Crocks	.18 3/4
Daniel Harrold	1 Dish	.25
Wm. Fearce	1 Sugar Barrel	.25
Chris. Fearce	1 Coffee Pot	.18 3/4
Ebzy Hudson	1 Tea Pot, 3 Cups & Saucers	.31 1/4
Daniel Harrold	1 Pitcher	.20
Ebzy Hudson	1 Table & Tea Spoons	.26
Andrew Dickson	1 Creamer	.06 1/4
Wm. Fearce	1 Tin Bucket	.50
Jane Fearce	1 Jar	.06 1/4
Henry Ferguson	5 Plates	.36
John Mc Kee	3 Plates & 1 Barrel	.25
Daniel Harrold	1 Wooden Bowl	.12 1/2
H. Freel	1 Dressing Iron	.37 1/2
Daniel Harrold	1 Bowl and 2 Pans	.16 3/4
John Mc Kee	1 Knife and Knife Box	.75
Daniel Harrold	1 Tin Pan	.18 3/4
Ira Kingsbury	1 Wooden Bowl & Bucket	.49
Ebzy Hudson	1 Bucket and Bottle	.12 1/2
H. Ferguson	Candle Moulds & Stick	.75
C. Moore	1 Lot of Viols	.75
Isaac Stevens	Hass & Steelyards	1.06 1/4
Andrew Dickson	1 Coffee Mill	.26
Ebza Hutson	1 Tin Cups	.33
Nick Zett	1 Tea Kettle	.70
Ira Kingsbury	1 Basket	.12 1/2
E. Holliway	1 Pot & Trammel	1.00

Joseph A. Right	1 Iron Wedge	$ .25	
Daniel Harrold	1 Clevis & Ring	.12	1/2
Wm. Ballard	1 Box & Irons	.20	
Ira Kingsbury	Stretchers & Chains	.13	
R. P. Hoddy	1 Box & Irons	.37	1/2
Ira Kingsbury	1 Hoe	.76	
Daniel Welshons	1 Hoe	.25	
William Fearce	1 Hoe	.06	1/4
R. P. Hoddy	1 Mattock	.56	1/4
Ira Kingsbury	1 Mattock	.18	3/4
Allen Cole	1 Half Bushel	.62	1/2
T. Murphy	1 Chair	1.50	
E. Fearce	1 Line	.25	
E. Fearce	1 Check Line	.75	
R. P. Hoddy	Horse Gears	1.50	
R. P. Hoddy	1 Horse Collar	.87	1/2
Ebza Hutson	1 Lot of Bridles	.46	
William Fearce	1 Bridle	.41	
Ira Kingsbury	Sickle Hoops	.50	
Jacob Colip	1 Box & 7 Bushels of Wheat	4.37	1/2
E. Fearce	1 Empty Box	.25	
Ira Kingsbury	1 Big Wheel	.75	
C. Fearce	1 Die Pot	.06	1/4
W. S. Dickson	1 Tarr Can	.06	1/4
Ira Kingsbury	1 Tarr Can	.18	3/4
Ira Kingsbury	1 Tub and Board	.42	3/4
William Fearce	1 Seive	.25	
Ira Kingsbury	2 Baskets	.35	
Daniel Harrold	3 Baskets	.60	
Joseph A. Right	1 Sythe	.62	1/2
Ira Kingsbury	1 Sythe	1.00	
R. P. Hoddy	1 Sythe	.81	1/4
E. Fearce	1 Ladys Ladle	3.06	1/4
R. P. Hoddy	1 Fire Shovel	.42	
Ebza Hutson	1 Old Saddle	.62	1/2
Ira Kingsbury	1 Stable Fork	2.00	
R. P. Hoddy	1 Shoval	.76	
C. J. Fearce	1 Little Wheel	.70	
Ira Kingsbury	1 Knot Maul	.35	
Ira Kingsbury	1 Barrel and Beans	.40	
Ira Kingsbury	1 Churn & Timothy Seeds	.57	
Ira Kingsbury	1 Empty Barrel	.06	1/4
William Fearce	2 Old Barrels	.06	1/4
James Dennen	1 Martin Box	.06	1/4
E. Fearce	1 Singletree	.18	3/4
Ira Kingsbury	1 Ox Yoke	.45	
Ebza Hutson	1 Shovel	.38	
Daniel Harrold	1 Bag	.17	
E. Fearce	1 Bag	.06	1/4
Daniel Harrold	1 Bag	.01	
Ira Kingsbury	1 Lot of Flour & Barrel	1.02	
James Dennen	Can and Lard	1.37	1/2
Harrison Freel	Barrel and Salt	.31	1/4
Pattrick Shields	Soap Grease	.50	

Pattrick Shields	Soap and Barrel	$ .25	
Ira Kingsbury	1 Meat Tub	.75	
Charles Freel, Sr.	12 1/2 lbs of Pickle Pork,12 3/4	15.87	1/2
Daniel Harrold	1 Bed and Bedding	6.00	
Daniel Harrold	5 Bed Covers	.50	
E. Holliway	1 Mantle Clock	12.69	
Andrew Dickson	1 Doz. Chickens	.93	3/4
Andrew Dickson	1 Doz. Chickens	.96	
Christian Stehman	1 Doz. Chickens	.90	
Christian Stehman	1 Doz. Chickens	.70	
Andrew Dickson	44 Lbs. of Potatoes	2.99	
Ira Kingsbury	2 Bee Gums	.18	3/4
William Fearce	25 Bushels of Corn, 31 cts.	7.75	
Hiram Stowel	25 Bushels of Oats, 31 Cts.	7.75	
R. P. Hoddy	25 Bushels of Oats, 30 cts.	7.50	
Daniel Welshons	Last Lot at .29 cts.	8.19	
Daniel Harrold	1 Waggon	20.62	1/2
R. P. Hoddy	1 Lot of Wheat in the ground	12.81	1/4
Ebza Hutson	1 Plough	3.06	1/4
Ebza Hutson	1 Plough	2.25	
Ira Kingsbury	1 Doubletree, Singletree and Clevis	2.38	
Ira Kingsbury	2 First Sires	10.00	
Ira Kingsbury	3 Hogs	11.37	1/2
T. Murphy	1 Hog	3.40	
Joseph Coens	1 Stack of Wheat	10.02	
R. P. Hoddy	1 Lot of Rakes & Forks	.51	
H. Ferguson	1 Lot of Hay in Barn	4.50	
Thomas Stafford	1 Wheat Fan	11.00	
Wilson Fearce	1 Gray Colt	22.25	
Thomas Caster	1 Sorrel Horse Colt	20.90	
Hiram Stowel	1 Bay Colt	16.00	
R. P. Hoddy	1 Bay Mare	57.50	
Scott S. Moore	1 Cow and Calf	16.75	
H. Stowel	1 Heiffer	5.77	
Ira Kingsbury	1 Bull	5.00	
Ira Kingsbury	1 Steer	5.08	
Hiram Stowel	1 Heifer	6.75	
Ira Kingsbury	1 Heifer	5.00	
Ira Kingsbury	1 Heifer	8.25	
J. S. Dickson	1 Keg and Tunnel	.62	1/2
T. Murphy	1 Bottle	.10	
N. Zett	8 Geese	2.62	
Ira Kingsbury	1 Lot of Sheep	26.50	
E. Fearce	1/3 of a Harrow	.50	
Ira Kingsbury	1/2 of a Grind Stone	.51	
Ira Kingsbury	1 Lot of Meadow Season	9.00	
Ira Kingsbury	1 Lot of Lower Meadow Season	13.50	
Ira Kingsbury	1 Jug	.15	
Daniel Harrold	1 Note On	2.68	3/4
Edward Ware	1 Note On	1.09	1/2
	Making in All	$442.66	

I, Jacob Colip, acting Clerk do hereby certify that the foregoing is a

True copy of the Inventory of the Goods, Chattles and Effects of Coonrod Fearce, late of Hamilton County, Indiana, Deceased, sold by Christopher J. Fearce on the 13th day of May, 1840 as by me kept on the said Day of Sale, Errors excepted in adding.

Jacob Colip, Clerk.

State of Indiana)
Hamilton County) June 5th, 1840
Personally appeared before me, William Wykoff, a Justice of the Peace of the County aforesaid, Jacob Colip, who being by me duly sworn, deposeth and saith that the above Inventory as by him, signed is Just and True to the best of his knowledge.

William Wykoff, (Seal)
Justice of the Peace

ROBERT P. HODDY'S ESTATE

An Inventory of the Goods, Chattles and Effects of Robert P. Hoddy, late of Hamilton County and State of Indiana, deceased. Taken by Elias Hoddy, Administrator of said Deceased, with the assistance of John Colip and Jacob Colip, Appraisors called and duly sworn for that purpose To WIT:

All of the Table & Cupboard Ware consisting of Buckets, Knives, Forks, Spoons, Plates, Tins, Coffee Pots, Tea Pots, including all Cupboard and Tableware _____ Milk Pans, Tin, Sugar Box, all the Tin Queens Potters, German Silver Ladle, Tea Spoons, Glassware, knife Box and Candle Molds.	$ 15.00
1 Cupboard	3.50
1 Table	2.00
1 Churn	.50
2 Wooden Bowls	.50
9 Split Bottom Chairs	3.00
1 Cradle	.37 1/2
1 Shoval and Hand Irons	1.50
1 Writing Desk	3.00
1 Chest	1.50
1 Old Trunk	.25
1 Mantle Clock	12.00
1 Bed and Bedstead, No. 1	15.00
1 Bed and Bedstead, No. 2	12.25
1 Trunnel Bed and Bedstead	4.50
3 Sheets and Bed Covers	13.75
3 Books and Slate	2.25
1 Man's Saddle	6.00
4 Bags	1.50
1 Tea Kettle	1.00
1 Stew Kettle	.75
1 Oven and Lid	.75

1 Skellet	$ .75
1 Little Skellet	.75
1 Wash Kettle	2.00
1 Wash Kettle	2.00
2 Wash Tubs and Wash Board	1.25
1 Meat Tub	.62 1/2
1 Half Bushel	.25
1 Frying Pan	.50
2 Old Barrels and Fat Can	.50
2 Empty Barrels	.25
4 Bee Stands	6.00
2 Mattocks	2.50
2 Hoes	1.00
1 Shovel	.25
1 Hammer	.50
2 Shovel Ploughs	4.00
1 Singletree and Clevis	1.50
1 Plough Harrow	2.50
1 Sythe and Hanings	.25
1 Manure Shovel	.50
1 Old Broad Axe	2.00
1 Rake and 2 Forks	.50
Steelyards	2.00
1 Grindstone	2.25
1 Log Chain	3.00
1 Steeple Ring and Newhoen Axe	1.50
1 Lot of Old Irons	.75
1 Box of Old Irons	1.00
Stretcher Chains	.50
2 Old Ox Yokes	.25
1 Iron Wedge	.50
1 Hand Saw	1.25
6 Augers	1.50
1 Shaving Knife and Old Saw	.50
2 Sets of Brick Chain Lines, 2 Collars, 2 Bridles, 2 Sets of Haims, 2 Set of Trams	12.50
1 Old Collar, Hames and Traces	1.50
1 Set of Blacksmith Tools	60.00
3 Gimblets	.18 3/4
1 Singletree, Clevis and Old Sled	1.00
1 Cary Plough	3.00
1 Waggon and Neck Yoke	35.00
1 Lot of Chair Coal	3.00
1 Doubletree and Clevis	1.00
2 Old Axes	1.00
1 Axe	.75
1 Old Scraper	.25
1/2 Harrow, whole owned by Hoddy and A. Cole	2.00
1/2 Wheat Fan owned by Hoddy and A. Cole	6.00
1 Sow and 7 Pigs	5.00
3 Hogs (Equal out of 6 Best in Flock)	13.50
3 Hogs	13.50
7 Shoat	15.00
1 Sow and Pigs	4.00

7 Sheep	$ 10.50
1 Lot of Oats in North End of Stubbs	5.00
1 Lot of Oats in South End	6.00
1 Hide	2.00
1 Hogs Head and Wheat	1.00
2 Flails, 1 Rake and 1 Spade	1.12 1/2
1 Axe Yoke Ring and Staples	1.25
1 Card and Brush	.06 1/4
1 Black Cow and Bell	10.50
1 Yearling Bull	3.25
1 Young Cow	9.00
1 Heiffer	8.50
1 Mare	50.00
1 Gray Horse	35.00
1 Bay Mare	29.00
1 Brown Colt	23.50
1 Sorrel Colt	5.00
8 Stacks of Hay at $6.00 per Stack	48.00
1 Stack of Hay	4.00
1 Large Stack of Hay	9.00
1 Stack of Hay	9.00
1 Calf	1.50
1 Half of 3 Stacks of Wheat, owned by R. P. Hoddy and Wm. Fearce	18.50
1 Stack of Wheat	7.50
1 Halter Chains	.75
1 Lot of Corn, supposed to be 3 Acres	15.00
1 Yearling Bull	4.00
1 Blind Bridle	.87 1/2
1 Book Hengels	.12 1/2
1 Little Stack of Wheat	2.81 3/4

Given under Our hands, this 19th day of September, 1840.

Jacob Colip)
John Colip) Apprs.

William Parkins, Due Bill Sept. 6th, 1836 for	$ 20.00
Nathan Kelly's, Note Due Dec. 24th, 1838	6.87 1/2
A. Carpenter, Due Bill, Nov. 17th, 1838	4.50
William James, Note Ballance	3.06 1/4
D. Willsons, Note Due, Feb. 3rd, 1835	5.18 3/4
Samuel Hamilton, Note, Sept. 22nd, 1839	.81 3/4
Charles Whitehead, Note Due, Sept. 9th, 1838	4.93 3/4
Wm. B. Hart, Note Due, Feb. 9th, 1839	.37 1/2
J. Colip, Note, Sept. 19th, 1839	5.00
Joseph Coens, Note, Nov. 6th, 1839	1.87 1/2
David Montgomery, Note, Nov. 4th, 1839	3.80
A. Dickson's, Note Due, May 2nd., 1840	60.00
M. Simpson's, Note Due, June 3rd, 1833	1.33
James Simpson,s Note Due, Jan. 3rd, 1840	1.50
Thomas Speaks, Note Due, Oct. 2nd, 1839	1.75
William Freel's, Note Due, June 5th, 1839	40.38
Making in All	$807.32 1/2

State of Indiana)
Hamilton County)   Personally appeared before me, Allen Cole, a Justice of
the Peace for said County, Elias Hoddy, Administrator of
the Estate of Robert P. Hoddy, deceased and John Colip
and Jacob Colip, Appraisors of said Estate and being duly
Sworn the said John Colip and Jacob Colip says that the
above Inventory and Appraisement assigned by them is a
Just and True Inventory and Valuation of the Goods, Chattles
and Effects of the said Robert P. Hoddy to the best of
their Judgement and the said Elias Hoddy, says that the
above is a True Inventory of the Personal Estate of the
said Robert P. Hoddy, so far as the same has come to his
hands to be administered.

                                    Allen Cole   (Seal)
                                    Justice of the Peace

     Invoice of the Goods, Chattles and Effects of Robert P. Hoddy, deceased
sold by Elias Hoddy, administrator of said Estate on the 19th day of September
1840 to Wit:

Josiah West	1 Clevis	$	.31 1/4
A. Palmer	1 Spade		.18 3/4
S. H. Colip	1 Sythe and Sned		.37 1/2
John Colip	1 Cole Rake		.25
John Murphy	1 Pitchfork		.31 1/4
Daniel Lester	1 Pitchfork		.18 3/4
S. H. Colip	1 Pitchfork		.68 3/4
J. Stenman	1 Shovel		.68 3/4
Daniel Lester	1 Lot of Old Irons		.45
S. Palmer	1 Shovel		.18 3/4
S. M. Smith	2 Old Axes		.31 1/4
A. Cole	1 Box of Old Irons		.50
A. Cole	1 Hoe		.25
Jno. Murphy	1 Hoe & Handle		.37 1/2
A. Cole	1 Axe		.43 3/4
S. M. Smith	1 Barr of Iron		.50
J. West	1 Ox Yoke Rings & Steeple		.75
S. H. Colip	1 Axe		1.06 1/4
John Mc Kee	1 Broad Axe		1.75
Jacob Colip	1 Card and Brush		.06 1/4
J. Murphy	1 Iron Wedge		.89
John Colip	3 Augers		.68 3/4
John Mc Kee	1 Shaving Knife		.37 1/2
S. H. Colip	3 Augers		1.06 1/4
Jacob Stehman	1 Hand Saw		1.30
Jesse Justice	1 Old Saw		.12 1/2
A. Cole	1 Ox Yoke and Ring		1.06 1/4
John Colip	Flails		.06 1/4
George Peck	1 Doubletree		.83
William Fearce	1 Plough		2.01
William Fearce	1 Shovel Plough		1.87
Abra. Teters	1 Shovel Plough		2.00
John Murphy	1 Half Bushel		.26

Harrison Stakesbury	1 Oven and Lid	$ 1.50	
Daniel Harrold	1 Frying Pan	.63	
Richard Sunner	1 Kettle	2.00	
A. Cox	1 Bee Stand	2.00	
A. Cox	1 Bee Stand	1.37	1/2
Jacob Colip	1 Bee Stand	.56	
John Murphy	1 Writing Desk	3.06	1/4
Abraham Teters	1 Grind Stone	2.14	
S. H. Colip	1 Chain	.28	
John Deaver	1 Book	.18	3/4
James Mc Real	Half Wheat Fan	5.31	1/4
W. Fearce	1 Bridle	.63	
George Peck	1 Rope	1.01	
William Fearce	1 Saddle	6.37	1/2
John Potts	1 Log Chain	4.00	
Henry Deavers	1 Set of Britching	7.75	
Thomas Murphy	1 Pair of Steelyards	2.56	1/4
Jonathan Shores	1 Set of Horse Gears	3.18	3/4
Daniel Lester	1 Set of Horse Gears	2.66	
A. Dickson	1 Halter Chain	.87	1/2
C. Fearce	Check Lines	1.50	
William Ballard	1 Anvil	2.25	
T. Beckwith	3 Gimblets	.31	1/4
T. Beckwith	1 Set of Blacksmith Tools	40.50	
S. M. Smith	1 Lot of Coal	3.00	
Jacob Crull	3 Hogs	13.37	1/2
Thomas Beckwith	1 Sow and Pigs	7.25	
A. Teters	7 Shoats	22.00	
A. Cole	1 Hogs Head and Stable	1.31	1/4
T. Beckwith	7 Hides	1.31	1/4
Jacob Colip	Oats in Northend Stable	4.00	
A. Palmer	Oats in Southend Stable	6.00	
C. Stehman	1 Waggon	29.50	
John Caster	1 Cow	13.06	1/4
A. C. Teters	1 Heiffer	12.31	1/4
A. C. Teters	1 Brown Yearling Bull	6.00	
A. C. Teters	1 Brown Yearling Bull	3.75	
George Peck	1 Gray Mare	38.50	
John Caster	1 Bay Mare	24.81	1/4
William Dick	1 Brown Mare Colt	25.25	
C. Shell	1 Hay Stack	7.00	
C. Shell	1 Hay Stack	5.06	1/4
J. Stehman	1 Hay Stack	8.25	
Richard Lemon	1 Hay Stack	6.12	1/2
A. Palmer	1 Hay Stack	6.75	
Jacob Colip	1 Hay Stack	4.37	1/2
A. Cole	1 Hay Stack	5.00	
A. Teters	1 Hay Stack	6.00	
A. Teters	1 Hay Stack	4.25	
The Widow	1 Large Stack	6.00	
A. Palmer	1 Large Stack	14.00	
John Murphy	1 Calf	2.37	1/2
The Widow	1/2 Wheat in Mow	16.00	
P. George	1 Stack of Wheat	5.12	1/2

John Murphy	1 Half Stack Wheat	$ 4.02
John Murphy	1 Half Stack Wheat	3.12 1/2
John Murphy	1 Half Stack Wheat	3.25
Jacob Colip	1 Little Stack	2.08 3/4
H. Stowel	1 Sled	.50
		$421.91

Amount of Property taken by the Widow at the Appraisement as allowed by Her to the amount of One Hundred dollars, To Wit;

All the Table and Cupboard ware consisting of Buckets, Knives, forks and Spoons, Plates Tin Coffee Pots, Tea Pots, including all Cupboard Ware, Table, Crocks, Milk Pans, Tin Sugar Box, all the Tins Queens Potters, German Silver, Table and Tea Spoons, Glass Ware and Candle Moulds, 1 Churn, 2 Bowls, and 1 Knife Box	$ 15.00
9 Split Chairs,	3.37 1/2
1 Shovel and Hand Irons	1.50
1 Chest	1.50
1 Mantle Clock,	12.00
1 Bed and Bedding	15.00
1 Bed and Bedding	12.25
3 Sheets, 9 Bed Covers	13.75
3 Books and Slate	2.25
1 Tea Kettle	1.00
1 Stew Kettle	.75
1 Oven and Lid	.75
1 Skettle	.75
	60.37 1/2
	$ 86.37 1/2
2 Wash tubs and Wash Boards	1.25
1 Meat Tub	..62 1/2
1 Fat Can and 2 Old Barrels	.50
1 Axe	.75
1 Black Cow and Bell	10.50

Given under ours Hands.

Jacob Colip
John Colip

Property taken by the Widow at the Appraisement and Bought, Bond and Security Taken To Wit:

1 Old Trunk and 4 Bags	$ 1.75
1 Sow and Pigs	5.00
3 Hogs (1st Choice)	13.50
7 Sheep	10.50
1 Trunnel Bed and Bedding	4.50
1 Kettle	2.00
1 Bed Stead	1.50

```
 1 Hoe                                $   .50
 3 Acres of Corn                         15.00
 1 Mare                                  50.00
 1 Collar and Haims                       1.50
 1 Blind Bridle                            .87 1/2
   Property Bought at Sale by
   The Widow, 1 Hay Stack                 6.00
   Wheat in Mow & 1 Bridle                4.62 1/2
                         In All $117.25
```

State of Indiana)
Hamilton County) Personally came before Me, Allen Cole, a Justice of the
                  Peace for said County, Jacob Colip, who being by Me duly
                  Sworn upon his Oath, deposeth and saith that the fore-
                  going is a True copy as kept by Him as Appraisor and
                  Clerk of Appraisement and acting Clerk of Sale as set
                  forth in the foregoing Schedule.

                                        Jacob Colip, Clerk

                  Subscribed and Sworn to before Me, the 13th day of
                  October, A.D. 1840.

                                        Allen Cole,   (Seal)
                                        Justice of the Peace

Book Accounts of Robert P. Hoddy, deceased

```
Peter Passwater                $  2.00
Samuel Neace                      2.06 1/4
Frederick Kemp                    1.00
Thomas Snider                     1.50
John Cox                           .50
William Handy                      .25
J. Goodrich                       1.75
Elias Hoddy                       2.87 1/2
Francis Booker                     .62 1/2
William Peck                     13.87 1/2
William Kelly                     3.12 1/2
John Lee                           .68 3/4
Ebenezer Fearce                  15.32
James Johnson                     6.62 1/2
Wm. S. Dickson                    3.37 1/2
Daniel Shepperd                    .25
Andrew Dickson                    2.00
Isa Dickson                       2.50
William Murphy                    2.75
Henry Hill                         .31 1/4
Charles Duncan                     .56 1/2
E. Lewark                         2.12 1/2
John Murphy                        .25
Chris. J. Fearce                  5.62 1/2
Henry Kemp                        3.56 1/4
John Potts                       10.12 1/2
```

John Whitehead	$ 6.93	3/4
John Colip	.81	1/4
John Fisher	.12	1/2
James Carey	.12	1/2
James Cochran	.37	1/2
Josiah West	1.87	1/2
Robison Stephenson	.62	1/2
Simon Cochran	.87	1/2
Amos Palmer	15.79	1/4
Daniel Harrold	5.00	
William Whitehead	.12	1/2
Wm. P. Heart	2.62	1/2
Parnick George	8.50	
James Mc Neel	.75	
Edward Ware	6.42	
James Hughey	1.00	
William Ward	.25	
Wm. Zett	4.25	
George Peck	7.87	1/2
Thomas Murphy	8.86	1/2
John Near	.12	1/2
Joseph Mc Cormick	.75	
Reubin Dillow	.12	1/2
Abraham Teters	.18	3/4
John Peck	1.16	3/4
Wm. Parker	.75	
Marshal Savage	6.50	
Jonathan Carey	1.75	
Daniel Martin	1.12	1/2
Jacob Wise	5.12	1/2
Solomon Wise	1.87	1/2
Peter Carey	.31	1/4
Cornelius Mc Kee	1.00	
Abraham Huffman	.37	1/2
Granville Gibson	.25	
Joseph Swracegos (?)	.56	1/4
Joseph Corns	5.43	3/4
Joshua Carey	1.56	1/4
Alexander Simpson	1.75	
Ebenezer Holliway	1.50	
Peter A. Temple	.75	
Isaac Montgomery	1.90	
William Mc Kee	.37	1/2
David Ware	1.75	
William Teter	.75	
Joshua Hamilton	.37	1/2
Christopher Shell	.50	
John Waring	2.25	
Wm. Hare	.25	
John Deaver	3.68	3/4
James Conner	.25	
Samuel Pickens	.37	1/2
Levi Allman	2.75	
Allen Ware	16.38	3/4

	Robert Dyer	$ 1.87	1/2
	James Gibson	1.50	
	Horrace Stowel	.68	3/4
	C. Brown	.50	
	Judah Leaning	.25	
	Joseph Teters	.25	
	Jacob Tyson	3.60	
	Jurden Paten	.18	3/4
	Robert Mc Kee	1.87	1/2
	Jacoh Mock, Jr.	1.06	1/4
	Cornelius Moore	.81	3/4
	Stephen Robinett	.12	1/2
	Samuel Sentry	1.25	
	Juben R. Blackenman	.50	
	Allen Cole	.37	1/3
	Semen Shots	.18	3/4
	Henry Stanbraugh	1.37	1/2
	Cottingham & Combs	20.00	
Croppray	Hezekiah Franks (Error)	2.50	
	John Fortner	.12	1/2
		$262.35	

JOHN LANDY'S ESTATE

An Inventory of the Personal Property of John Landy, late of Hamilton County, Indiana, Deceased, December 28th, 1840.

1 Mall	$ .25	
1 Mall and Iron Wedge	.50	
1 Sythe and Hanings	.50	
1 Shovel	.25	
1 Log Chain	1.50	
1 Singletree	.50	
1 Drawing Knife & Chisel	.50	
1 Auger	.37	1/2
1 Bake Oven	.75	
1 Grubbing Hoe	.75	
1 Small Tub	.12	1/2
1 Large Tub	.25	
1 Basket	.12	1/2
1 Chopping Axe	1.00	
1 Sled	.25	
1 Shovel Plough	3.00	
1 Barsheer Plough	8.00	
1 Kettle	1.00	
1 Kettle	3.00	
2 Flour Barrels	.50	
1 Churn	.25	
1 Pickle Stand	.25	
1 Fat Stand	.25	
1 Bell	.25	
1 Bag	.37	1/2
2 Old Bags	.25	

```
1 Pair of Haims & Etc.        $  2.00
1 Collar                         1.00
1 Blind Bridle                    .50
1 Halter                          .37 1/2
1 Neck Band                       .75
1 Bell and Strap                  .75
1 Neck Band and Rope              .25
1 Curry Comb                      .12 1/2
1 Lot of Potatoes at 12 1/2
           cts per lb.           1.31 1/4
1 Rifle                         12.00
1 Pouch                           .25
2 Cows $10.00 each              20.00
2 Calves $3.00 each              6.00
1 Calf                           2.00
1 Colt                          12.00
1 Colt                          30.00
1 Mare                          45.00
1 Fat Hog                        3.50
1 Lot of Hogs                   10.50
1 Lot of Pork                    3.50
  Boards 750 Feet                6.56 1/4
8 Chois, 16 Fat Logs 3 by 8      1.00
4 Crocks                          .25
1 Lot of Cupboard Ware           3.00
1 Pot, 1 Smoothing Iron and
         Fire Shovel             1.50
1 Skellet                         .50
1 Clock                          5.00
1 Looking Glass                   .06 1/4
4 Chains                         1.00
2 Rocking Chairs                  .25
1 Tub for Crout                   .37 1/2
1 Beaureau                       6.00
1 Table                          2.00
  Steelyards                     1.00
1 Sive, 2 Bedsteads, Bedding
  for 3 Beds, 1 Bag and 3 Acres
  of Wheat in the Ground        31.75
1 Apple Butter Stand, 1 Lot of
  Hogs, Shoe Making Tools       10.37 1/2
1 Vinager Barrel, 1 Spinning
  Wheel, 1 Reel, 1 Hagel and
  Tobacco                        5.37 1/2
1 Axe Handle, 1 Umbrella, 2
  German Books                    .65
                              -----------
                              $246.00 3/4
```

George Kloepper)
) Apprs.
Peter Schenbach)

Now on the 26th day of December, 1840, comes Peter Schenbach and George Kloepper and was duly Sworn to Appraise the Personal Property of John Landy, Deceased, according to its true Value.

Given under my hand and Seal the date above.

Henry Jones   (Seal)
Justice of the Peace

Account of Sales of the Personal Property of John Landy of the County of Hamilton and State of Indiana, deceased at a Public Auction held at the late Dwelling House of the Said Deceased on the 15th day of January, 1841.

Jesse Brown	1 Mall	$ .18 3/4
Peter Landy	1 Mall & Wedge	.75
John Emehiser	1 Sythe	.50
H. Badowner	1 Shovel	.32
J. Brown	1 Log Chain	3.00
H. Shivy	1 Singletree	.57 1/2
D. Webbert	1 Sickle & Drawing Knife	.75
A. Smith	1 Auger	.29
J. Whisler	1 Mattock	.87 1/2
A. Smith	1 Tub	.60
M. Tucker	1 Basket	.11
C. Sparger	1 Sled	.12 1/2
T. Miller	1 Shovel Plough	4.50
D. Robertson	1 Barnshine Plough	7.25
G. Kloepper	1 Kettle	1.00
H. Shiry	1 Kettle	4.06 1/4
J. Aman	2 Barrels	.18 3/4
A. Herrington	1 Churn	.45
J. Emehiser	1 Bag	.25
D. Smith	1 Stand (Pickle)	.18 3/4
J. Emehiser	1 Bell	1.31 1/4
J. Whisler	1 Pair of Gears	2.06 1/4
J. Emehiser	1 Collar	1.46
J. Whisler	1 Blind Collar	.70
G. Tucker	1 Halter	.65
F. Smelser	1 Bell	1.87 1/2
E. Beard	1 Curry Comb	.18 3/4
D. Welbert	10 3/4 Bushels of Potatoes	2.53
H. Badowner	1 Rifle Gun	13.50
H. Badowner	1 Pouch	.75
F. Ophilder	1 Cow	12.00
J. Egler	1 Cow	13.18 3/4
J. Aman	1 Calf	4.75
J. Emehiser	1 Calf	3.62
A. Smith	1 Calf	4.41
H. Achenbach	1 Colt	13.81 1/4
J. Aman	1 Colt	34.25
T. Miller	1 Halter Chain & Band	1.33
G. Motes	1 Halter Chain & Band	.50
T. Roads	750 Feet of Plank	6.15
J. Miller	1 Joist	1.12 1/2
A. Goodpasture	1 Wash Board	.13

J. Parker	1 Lot of Crocks	$	.32
M. Tucker	1 Looking Glass		.50
J. Parker	2 Chairs		1.50
G. Motes	2 Chairs		1.40
D. Webbert	1 Crout Tub		.95
E. Parker	1 Beaureau		7.56 1/4
J. Fifer	1 Table		2.69
J. Parker	1 Pair of Steelyards		1.26
J. M. Thompson	1 Bedstead		3.56 1/4
J. Emehiser	3 Acres of Wheat in Ground		7.87 1/2
D. Webbert	1 Lot of Hay		6.62 1/2
F. Smelbzer	1 Stand of Apple Butter		2.06 1/4
F. Coapman	Shoe Makers Tools		1.62 1/2
G. Motes	2 Casts		.37 1/2
W. B. Quick	1 Lot of Lasts		.37 1/2
W. B. Quick	1 Lot of Lasts		.70
J. Fifer	1 Vinegar Gag		1.25
N. Zett	1 Spinning Wheel		3.00
P. Landy	Books		.90
A. Smith	300 Cupboards		.36
D. Webbert	1 Trough		.25
N. Zett	2 Planes		1.00
P. Landy	1 Axe Handle		.12 1/2

Whole Amount	$191.11
Book Account	16.05 1/2
Sum Total	$207.15 1/2

George Kloepper, Clerk   Jacob Whisler, Administrator

State of Indiana)
Hamilton County)   Personally Appeared before me, a Justice of the Peace in
and for said County, George Kloepper, Clerk of the Person-
al Estate of John Landy and after being duly sworn says
the above Inventory is True.

Given under my hand and Seal this 8th day of February, 1841.

Samuel Dale, (Seal)
Justice of the Peace

SAMUEL POWEL'S ESTATE

An Inventory of the Goods, Chattles and Effects of Samuel Powel, late of
Hamilton County, State of Indiana, deceased taken by Joseph Powel, administra-
tor of the Estate of said Deceased with the assistance of Caleb Carson and
James George, Appraisors called and duly qualified, to wit:

1 Sorrel Mare	$ 30.00
7 Sheep	10.00
Thirty Five Hundred	10.50
1 Sickel	.25
1 Set of Chairs	3.00

<pre>
            Also Cash $ 65.37 1/2
            Sundries Notes   69.62 1/2
                                   $188.75
</pre>

Given under our hands this ____ day of _____, 1840.

<pre>
State of Indiana)
Hamilton County)   Personally came before me Stephen Carey, a Justice of the
                    Peace of said County, Joseph Powel, Administrator of the
                    Estate of Samuel Powel, deceased, Caleb Carson, James
                    George, Appraisors of said Estate and being duly qualified
                    the said Caleb Carson and James George says that the above
                    Inventory and Valuation of the Goods, Chattles and Effects
                    of the said Samuel Powel to their best of their Judgement
                    and the said Joseph Powel that the above is a True Invent-
                    ory of the Personal Estate of the said Samuel Powel, so far
                    as the same has come to his hands to be administrated.

                                            Caleb Carson
                                            James George
</pre>

Signed and affirmed to before me, this 19th day of December, A.D. 1840.

<pre>
                                            Stephen Carey (Seal)
                                            Justice of the Peace
</pre>

Sale Book of Samuel Powel, deceased:

<pre>
        Nathan Fisher   2 Chairs $ 1.12 1/2
        Martin Gunner   2 Chairs   1.12 1/2
        Nathan Fisher   2 Chairs   1.12 1/2
        William Pearce   1 Sickle   .30
        John Carson   350 Bricks   3.12 1/2
        Daniel Griner   2 Sheep (1st Choice)   6.00
        Daniel Griner   2 Sheep (2nd Choice)   6.00
        William Pearce   2 Sheep (3rd Choice)   5.00
        James Edwards   1 Sheep (Last Choice)   2.18 3/4
        Daniel Fisher   1 Mare   30.25
                                         Amount $ 56.18 3/4
</pre>

<pre>
State of Indiana)
Hamilton County)   Before Me, came this day, Nathan Fisher and being duly
                    Sworn by me, says the above is a True Account of the Sale
                    of the Property of the Estate of Samuel Powel, late of
                    said County, December 19th, 1840.

                                            Stephen Carey, (Seal)
                                            Justice of the Peace
</pre>

WILLIAM BROWN'S WILL

In the name of God, Amen. I, William Brown of Hamilton County in the

State of Indiana, being sick and weak in body, but of sound and deposing mind, memory and understanding and considering the certainty of death and the uncertainly of the time thereof and being deserious to settle my worldly affairs and thenly to the better purpose to leave this world when it shall please God to call me hence do therefore make, publish this my Last Will and Testament in the manner and form following that is to say.

First and principally I commit my soul into the hands of Almighty God and my body to the earth to be decently buried at the desretion of my executor herein after named and after my debts and funeral charges are paid.

I devise and bequeath as follows:

First: I give and bequeath unto my son, John Brown the sum of one Dollar with what he has received of me as his full share of my Estate both real and personal.

Second: I give and bequeath unto my Daughter, Nancy Lewis and Polly Olvey and my Son, Nelson Brown by _____ share and share about after deducting Ten Dollars for each of the Children of Silas Brown, deceased: To Wit:

Charles H. Brown
Meicajah Brown
Lewis Nelson Brown
Rhoda Brown

Third: It is my desire to have all my property in my possession at the time day of my decease appraised and sold the Personal property on a credit of Twelve Months and the real property sold at one third of the price there of to be paid in Twelve Months after the day of Sale and the remainder in Ten installments, one half in Two Years after said Sale and the last to be paid in three years from day of sale.

Fourth: And whereas My son Nelson Brown is indebted to Me for Forty Five Dollars which is to be taken out of his share and whereas I hold a note on James Lewis for Fifteen Dollars which I give him for his trouble with me, which is not to be and with my estate and lastly I do hereby constitute and appoint my worthy friend, James Lewis and John L. Kinnaman to be Executors of this My Last Will and Testament, by me made.

In Testimony whereof I have hereunto set my hand and seal this 21st day of June, in the year of Our Lord, Eighteen Hundred and Forty One.

William X Brown (Seal)
(his mark)

Signed, Sealed, published and declared by William Brown the above named Testator as his Last Will and Testament.
In Presence of Us:

John F. Helms
Isiah Whelchel

State of Indiana)
Hamilton County) Be it remembered that on the 28th day of March, A.D. 1844, Personally came before Me the undersigned Clerk of the Hamilton County Probate Court, John F. Helms, of lawful

age, one of the subscribing Witnesses to the within Will of
William Brown, late of said County, deceased who after being
duly Sworn upon his oath says that the within instrument of
Writing was made signed, sealed and declared by the within
named William Brown to be his last Will and Testament and
that he this and affirmed. and Isaiah Whelchel of lawful
age was called upon by the Testator as witness thereof and
that they the said Witnesses subscribed their names thereto
as Witnesses in the presence of the said Decedent and in
the presence of each other and that said William Brown the
Testator at the time of making said Will was of SOund mind
and memory and that the said William Brown was an inhabitant
of said County of Hamilton at the time of his death and died
in said County of Hamilton and that said Testator at the
time of making and executing said Will was past the age of
Twenty one years and was not under Cocrcion or restraint as
the affiant believes and that the particular facts and
circumstances of the executing subscribing and attesting
said Will not herein alive States and as follows that is
that on oralact the 25th day of June, A.D. 1841 this
affiant and said Witnesses were called upon at the request
of the said Testator to attest said Will that Said Testator
at that time was sick and said County of Hamilton and the
subscribing of said Will by Testator _____ _____ the presence of this affiant and said Whatsoever and that said
Will has been since the making executing and testing of
the same as this affiant believes attend as follows that
is the word _____ being the last word in the first with
him of _____ will has been erased and the words ten
intestment in the steace thereof.

                                    John F. Helms

Sworn to before me the undersigned Clerk of the Probate
Court of the County of Hamilton, State of Indiana, this
28th day of March, A.D. 1844.

         (S E A L) Given under my hand and seal of said
                      Court at Noblesville in said County of
                      Hamilton.
                                 Jno. G. Burns, Clerk.

INDEX
NAME MAY APPEAR MORE THAN ONCE ON ANY GIVEN PAGE

INDEX
NAME MAY APPEAR MORE THAN ONCE ON ANY GIVEN PAGE

COOPER, 129.
COPPOCK, 67;68;86.
CORNS, 116;117;148.
COSTOLLER, 84.
COTTINGHAM, 12;13;14;
21;22;25;26;28;29;30;
31;32;37;39;50;95;118;
136;137;138;149.
COUOP, 38.
COVERDALE, 38;50;51.
COX, 117;145;147.
CRAIG, 70;71;85.
CREEKMORE, 107.
CRISWELL, 116;119;120;
124;125;126.
CRULL, 116;125;145.
CRUSE, 7.
CURRY, 38.
CUSTER, 103;109.

D.
DALE, 9;20;31;37;38;
49;51;53;61;67;72;74;
76;82;84;131;152.
DARROW, 135;136.
DARSON, 50.
DAVIS, 4;6;7;8;9;20;
26;36;37;40;66;75;81;
96.
DAVIDSON, 12;13.
DAWSON, 81.
DAYTON, 85.
DEAL, 117;125.
DEAN, 46;47.
DEAVER, 134;145;148.
DENNAND, 63.
DENNEND, 118.
DENNEN, 139.
DEMOSS, 31;34;37;51.
DICK, 113;121;122;145.
DICKERSON, 129.
DICKSON, 38;50;51;138;
139;140;143;145;147.
DILLOW, 148.
DOAN, 41.
DODSON, 130.
DUMGS, 25.
DUNCAN, 141.
DUNING, 129;130.
DUNNING, 79.
DYER, 149.
DYRE, 112.

E.
EARL, 103.
EDWARDS, 55;153.
EGLER, 151.
ELLER, 127;128;129;
130;131.
ELLIS, 6;122.
EMEHISER, 151;152.
EMMONS, 29;38.
ESSEX, 5;6;7.
EVANS, 88;89.

F.
FALLIS, 21;25;26;40;
80;81.
FARLOW, 70.
FEARCE, 136;137;138;
139;140;144;145;147.
FEAKWAY, 34.
FERGUSON, 33;63;116;
117;118;138;140.
FIFER, 152.
FINCH, 41;48;49;50;51.
FISHER, 22;38;51;64;
65;74;91;96;97;98;148;
153.
FLANIGAN, 128;130.
FLANNAGON, 128.
FLEETWOOD, 63;116;117;
134.
FLETCHER, 109;110.
FLOWER, 22.
FOLAND, 109;110;112;
113;117.
FORE, 134.
FORTNER, 149.
FOUTS, 35;45;46;47;48.
FOX, 51;82.
FRANKS, 149.
FRAZER, 109.
FREEL, 47;48;63;109;
113;114;115;116;117;
118;138;139;140.
FROMAN, 34.
FROMER, 34.
FRYBARGER, 12;13;21;
26;28;30;31;32.
FUKEWAY, 47.
FURL, 50.

G.
GARDNER, 116;121;122;
125.

GARRIOT, 37.
GARRIOTT, 38.
GATES, 82.
GEORGE, 8;9;31;34;46;47;
48;129;134;145;148;152;
153.
GREENING, 23.
GIBSON, 148;149.
GILBREATH, 23;25.
GILKEY, 50.
GLASGO, 8;9;10.
GOE, 39;51;52;53.
GAIN, 134.
GOLEY, 130.
GOODEN, 23.
GOODING, 25.
GOODPASTURE, 47;48;117;
151.
GOODRICH, 147.
GOUGH, 113;117;132.
GRANGER, 13.
GRAVES, 25;104;112.
GREENING, 20;22;23;25;40;
79;80;81.
GRIFFITH, 52;53.
GRILBY, 13.
GRIVER, 153.
GROVES, 10;20;21;23.
GUILKCE, 48.
GUILKEY, 49;50.
GUNGON, 29.
GUNNER, 153.

H.
HACKER, 14;15;16;104.
HAINES, 105.
HAINS, 56;57;58.
HAIR/HAIRE, 12.
HALE, 57.
HALL, 13;58;88.
HAMBLE, 12.
HAMER, 6.
HAMILTON, 63;116;117;
143;148.
HAMMEL, 25.
HANDY, 147.
HANNAMAN, 32;33;34;35.
HARDIN, 7.
HARE, 14;37;38;114;115;
148.
HAROLD, 92.
HARRISON, 7.

157

INDEX
NAME MAY APPEAR MORE THAN ONCE ON ANY GIVEN PAGE

HARROLD, 116;117;138;
139;140;145;148.
HART, 143.
HAWL, 87.
HAYS, 38.
HAYWORTH, 65;66;74;
75;92;96;97;98.
HAZLE, 15.
HEAD, 23.
HEADY, 23.
HEART, 148.
HEATON, 38;40;55;56.
HEDDY, 110.
HEDY, 25.
HEFFER, 107.
HELMS, 106;154;155.
HERRINGTON, 151.
HIATT, 66;91;92;96;
97.
HILDEBRANDT, 127.
HILL, 39;147.
HILLORY, 39.
HOCKET, 66;89;90;91;
92;93;95;97;98.
HODGIN, 106;109;110;
114;115;116;131;139;
140;141;144;147.
HOKSON, 25.
HOLLIWAY, 134;138;140;
148.
HOOVER, 6;95;109;130.
HOPPER, 28.
HORNE, 37.
HOUGH, 125.
HOUGHAM, 38.
HOUOWAY, 117.
HOW, 21.
HUCHEN, 82.
HUDSON, 117;118;138.
HUFFMAN, 87;148.
HUGHEY, 39;110;112;
113;114;134;135;148.
HUMPHREY, 116.
HUMPHREYS, 116.
HUMPHRIES, 117.
HUNT, 108.
HURLOCK, 16;39;50;51;
70;75.
HUSHMAR, 9.
HUTCHENSON, 31.
HUTSON, 63;138;139;
140.

I.
IRWIN, 15;40;79;80;81.

J.
JACKSON, 23;25;39;66;
104.
JAGOE, 10.
JAMES, 143.
JASPER, 20.
JELLY, 34.
JOHN, 136.
JOHNSON, 21;23;38;39;
51;72;135;147.
JONES, 13;31;34;38;39;
51;70;87;88;89;151.
JUSTICE, 134;144.

K.
KARR, 13;126.
KECK, 121;122;123;124;
125;126;127.
KELLER, 10;12;21.
KELLY, 34;58;61;62;63;
64;143;147.
KEMP, 117;125;147.
KENDAL, 70.
KENDLE, 15.
KESTERSON, 88.
KICKSON, 138.
KIMBERLIN, 130.
KINDER, 121;122.
KINDERS, 116.
KINEAMAN, 71.
KING, 67;68;85;86;87.
KINGSBURY, 34;35;45;46;
113;118;138;139;140.
KIRKENDALL, 15;21;23;
25;37;39;54;55;75;78;
80;81;95.
KIRKPATRICK, 50;113.
KINNAMAN, 84;106;107;
154.
KLOEPPER, 120;121;122;
124;126;127;150;151;
152.
KOMER, 34.

L.
LACKY, 71.
LACY, 16;17;20;21;23;
25;26;39;53;76;79;80;
81.

LAMBERTON, 71.
LANDY, 149;151;152.
LANHAM, 55;80.
LAREW, 113.
LEARNING, 149.
LEARNING, 47.
LEDMUN, 107.
LEE, 47;48;147.
LEMAN, 145.
LEMHAM, 76.
LEMMING, 38;67.
LENHAM, 79.
LEMON, 107;108.
LENUN, 107.
LEONARD, 116;117;127.
LESTER, 117;118;144;145.
LEWARK, 147.
LEWIS, 10;154.
LINDLEY, 104.
LOW, 70.
LOWERY, 70;71.
LUTZ, 53.

M.
MACUSTRY, 71.
MAHIN, 10;12;13;14;30;
38;51;135.
MALLERY, 39.
MANSHIP, 85;106;107.
MAPPIS, 44;45.
MARROW, 66;74.
MARSHALL, 75.
MARSHILL, 1;3;4;5.
MASTER, 34.
MARTIN, 148.
MATER, 113;119;120;121;
122;123;124;125.
MATHEWSON, 116;118.
MATHISON, 38.
MEDSKER, 20;55;79;80.
MENDENHALL, 44.
MESSICK, 20;26;29;30;31.
METSKER, 21;25.
MIDSGAR, 38.
MILLERS, 112;122;123;126;
151.
MILLS, 20;129.
MINCER, 50.
MINNER, 50.
MITCHELL, 20.
MOCK, 34;103;129;149.
MOFFIT, 20.

158

Heritage Books by Frances T. Ingmire:

Arkansas Confederate Veterans and Widows Pension Applications

Citizens of Missouri Territory: 1787-1810, Grants in Present Day Missouri, Arkansas and Oklahoma, Vol. 1

Citizens of Missouri Territory: 1810-1812, Grants in Present Day Missouri, Arkansas and Oklahoma, Vol. 2

Citizens of Missouri Territory to-1835, Grants in Present Day Missouri, Arkansas and Oklahoma, Vol. 3

Hamilton County, Indiana Marriage Records Book A, 1833–1843

Hamilton County, Indiana Naturalization Certificates, 1855-1905

Hamilton County, Indiana Will Book B, 1835–1844

Hardin County, Kentucky Will Book A, 1793–1809

Hardin County, Kentucky Will Book B, 1810–1816

Hardin County, Kentucky Will Book C, 1816–1821

Laurens County, South Carolina Will Book A, Volume II, 1840–1853

North Carolina Marriage Bonds and Certificates Series: Craven County, North Carolina, Marriage Records, 1780–1867

North Carolina Marriage Bonds and Certificates Series: Cumberland County, North Carolina, Marriage Records, 1803–1878

North Carolina Marriage Bonds and Certificates Series: Guilford County, North Carolina, Marriage Records, 1771–1868

North Carolina Marriage Bonds and Certificates Series: Lincoln County, North Carolina, Marriage Records, 1783–1866

North Carolina Marriage Bonds and Certificates Series: Orange County, North Carolina, Marriage Records, 1782–1868

North Carolina Marriage Bonds and Certificates Series: Randolph County, North Carolina, Marriage Records, 1785–1868

North Carolina Marriage Bonds and Certificates Series: Rowan County, North Carolina, Marriage Records, 1754–1866

North Carolina Marriage Bonds and Certificates Series: Stokes County, North Carolina, Marriage Records, 1783–1868

North Carolina Marriage Bonds and Certificates Series: Surry County, North Carolina, Marriage Records, 1783–1868

North Carolina Marriage Bonds and Certificates Series: Wake County, North Carolina, Marriage Records, 1781–1867

North Carolina Marriage Bonds and Certificates Series: Wilkes County, North Carolina, Marriage Records, 1779–1868

Texas Ranger Service Records, 1838–1846

Texas Ranger Service Records, 1847–1900, Volume 1: A-C

Texas Ranger Service Records, 1847–1900, Volume 2: D-G

Texas Ranger Service Records, 1847–1900, Volume 3: H-K

Texas Ranger Service Records, 1847–1900, Volume 4: L-N

Texas Ranger Service Records, 1847–1900, Volume 5: O-S

Texas Ranger Service Records, 1847–1900, Volume 6: T-Z

www.ingramcontent.com/pod-product-compliance
Lightning Source LLC
Chambersburg PA
CBHW080241270326
41926CB00020B/4328